Resource Focused Counselling and Psychotherapy

An Introduction

Michael Wilson

Routledge
Taylor & Francis Group

LONDON AND NEW YORK

First published 2017
by Routledge
2 Park Square, Milton Park, Abingdon, Oxon OX14 4RN

and by Routledge
711 Third Avenue, New York, NY 10017

Routledge is an imprint of the Taylor & Francis Group, an informa business

British Library Cataloguing in Publication Data
A catalogue record for this book is available from the British Library

Library of Congress Cataloging in Publication Data
A catalog record for this book has been requested

ISBN: 978-1-138-91579-4 (hbk)
ISBN: 978-1-138-91581-7 (pbk)
ISBN: 978-1-315-68384-3 (ebk)

Typeset in Times New Roman
by Taylor & Francis Books
Printed and bound by CPI Group (UK) Ltd, Croydon, CR0 4YY

Resource Focused Counselling and Psychotherapy

Therapists sometimes ask: What supports you in life? What gets you through difficult times? Our 'journey' in life relies on a range of resources to equip and fulfil us. Knowing about these resources, however, is not enough: for lasting benefits, they must be bodily felt experiences. The aim of this book is to illustrate the holistic purpose of therapy to resource integration of the client. It draws upon extensive material to affirm that the practice of contemporary therapy benefits from insights gained from evolving neuroscience. Particular emphasis is put on the benefits of drawing on the *dimensions of experience* to strengthen ego processes like self-awareness and self-regulation, and engage with the depths of being, including 'soul'.

Resource Focused Counselling and Psychotherapy provides professionals with a comprehensive and integrative model of resource focused therapy, drawing upon clinical examples and the current range of research and theory surrounding this emerging approach. Additionally, the book contains a range of self-resourcing exercises and practices for each part of the integrative model, enabling individuals to develop self-resources for greater resilience and well-being in their own lives.

This book is an important read for psychotherapists, psychologists and counsellors, including those working with trauma. It also provides valuable insights for modalities practising from a psycho-spiritual perspective, including Jungian and transpersonal psychotherapists.

Michael Wilson is a psychotherapist (UKCP reg.) in private practice in Edinburgh and Berwick-upon-Tweed, UK. He is the co-author of *Creative Ethical Practice in Counselling and Psychotherapy* (2012, Sage).

For my mother Johanna Kraus Wilson

Contents

Acknowledgements

The resources available to me during the writing of this project were numerous, and often deeply validating when they came in the form of dreams.

Particular thanks go to Lyn Phillips for his enduring commitment at every stage of this book. My thanks, too, go to Bridget Grant for offering valuable feedback on the later stages of this project as a whole, and to Jenny Pearson for thoughts on Chapter 9. Appreciation also goes to Jorge N. Ferrer and Michael Washburn for their reflections on my representation of some of their ideas at earlier writing stages. Within the participatory nature of reality where time present contains something of time past, and anticipates time future, I thank my Jungian analyst Bani Shorter (1923–2010).

One of the deepest resourcing experiences is the Northumberland country-side, in particular the River Tweed, College Valley, Holy Island, the coastal pathways and wooded areas, and the inhabitants of these places. Thank you.

Permissions

Washburn, M. (1999) 'Embodied Spirituality in a Sacred World', *The Humanistic Psychologist*, 27(2): 133–172. Extracts reprinted by permission of Division 32, Society for Humanistic Psychology (http://www.apadivisions.org/division-32).

McGilchrist, I. (2009) *The Master and His Emissary: The Divided Brain and the Making of the Western World*, New Haven and London: Yale University Press. Permission granted by David Higham Associates.

Schore, A. N. (2014) 'The Right Brain is Dominant in Psychotherapy', *Psychotherapy*, 51(3): 388–397. Extracts reprinted with permission from APA.

Introduction

The stillness of the morning is for me one of the most resourcing experiences. Everything is just coming into animation, beginning with the birds. There is something about the quality of this stillness, like the earth presencing itself to us and witnessing everything coming to wakefulness. On occasion this is worth waking up so early for. I imagine, too, that I have felt supported by stillness from the moment of my 'first breath', which is where I may have learnt to value times of stillness thereafter. I hope I will carry this tacit knowing to my last breath, for it brings a deep felt acceptance of the way things are; a profound bodily felt sense that everything is ultimately alright.

The resource seeking self-system is continually looking for ways to establish times of rest, safety, comfort and contentment in our relationships, and satisfaction in what we aspire to achieve in life, as experiences in themselves, and also to find and deepen meaning and purpose in life and widen a sense of self.

One of our basic abilities is to regulate our inner life, namely our thoughts, feelings, imaginings, sensations, energy and even some of our bodily functions. Mastery of this begins early on in life in relation to our primary caregivers who are able, hopefully, to facilitate our self-regulation through the nurturing quality of the regulating relationship itself. Such caregivers enable the one first accomplishing step in our earliest experience of feeling safe and at ease in our body and in our immediate environment. Hence, self-regulation is one of our most rudimentary resources. Boundary-making is also a coemerging basic ability, not only physically, but also psychologically and emotionally, in our ability to keep 'things' at 'wanted' distances from ourselves bodily, as well as psychically or inwardly, from the core sense of our emerging self, by, for example, repression of the 'unwanted'. Following a period of 'magical' ability to resource ourselves in a range of ways through our relationship with mother as a symbiotic part of ourselves, boundary-making possibly first arises out of our felt sense awareness of separateness or autonomy from her. In this way, we experiment with creating experiences of feeling safe on our own for variable periods of time. We may say, therefore, that there are at least two aspects to regulation: self-regulation of inner processes, and the regulation of our environment which includes what is other. Thus for the whole of our lives we seek to influence both inner and outer realities to establish and maintain regulation, and draw upon other resources to keep this going. This can be time spent relaxing in a resourceful setting (e.g., garden, park, art gallery), or engaging in a resource-making activity (e.g., exercising, enjoying social time with friends, going to college), or cultivating values to live by, or identifying with positive attitudes to increase resilience (e.g., optimism, gratitude), or adapting and making changes to our lives to bring about a greater sense of felt satisfaction, especially in our relationships.

However, many people struggle with self-regulation and boundary-making. Sometimes they find thoughts and feelings intrusive, including empathy from others, deeming these as 'unwanted' or fear-evoking, and are unable to resource themselves to alleviate and bring meaning to these experiences. Likewise, many people feel responsible for their experiences of unsupportive, toxic or even abusive relationships and environments, not knowing where responsibilities belong or how to establish resourceful boundaries by placing limits on what they are responsible for, or learning to avoid situations which give rise to negative experiences. Often the template for our boundary-setting, or lack of this, is determined early on in life through boundaries first being given (or not given) to us, often to protect (or not protect) us.

The absence of a consistent ability to regulate inwardly can bring us to regulate by the degree of satisfaction or comfort gained by certain relationships (e.g., when leaning towards co-dependency or reassurance-seeking), or by the acquisition of 'things' (e.g., mobile devices, computer games, designer labels, food), including addictions of all kinds. Many people, it seems to me, place the source of regulation in the 'power' of 'things' or the 'other' alone to bring about a sense of contentment, or to transform discontent or misery into pleasure or delight, and so on. My point is that, if we look for resources only as 'things out there' or 'others', then we neglect our ability to resource from within, because 'others' or 'things out there' will never alone satisfactorily resource us. For example, rampant consumerism does not help in this, but rather encourages us to find satisfaction in a limitless range of 'things' with bold promises of a better quality of life when we acquire these. We forget to consider the consequences of our omnipotent longing for more, and rarely take into account the impact of this on other people, and the disturbing environmental costs of our insatiability. Similarly, too much co-dependence or reassurance-seeking tends to put the responsibility for our lives on others. None of this answers the perennial questions about meaning and purpose, which often return as dark experiences of emptiness and a persistent longing for a panacea, especially with the decline of the regulating influence of religion in our society. Mindfulness may help to restore the balance by bringing our attention to the resourcefulness of the present moment and away from longing. However, mindfulness itself is also in danger of now becoming another consumable.

When symptoms like melancholy (e.g., Horwitz and Wakefield, 2007), anxiety (e.g., Stossel, 2014) and worry (e.g., O'Gorman, 2015) begin to appear, rather than engage in these as information or indicators that our life or an aspect of it is far from satisfactory, or as invitations for meaning-making, we resort to fretting that 'something is *wrong* with me' and are quick to find labels and seek to affirm this (e.g., 'depression', 'anxiety disorder', 'bipolar', 'PTSD' or 'trauma', or even 'ADHD'). These labels are now part of ordinary vocabulary and are often used without true understanding of the underlying issues or conditions from which they give rise, and can be treated too easily as 'unwanted' enemies; even GPs can be quick to label and prescribe. For example, regarding the diagnosis and drug treatment of Attention Deficit Hyperactivity Disorder (ADHD) among American children, youth and adults, the rate of 'diagnosis now exceeds all reasonable estimates of the true prevalence of the disorder' (Watson et al., 2014: 50). In addition, Allan Horwitz and Jerome Wakefield (2007: 225) powerfully demonstrate how psychiatry transformed ordinary sadness as an 'inherent part of the human condition' into a depressive disorder. In contrast, the legitimate use of diagnosis can liberate clients from feeling that conditions are their 'fault' through the explanation diagnoses offer, and provide opportunities for treatment and support, which in themselves are resources. But, 'a drug will not provide a growth-facilitating environment' to promote deeper healing and resourcefulness (Schore quoted in Sieff, 2015: 135). The argument throughout this book is that, as therapists, we must not only support clients to come into meaningful relationship with these and other symptoms when they arise, but also bring attention to and nurture our capacity for self-resourcing in times of difficulty and struggle, by accessing a combination of available inner and outer resources. Therapists may want to keep sight of the probability that effective therapy is about more than exploration and meaning-making, but has a resource focus as well. Michael Lambert (1992), for example, suggested that forty per cent of the transformative factors in therapy are attributable to client *strengths, resources, abilities* and *resilience.* And while thirty per cent of the outcome of therapy was attributable to *relational factors* of warmth and the Rogerian Core Conditions of empathy, acceptance and congruence, only fifteen per cent was respectively attributable to mutual *expectations of a positive therapeutic outcome* and *hope* (cf. Wampold and Imel, 2015 [2010]: 212, 'the power of expectations' in psychotherapy), and the therapist's theoretical orientation and methodology. Even if findings were different now, Lambert's study highlights the importance of resourcing in therapy; my emphasis indicates the bringing together of these factors under a single 'resources' umbrella.

Moreover, this book is a response to the seemingly obvious question 'What is it that we are resourcing?' and opens up discussion into the wider nature of being human to consider intelligences other than thinking (IQ), such as the intelligence of feeling or emotion (EQ), imagination (IMQ), spirituality (SQ), of sensation or the body (BQ), or physical intelligence (PQ), and so on, as resourcing pathways. Thus the book also addresses the role of therapy in resourcing the brain/mind/body as a whole, including the egoic and deeper aspects of the self-system. I further argue that our resourcing sits within the context of a wider picture of lives other than our own, even other-than-human. While we ourselves are often resourced by these others, they too require resourcing by us, even possibly the earth itself. For to become fully ourselves is in some way reliant on our enabling the other to also become themselves, as *the whole resources the part and the part resources the whole* in a dynamic participatory, coinfluencing, cocreating exchange. In this sense, therefore, we are not entirely separate from this coinfluencing whole. Although it is often enough for therapists to draw attention to the impact on clients of their life context, sometimes the wholeness 'project' requires more proactive engagement to take this wider context more fully into account, even if only to notice those resourcing aspects in our immediate surroundings and find ways to experience the qualitative feel of them. For I suggest that more than a thought, *a resource is an experience.* My intentions in writing this book, then, are, first, to begin to examine what 'resourcing' in therapy means and, second, to begin to explore what this might look like in practice.

To this end, Chapter 1 offers an overview of resourcing by considering the resource areas of therapy within the context of a brief review of therapies. The chapter also looks at how resources are both inner and outer, innate and cultivated over time. Based on the principle that the part influences the whole and *vice versa*, I reflect on ways in which resourcing also benefits others, including the therapist. Resourcing the emotional regulating systems is also introduced, as well as the dimensions of experiencing (e.g., thinking, feeling, physical, interpersonal). This opens up discussion on the neuroplasticity of the brain and the benefits gained from cultivating positive experiences, which includes the resourcing experience of the therapeutic relationship itself.

With Chapter 2 I take a comprehensive view of the origins of resourcing, building on the earlier view of inner/outer/innate/cultivated ways of resourcing, to consider purposeful and inadvertent resourcing experiences, and explore the view that *resource is an experience.* The chapter also focuses on the importance of strengthening self-awareness and self-regulation as core capacities, and looks at 'will' as a core resource alongside those of the imagination, breath and (in its widest sense) relationship. Drawing upon the writing of Michael Washburn this chapter puts the origins of resourcing within a developmental perspective with the Ground of Being as our deepest and most profound resource.

Turning then to consider resourcing of the emotional systems (safety, achievement and connection seeking), Chapter 3 looks at bottom-up–top-down and left–right brain hemispheres processes in relation to this, and the 'negativity bias' of the mind in its frequent tilt towards rumination. I also consider ways of increasing positive experiences in these systems, and highlight how focus on emotion is fundamental in therapy as a predominantly right brain of client to right brain of therapist communication (Schore, 2014), and consider the process of coming into the present moment as key to effective practice (Siegel and Solomon, 2013).

Central to this book is consideration of the *eight dimensions of experiencing* for resourcing clients, and this is the focus of Chapter 4. These dimensions are: thinking, feeling, physical, energetic, imaginal, behavioural, interpersonal and spiritual. While reflecting on the distinctive nature of these, the chapter argues that these dimensions are sometimes taken for granted and neglected as intelligences and pathways of development in their own right. I consider these intelligences and suggest ways in which they can resource us, and how they can in turn also be the focus for resourcing within the 'language' of their own modality.

Chapter 5 considers how psychotherapy and counselling can combine understanding of emotional systems and related bottom-up–top-down and left–right brain integration of inner processes and memories (i.e., the theme of Chapter 3) with the dimensions of experiencing (i.e., the theme of Chapter 4). I also take into account a bipolar view of the self-system as consisting of egoic and nonegoic processes, often referred to as 'ego' and depth or 'soul'. I then suggest that resourcing this unified whole is of prime importance, not only egoic processes and functions, though I acknowledge that this is not always possible in therapy. The chapter proposes three resourcing orientations or categories, namely, pseudo resources, protective resources, and growth facilitating or authentic resources, and also looks at the resourcing focus at different stages of therapy, namely assessment, beginning, review and ending.

With Chapter 6 we look at therapy as inherently an educative process, and reflect on the implicit and explicit nature of education, as well as suggest principles which can be taken into account to increase educative effectiveness. Drawn from neuroscience, these principles include: neurons that wire together, fire together, use it or lose it, use it or improve it, regulation, specificity, repetition, intensity, time and transference. I also consider the therapeutic implications of explicit education, and the ethics which inform this, namely, non-maleficence, beneficence, justice, autonomy, fidelity and self-care.

Then in Chapter 7 I consider the resourcing potential of the therapeutic relationship, with its emphasis on empathic engagement, and the idea of therapy as largely a right brain hemisphere activity (Schore, 2014). The resourcing nature of the relationship is examined with reference to modern attachment theory (e.g., Allan Schore), the development of the core related abilities of self-awareness and self-regulation, as well as transference and projective identification phenomena, the resourcing nature of self-disclosure, love and the transpersonal aspect of therapy with its potential for further expansion of awareness. This leads our discussion on to resourcing from the 'shadow' which can bring into awareness hitherto unacknowledged potentials, capacities and strengths, before reflecting on why resourcing in the thinking dimension alone is often not enough.

Chapter 8 turns our attention to trauma as an example of resourcing for complex processes, and shows how effective resourcing can support clients to make the transition from self-protective to more expansive authentic resourcing in different ways; for example, by establishing a 'safe place' and other inner resources, and helping clients increase self-regulation and stress-reduction by learning to down-regulate the amygdala (the threat protect area of the right brain hemisphere) through the use of ritual, and to integrate right–left brain hemispheres, and to be empowered by the healing potential of the therapeutic relationship, and meaning-making.

Chapter 9 reflects on the importance of protecting empathy as a fundamental transformative resource – as a factor 'more highly correlated with outcome than any other variable studied in psychotherapy' (Wampold and Imel, 2015 [2010]: 211). I examine some of the consequences for therapists and therapy when this resource becomes depleted, for example, by looking at factors contributing to empathy fatigue, experiencing trauma through transference, vicarious trauma and therapist burnout. I also consider a novel view of how working with trauma can be beneficial for the therapist before looking at the therapist's own self-awareness and self-regulation, the embodiment of self-care, and establishing equilibrium as aspects in a quaternal self-care cycle. The chapter then reflects on what it means to talk of therapist commitment to therapy.

Finally, you will have already noticed my use of the term 'client' rather than 'patient'. This is to avoid the connotation of sickness that the term 'patient' tends to imply. However, in using the term 'client', I am retaining the meanings often associated with 'patient', namely, the emphasis on the healing aspect of therapy as a wholing activity, in that patients are those who suffer in some way (as the classical root of the word 'patient' denotes) and seek wholeness by coming for treatment. In this sense we are all patients. The term 'patient' locates the activity of therapy firmly within the healer archetype, as does the term 'client' when understood in this way.

References

Horwitz, A. V. and Wakefield, J. C. (2007) *The Loss of Sadness: How Psychiatry Transformed Normal Sorrow into a Depressive Disorder*, Oxford: Oxford University Press.

Lambert, M. J. (1992) 'Implications of Outcome Research for Psychotherapy Integration', in *Handbook of Psychotherapy Integration*, J. C. Norcross and M. R. Goldstein (eds), New York: Basic Books, pp. 94–129.

O'Gorman, F. (2015) *Worrying: A Literary and Cultural History*, London: Bloomsbury.

Schore, A. N. (2014) 'The Right Brain is Dominant in Psychotherapy', *Psychotherapy*, 51(3): 388–397.

Sieff, D. F. (2015) *Understanding and Healing Emotional Trauma: Conversations with Pioneering Clinicians and Researchers*, London and New York: Routledge.

Siegel, D. J. and Solomon, M. (2013) *Healing Moments in Psychotherapy*, New York: W. W. Norton.

Stossel, S. (2014) *My Age of Anxiety*, London: Windmill.

Wampold, B. E. and Imel, Z. E. (2015 [2010]) *The Great Psychotherapy Debate: The Evidence for What Makes Psychotherapy Work*, New York: Routledge.

Watson, G. L., Arcona, A. P., Antonuccio, D. O. and Healy, D. (2014) 'Shooting the Messenger: The Case of ADHD', *Journal of Contemporary Psychotherapy*, 44(3): 43–52.

Chapter 1

Overview of resource focused therapy

Defining 'resource'

The word 'resource' itself is interesting. If we follow a dictionary definition we can say a resource indicates something to increase effectiveness or functionality, and also something to resort to in difficult circumstances. Resources are life enabling strengths, fortitudes, abilities, qualities and capacities. The etymology of the word 'resource' originates in the Old French word 'resourdre' meaning to 'rise anew' or 'spring up again'. If we also think of a resource as a temporarily lost capacity, something the brain knows how to access through millions of years of evolution, then in keeping with its etymological roots we could say 'resource' also means to 're-establish the source' or 're-source'; to connect back to the origin, or re-connect to the brain/mind/body wisdom so the resource can spring up, as if anew. Christoph Flückiger and Martin Grosse Holtforth (2008), in writing about resource activation, present a way to use clients' own strengths in therapy to increase well-being. This view suggests the activation of something known then forgotten, taken-for-granted, neglected, hidden by modesty, not recognised or innate; *inner resources*. To put emphasis on inner capacities, including innate strengths, takes the focus away from problem-solving, 'fixing' or 'prescribing' resources to clients (e.g., as in some solution-focused approaches) which often fail to acknowledge the pre-existing resources utilised by clients before engaging in therapy. Rather, in my view, effective therapy first seeks to discern inner resources already available to clients, before seeking to collaboratively cultivate resources in other ways. Examples of inner resources include the ability to ease worry or anxiety, to avoid rumination, and to activate a range of positive feelings (e.g., joy, enthusiasm, contentment, optimism).

The term 'resource' also refers to engaging with something *outer* to increase functionality and effectiveness. Examples of outer resources include going on retreat, enjoying a quiet day, spending time in nature, meeting with a friend or sitting with a therapist. These resources can support the development and maintenance of capacities across the dimensions of human experience (e.g., thinking, emotional, physical, interpersonal, spiritual), increase well-being in these dimensions, and potentially enable the realisation of our fullest aspirations in life. This may even include the activation of exceptional human experiences (Palmer and Hastings, 2013) and non-ordinary states of consciousness (Grof, 2012; Garcia-Romeu and Tart, 2013). While these are rare occurrences, such possibilities point to the extraordinary range of experiencing. So, for example, in this sense the practice of meditation is a resource to gain greater mastery for self-regulating thoughts (thinking dimension) and feelings (feeling dimension) and increase spiritual awareness (spiritual dimension).

The engagement with both *inner* and *outer* resources is necessary then for effective change and to enable clients to reach their goals through therapy – whatever they may be in terms of potential.

Areas of resource focus in therapy

Yet while the term 'resource' may be relatively easy to define, therapists will not always agree on which areas to resource in therapy. Views are likely to depend on therapeutic orientation and firm ideas and beliefs about the aims of therapy. For instance, these include such broad aims as to transform suffering, reduce distress, support the emergence of identity, facilitate and enable self-actualisation (Abraham Maslow and Carl Rogers) or individuation (Carl Jung), engage in meaning-making, support decision-making, reduce depression and anxiety, work through trauma (Chapter 8), or more generally increase satisfaction in life. Others support the view that therapy aims to strengthen ego and to minimise a propensity for ego-depletion. William Goldstein (1993: 173), for example, suggests such an aim increases at least a number of relative strengths: 'the relative intactness of reality testing; the relative intactness of thought processes; the relative intactness of interpersonal relations; the relative intactness of the adaptation to reality'. In brief, such a focus aims to support the relatively stable part of consciousness (ego) to achieve greater buoyancy and to increase secure relationships in life, and therefore place emphasis largely on the thinking (cognitive left brain thinking), feeling, and interpersonal dimensions. A similar aim is offered in Samuel Rubin's (1986) 'ego-focused psychotherapy' which seeks to reduce guilt and to constructively satisfy drives (e.g., control impulses, release of anger) in order to strengthen ego functions, thus focusing primarily on the thinking and feeling dimensions. Yet there is no consensus amongst therapists as to what the term 'ego-strength' actually means (Bjorklund, 2000; Ando, 2009; Hagger, Wood, and Stiff, 2010).

Alternatively, if we take the view of ego as a *process* rather than a *structure* we avoid the thorny issue of trying to figure out what it is about ego that requires strengthening, given the mutable and variable nature suggested by the word 'process'. Also to understand *ego-process* as requiring *resourcing* rather than strengthening does away with the term 'ego-strength' altogether. In this view resourcing supports ego-*process* rather than ego-*strength*, as there may be nothing to strengthen; no structure, nothing fixed or static. Yet resourcing ego-process *does* include strength but embraces this within a wider capacity-making frame. This allows a view that moves away from the polarisation and judgement implied by the term 'ego-strength', such as in 'strong ego' and 'weak ego', and helps to soften the idea of an ego that requires propping up, in favour of a more fluid and expanding-contracting part of identity. So we can play with the idea of bracketing the concept 'ego-strength' without letting go of strength capacity. Further, while resources may be abundant, scarce, or insufficient, there is no judgement implied in describing a resource as either 'weak' or 'strong'. We therefore avoid evaluating ego in critical terms and look to the resilience found in the experience of strength itself. In addition, to overly preoccupy oneself with ego-strengthening mistakenly lays full weight on only one part of consciousness; one part of identity. My focus on the dimensions and depth or 'soul' in this book aims to broaden the view of what identity is.

Resourcing, then, aims to identify and increase 'both (a) primarily consciously accessible *ego resources* for constructive ways to relate to others and to tasks and (b) generally non-consciously accessible *self-capacities* to maintain a cohesive sense of self, identity, and self-regulation' (Leeds, 2009: 152). Here the term 'self-capacities' is viewed differently from ego resource in that self-capacities 'allow the individual to maintain a consistent sense of identity and positive self-esteem' (Kohut quoted in Leeds, 2009: 152), whereas ego-resources include 'conscious abilities which are used to relate to the world outside oneself, including other people and tasks, in a constructive way' (McCann and Pearlman quoted in Leeds, 2009: 152). In this way developing and maintaining resources strengthens intrapersonal and interpersonal capacities and abilities. Another way of putting this is to talk about the surface and ground of identity, with ego as the surface and self as the ground, albeit the meanings of these concepts differ and comparisons are not always useful. Therefore, in summary, the aims of therapy are various, and what is meant by the term 'ego-strength' cannot be agreed upon. However, if we think in terms of 'ego-process' rather than 'ego-strength' we may resolve a number of issues, without abandoning strength. We can also dispense with polarising and judgemental language altogether as not being conducive to holistic thinking.

Thus far I generally agree with Flückiger and Grosse Holtforth's (2008) position which supports resource activation of clients' strengths, but I differ from these authors in that my own focus on the dimensions of human experiencing offers more than merely avenues for *inner* strength building. My interest lies in developing in-built, innate, hidden, *in potentia*, under-developed capacities in these dimensions, as well as known or half-forgotten capacities, including intrinsic strength and wisdom. This takes the focus away from a preoccupation with inner or intrapersonal (we even might say a narcissistic over preoccupation with ego) to include interpersonal and transpersonal perspectives.

On this point, other practitioners and theorists locate the aim of therapy within a larger explorative context of nonegoic influences, for instance

Sigmund Freud's id, or Carl Jung's view that reality consists of both personal and collective unconscious processes (beyond the personal and boundless) accessible to the individual, and that the field of consciousness has no limits (Jung, 1981 [1959], para. 2), whilst transpersonal psychology also locates egoic processes within a larger consciousness perspective. Therapists in this field aim to widen awareness and expand the perceived limits of the field of con-sciousness (e.g., Rowan, 2005 [1993]; Walsh and Vaughan, 1993; Friedman, 2013), and view ego consciousness as a fragment of psyche as a whole, and a key, but not sole, focus for therapy. From this perspective, therapy also offers the opportunity to look beyond ego-strength and ego function to explore ways to live more contemplatively, and to trust and be guided more by latent creative capacities and depths of psyche. This can mean to engage with whatever might lie below the surface of ordinary awareness and existence, with what might be called 'soul', and to live more fully with the content arising from these depths, and even to discern the nature of consciousness itself. Here the focus is on resource-making that supports both egoic development as well as the spiritual, imaginal, and energetic dimensions of human experience. I am suggesting, then, that effective resource focused therapy relies on therapists' training(s), professional interest, and practical experience, as well as the openness of clients to actively engage in resource-making while engaging with the full range of the dimensions to do this. It is unfortunate that in some instances, exploration into areas such as the spiritual, imaginal, and energetic dimensions is seldom given adequate credence as having therapeutic value. But a certain deficiency and lop-sidedness of personhood are often the result of neglect in these and other areas.

So, resource focused therapy not only aims to support clients to develop and cultivate *inner* and *outer* resources, it also aims to help clients self-resource the whole brain/mind/body neurobiological and neurophysiological systems as well as the full spectrum of intrapersonal, interpersonal, and transpersonal dimensions of human experiencing as this relates to this whole, thereby widening identity and the parameters of possibility. This may be familiar, but less so may be the idea of *developing each dimension of human experiencing in its own right*. This theme will be developed more fully in Chapter 4.

Vignette: Avril

During the most difficult time in her life when she was battling with the same illness from which her mother died a few years earlier, Avril (aged fifty-four) found ways of not only 'getting through' from day to day, but also 'life enabling practices and processes' to remind her of what was important when things in life were beginning to fall apart. Perhaps the most significant of these processes was to continue in therapy; to allow herself space to talk, to grieve, and to prepare for her own death. Alongside this, Avril found strength in simple things like sitting in her cottage garden, sometimes for a few minutes at night while gazing up at the moon. Frequently, the evening song of the blackbird found its resonance deep within her. Also, morning walks, evening walks, tea with friends, and long periods of quiet contemplation were some of Avril's resourcing 'practices and processes'. When telling me about these in therapy I would often notice how, quite naturally on the in-breath, she would breathe these experiences in, allowing them to drop down into a place deep inside her. Subtly at first, then with increasing vigour, but still subtly. 'Yes', I said, 'keep breathing it all in. These experiences are a part of you' (while I pondered about the amazing capacity many people have to find resources in difficult times).

Literature review of resource focus in therapies

Literature on resource focused approaches to therapy highlights many orientations and themes. In ordering these into seven categories, I acknowledge they are somewhat arbitrary divisions – given the significant overlaps on focus between modalities. Presenting the therapies in this way helps map their general focus areas, and gives a view of similarities, differences, and specialisms:

1   Where the focus relates to specific conditions, such as working with trauma and emotional and relational trauma (e.g., Levine, 1997; Rothschild, 2000; Ogden, Minton and Pain, 2006; Leeds, 2009; Levine, 2010; Heller and LaPierre, 2012; Grand, 2013; Ogden and Fisher, 2013), with cancer clients (e.g., Diegelmann and Isermann, 2006), with depression (e.g., Williams, 2007), anxiety (e.g., Levy Berg, Sandell and Sandahl, 2009; Flückiger et al., 2014), panic, grief, addiction, a range of symptoms as in symptom focused psychotherapy (e.g., Connors, 2010), personality disorders (e.g., Yeomans, Levy and Caligor, 2013), psychosis, and so on.
2   Where the focus aims to support ego-strength (Rubin, 1986), and strength activation (Flückiger and Holtforth, 2008; Flückiger et al., 2010).
3   Where the focus aims to resource clients *via* the dimensions such as in emotion focused therapy (Greenberg, 2014), affect-focused psychotherapy (Dornelas et al., 2010), affect focused body psychotherapy (Levy Berg, Sandell and Sandahl, 2009), spirituality focused interventions (Bowland, Edmond and Fallot, 2012), psychoanalytic energy therapy (Mollon, 2008), and cognitive-behavioural therapy.
4   Where the focus aims to increase particular attitudes such as in hope focused therapy (Larsen and Stege, 2010a, 2010b).
5   Where the focus is mindfulness-based such as in Compassion Focused Therapy (Gilbert, 2010), Mindfulness-Based Cognitive Therapy (MBCT) and the Buddhist orientated Core Process Psychotherapy (Sills, 2009), Acceptance and Commitment Therapy (Hayes, Strosahl and Wilson, 2011 [2003]), and mindfulness-based practices across therapeutic approaches (e.g., Germer, Siegel and Fulton, 2013; Pollak, Pedulla and Siegel, 2014).

6   Where the focus aims to support functionality such as in job focused
     therapy (Riordan and Kahnweiler, 1995), solution focused (de Shazer,
     2007), and narrative and solution-focused approaches (Chang and
     Nylund, 2013).
7   Where the focus is on working with family systems (Ray and Keeney,
     1993).

From these categories, we find the therapeutic focus is usefully applied to
specific areas (e.g., ego-strength and functioning, trauma), but not necessarily
in ways to encompass the whole dimension spectrum put forward by my
thesis (Chapter 4). I offer this as an observation rather than a critique of
therapies which confine therapy to only a few dimensions, (e.g., thinking and
behavioural dimensions in CBT), and acknowledge the value of these therapies
as often necessary for effective change (there is also reference in Chapter 3 to
the limitations of left brain cognitive focus in therapy). My suggestion is that
it is beneficial to simultaneously draw upon multiple dimensions to increase
therapeutic benefit.

Traditionally, resourcing in therapy was intrinsically linked to the process
and outcome of what goes on in the therapeutic relationship. While this
remains crucially the case, since the 1960s (if not earlier) therapists increasingly
turned their attention toward the clients' role in therapy, and finding that
effective therapy supports clients to self-resource. Eugene Gendlin (1969)
offers a prime example of this in his focusing-orientated approach to therapy
in which he invites clients to trust their introspective processes and pay particular
attention to felt-sense phenomena as self-guiding wisdom. Clients thereby
open themselves to the 'great bodily resource'; he also viewed 'openness' as a
significant resource by the cultivation of openness to bodily felt experience in
the here-and-now (Gendlin, 1981). While emphasis on the felt-sense is a primary
route of enquiry in many humanistic therapies (e.g., person-centred, transpersonal) this emphasis is now found in the analytic therapies (e.g., Mollon,
2008) and Art Psychotherapy (Rappaport, 2008), and characterises many
Buddhist orientated and mindfulness-based approaches (e.g., Core Process
Psychotherapy). Clients' capacity to pay attention to felt-sense phenomena
helps further self-understanding of the organic movement of the selving-process,
as well as develop an ability to self-regulate difficult felt-sense experiences
such as when processing trauma (Chapter 8).

Partly as a result of the increasing emphasis on evidence based practice, the
past two decades have witnessed a growth in interest in the relationship
between the brain/mind/body's self-regulating capacities and psychotherapy,
and with this, an interest in the dialogue between neuroscience and therapy (e.g.,
Corrigall and Wilkinson, 2003). This dialogue continues to gain momentum as
indicated by a growing volume of papers and texts emerging from academic
institutions and elsewhere on this subject. I am particularly interested in and
enthusiastic about how therapy can usefully bring together developments in our

understanding of the correlation between brain, mind and body, and take the view that therapy is largely a relational and embodied-felt-sense activity.

The emergent traditions of brain/mind/body psychotherapies include Eye Movement Desensitisation and Reprocessing (EMDR), Sensory Experiencing (SE), Brainspotting (BSP), Comprehensive Resource Model (CRM), Sensorimotor Psychotherapy, Somatic Trauma Therapy, Neuro Affective Relational Model (NARM), and the Energy Psychology umbrella of therapies perhaps most notably Psychoanalytic Energy Psychotherapy (PEP). These approaches were primarily developed to work through negative experiences and trauma, and also to support the 'greening' or stabilising of brain/mind/body functions and processes. These are the regulatory functions in the brain, namely, the avoid-threat system in the brain stem, the 'curiosity-interest-expectancy' system (Turnbull, 2003: 141) in the mid-brain, and the attaching system in the modern brain. Within this context the idea of 'greening' follows Rick Hanson (2009, 2013) who coined the term to mean the ability to relax these regulating systems when they become 'reddened' through excessive activation; fostering responsive rather than reactive behaviours. For example, fear is the activation or 'reddening' of the avoid-threat system and relaxation is the responsive or 'greening' state of this system.

The wider context of resourcing

Resource focused therapy supports clients to build resources in a context of a number of positive or negative influences from relationships, work life, gender and sexuality, dis(ability), religion, race, and other factors. Naturally, influences often extend beyond obvious immediate self-concern to include equally impactful influences, such as concern about the environment, poverty, persecution, terrorism, and the threat of war; concern about others and the Other. Resource focused therapy must take these factors into account by enabling clients to develop resources to self-support when negative influences (actual or construed) feel pressing.

We are not immune from the influences of being part of a coinfluencing whole. For example, something that happens across *there* can be felt *here*, regardless of distance. Of course, the converse is also true. David Abram (2010: 63; my emphasis) helps further our understanding of this coinfluencing picture when he writes: 'We can sense the world around us only because we are entirely a part of this world – by virtue of our carnal density and dynamism – we are wholly *embedded* in the depths of the earthly sensuous.' Also, 'Sentience was never our private possession. We live *immersed* in intelligence, enveloped and informed by a creativity we cannot fathom.' Immediately, we find ourselves thrown into a coinfluencing participatory view of reality (cf. Ferrer, 2000, 2002; Adams, 2010) where nothing occurs without the impact or influence of this on something or someone else. For instance, a change in attitude towards someone can often be felt by that person, or even by others.

Therefore, the focus of therapy is not only resourcing clients but also, indirectly, resourcing the immediate context in which the person lives as well as the wider context, over there – those potentially far-reaching ripples set in motion by bringing empathic attention to clients. The part cannot be separated from the whole; and the benefit of therapy then potentially becomes of benefit to wider circles (Martin Heidegger cited in Levin, 1985: 17). We might emphasise this point with reference to David Michael Levin (1985: 289) who notes 'the earth ... is the source of our individuation, since it let us stand becoming ourselves'. This puts the task of resourcing firmly on the ground, even embedded in the living earth. The benefit of resourcing extends beyond the individual to others, and may (for some) even include the Earth itself. Furthermore, I suggest the effective task of therapy focuses on the part as it relates to the whole, and holds in pointed awareness this fact in a participatory coinfluencing reality. This crucial point makes most sense when we root our identity in being in some way inseparable from the whole and less confined to only egoic existence. The dimensions, I propose, are primary routes of connection to a groundedness in the whole, a view which does not separate the person from a wider context. Given the mutuality of resource-making, the lives of both clients and therapists are subject to influence in the consulting room.

Resourcing the brain/mind/body's emotional systems

Though often regarded by neuroscience as simplistic, Paul MacLean (cited in Holden, 1979) put forward the widely acknowledged view, as mentioned above, that there are three major affect regulating systems in the brain. These are often referred to as the *avoid-threat self-protect system*, the *resource or achieving seeking system*, and the *attachment seeking system*. By understanding the ways in which these affect regulating systems correlate with different experiences, we are potentially able to respond more directly to these areas, and resource them, as in trauma therapies. For example, fear is activated by the avoid-threat self-protect system in the brain stem when the feeling of threat and of not feeling safe has arisen. Bringing psychophysiological and psychotherapeutic understandings to this activation can ultimately facilitate the regulation of fear when it arises in clients, through the supportive and enabling space in the therapeutic relationship (Chapter 7). My suggestion is that this can effectively happen by engaging multiple dimensions, and through education (Chapter 6). So, for example, alongside sensitive therapeutic exploration of fear, experiences of worry, anxiety and panic can be regulated by cultivating feelings of safety; the feeling dimension. We could also draw upon the imaginal dimension to evoke a picture of safety, or imagine breathing into areas of activation with the aim of relaxing these, as well as inducing an embodied felt experience of this through the windows of the five senses in the physical dimension. And further, because fear often arises in relation to others, cultivating safety in the interpersonal dimension through the therapeutic relationship opens up further possibilities for resource-making, especially where the activation of unmanageable amounts of fear, worry and anxiety originates in trauma. The more dimensions we are able to access to generate this experience of safety the more effective the resource-making activity becomes (Chapter 8; embodied imagery, Appendix).

The resource or achievement seeking system, in the mid-brain (which includes the limbic system) seeks contentment, and is sensitive to experiences of failure, while the attachment seeking system rooted into the neocortex seeks secure belonging, and is susceptible to experiences of rejection. As is well documented (e.g., Gilbert, 2009, 2010), the three affect regulation systems interact. Vulnerability in one system potentially creates vulnerability in others, while resilience in one system also influences others.

Vignette: Robert

> The fear of loss was always present in therapy, but Robert (aged thirty-eight) found it difficult to allow this feeling in. It was easier to talk 'about it', rather than to dip into it and experience it. This was quite understandable, as it was difficult to face the fear of his sexuality; especially for a man in a loving relationship with a woman, with twins coming up to their fifth birthday. We both needed to wait. Over the months Robert spoke about many things, both good and bad, both easy and difficult, while knowingly avoiding the fear of loss. It was only when the news of the 7/7 bombing in London in 2005 broke on the Thursday of Robert's appointment that he finally wept. First for 'them', but then for himself, his wife and daughters. It was as if it took some awful event to allow Robert to open up and more fully explore his sexuality. It was as if 7/7 was a 'dark resource' which enabled Robert to finally let go, supported by the resourcing experience of being in the therapeutic relationship.

Dimensions of human experiencing

Following this overview of some of the resource focus areas in therapy, we now come to consider further what I mean by the term 'dimension'. I will argue that the specific exploration of these dimensions reveals their potential for therapy and how they are worthy of being resourced as areas of growth in their own right, and how conjointly they can influence personal development and transformation. And so we come now to look briefly at the multiple dimensions of human experience through which effective resourcing can be harnessed (see Chapter 4 for more detailed discussion).

The concept 'dimensions of human experience' arises out of research into Integral Transformation Programmes (ITP), sometimes referred to as Integral Experiential Learning (IEL), and began with Michael Murphy (1992), George Leonard and Michael Murphy (1995), in Esalen, Big Sur, California, in the 1960s as part of the emergent Human Potential Movement. Based on the assumption 'we live only part of the life we are given' (Murphy, 1992: 3),

ITP engaged the individual in a range of potentially transformative dimension-related practices (e.g., in the thinking, emotional, physical, energetic, etc., dimensions). These practices brought further development of these dimensions, and evoked a fuller embodied life experience (Amiras, 2008). The view was that by simultaneously developing these dimensions one area would positively impact on the other.

Taken a step further, and in the context of our earlier discussion on the wide spectrum of consciousness, Ken Wilber (2000: 39) asserts how ITP facilitates 'nondual enlightenment' or 'nondual One Taste' experiences, that is, experiences of nonseparation from the participatory resourcing whole of reality. ITP make us more prone to the 'accident' of enlightenment, as well as a variety of other spiritual states and experiences (Wilber, 2000: 39; cf. Ferrer, 2003). Here the term 'enlightenment' means awakening to the nature of reality; knowing things *just as they are*. It is as if we experience life from a holistic right brain perspective, which sees no separation or divisions between things. Within this view, therefore, 'the more dimensions of the human bodymind [or brain/mind/body] that are exercised, then the more transparent to the Divine [or Mystery] they become, and thus the more accident prone the individual is' (Wilber, 2000: 39) to experiences of non-separation from the resourcing whole.

Wilber (2000: 39; my emphasis) further points out that 'The idea of ITP is simple, [in that you] pick at least one practice from each [dimension] and practise them concurrently. The more dimensions you practise, the more *effective* they all become, the more you become one big accident-prone soul.' This appears to reinforce the view that development of the parts affects development of the whole, and *vice versa*, and supports an aim of resource focused therapy to increase effectiveness and integration of the dimensions as modalities of experience. The popularity and effectiveness of ITP has given rise to a range of similar programmes, for instance, Jorge Ferrer's (2003) participatory perspective and his emphasis on integral growth, Frederic Luskin's (2004) transformative practices for integrating brain/mind/body, as well as deliberations from Ferrer and colleagues (2004, 2005, 2006) on embodied participation in Mystery and integral transformative education. Thus the effectiveness of integrating practices is well documented. It is worth noting that I am in agreement with Ferrer's (2014: 168) view that 'the mystery [or source of all] cocreatively unfolds in multiple ontological directions' rather than in 'objectifiable pregiven attributes (e.g., personal, impersonal, dual, or nondual)'. This means that there is no limit to the modes of expression of Mystery.

While resourcing in therapy does not set out to facilitate 'One Taste', non-dual, or other exceptional human experiences, I emphasise the value gained from resourcing the full range of the dimensions of human experience, and view this as developing a wide scope of resource-making pathways, even if (or especially if) this enables the person in ways beyond the agreed goals of therapy. To this end I am suggesting eight dimensions of human experience as modalities for resource-making: thinking, feeling, physical, behavioural, interpersonal, spiritual, imaginal and energetic. The more we develop the dimensions the more available these become as resource pathways for healing. Further integration of the person is likely to follow on from this.

Potency in having positive experiences

Fundamental to the process of resourcing are the untold and obvious benefits gained by having positive experiences. This fact is largely built upon a single premise: *the development of neurostructure is experience dependent*. As Jeffrey Kleim and Theresa Jones (2008: 225) point out, 'the adaptive capacity of the central nervous system (*plasticity*)' is supported by a burgeoning amount of evidence (e.g., May, 2011; Fields, 2013; Lovden et al., 2013; Scaer, 2014 [2001]) which 'strongly suggest[s] that neurons, among other brain cells, possess the remarkable ability to alter their structure and function in response to a variety of internal and external pressures'. As Hanson (2009) notes, if we change the mind we change the brain, and if we change the brain we change the mind, which then changes the brain, and so on. The brain/mind/body is a coinfluencing system. For instance, regular relaxation increases activity of genes that reduce stress reactions. Findings suggest the benefits of training the physical dimension positively influence other dimensions, as will be considered in the following chapters. For the moment, suffice to say neuroscience offers principles supported by numerous studies which suggest neuroplasticity of the brain occurs in at least the following ways; I include here the most relevant to our discussion:

Neurons that fire together, wire together: Donald Hebb (2009 [1949]) discovered that neurons that fire together, wire together. In other words, Bessel van der Kolk (2014: 56) informs us, 'When a circuit fires repeatedly, it can [most likely] become a default setting.'

Use it or lose it: It follows on from the last principle that 'the brain is formed in a "use-dependent manner"' (van der Kolk, 2014: 56; cf. Hanson, 2009, 2013) and that 'neural circuits not actively engaged in task performance for an extended period of time begin to degrade' (Kleim and Jones, 2008: 227). For instance, a study of London taxi drivers found an increase in the size of the posterior hippocampi in the medial temporal lobe of the brain of drivers who acquired 'The Knowledge' (Woollett and Maguire, 2011). I infer from this that to cultivate positive experiences in therapy also positively influences the brain, such as through therapeutic resonance or significant moments of meeting (i.e., feeling and interpersonal dimensions).

Use it or improve it: This principle asserts 'plasticity can be induced within specific brain regions through extended training' (Kleim and Jones, 2008: 228). In their review of studies on plasticity Kleim and Jones point out there was 'profound plasticity within the cerebral cortex' (p. 228) following skills training in people with brain damage (cf. Green and Bavelier, 2008). I infer from this a similar influence is achieved in therapy, again through cultivation of positive experiences, especially through the empathic quality of the therapeutic relationship, and also through increased self-regulation. For instance, Katie Witkiewitz and colleagues (2013) suggest mindfulness training increases the capacity to self-regulate in people with substance abuse addictions, who were particularly vulnerable to relapse during periods of craving and the rise of negative affect. Hence we can change the brain by changing the mind, and so on.

Regulation: As Allan Schore (2003: 27) points out, all psychotherapies demonstrate similar aims to increase affect regulation in clients through the experience of being in the therapeutic relationship, with the therapist's resonance being significant as an affect regulatory force in this (Chapter 7); while self-regulation develops with the increase of self-awareness from the frequent contemplative feel of therapy. The regulation principle is also of particular importance to help clients regulate negative feelings such as those associated with trauma (Chapter 8).

Specificity: This principle demonstrates that 'learning-induced brain changes also show regional specificity', therefore 'specific forms of neural plasticity and concomitant behavioural changes are dependent upon specific kinds of experience' (Kleim and Jones, 2008: 229). Particular types of experience like empathy, and the experience of self-compassion (Neff, 2008) and mindfulness (Pollak, Pedulla and Siegel, 2014) positively affect different regions of the brain. Following the work of Hanson (2013), to cultivate positive experiences targeted to specific functions of brain regions increases capacity in these regions, so that for instance, cultivating the experience of peace can develop relaxation of the avoid-threat activating system, while cultivating the experience of satisfaction can placate 'reddening' of the achievement seeking system, and the experience of feeling cared for can develop 'greening' of the attachment seeking system.

Repetition: This principle relates to the importance of repetition, for example in the behaviour dimension, to increase the likelihood of inducing lasting neural changes (Kleim and Jones, 2008: 229). Also, repetition of immersion in the healing experience of being in a therapeutic relationship (feeling and interpersonal dimensions).

Intensity: This principle supports the previous principle in that often intense activity can positively increase plasticity (Kleim and Jones, 2008: 230) as, for example, being in once-weekly or more than once-weekly open-ended therapy.

Time: This principle reminds us of the value of the accumulative effects of the process of learning through time rather than as a result of a single event as bringing about stable consolidation of wanted change (Kleim and Jones, 2008: 230). For instance, if you were to allow your mind to rest on the knowledge of good events, situations and experiences, good intentions and qualities, 'then over *time* your brain will take a different shape, one with strength and resilience hardwired into it, as well as a realistically optimistic outlook, a positive mood, and a sense of worth' (Hanson, 2013: 12; my emphasis).

Transference: This principle supports my view of the coinfluencing nature of resourcing *via* the dimensions and brain functions in the therapeutic relationship, and affirms the fact of the holistic functioning of the brain where benefits in one region can be of benefit in others (Kleim and Jones, 2008: 232). For instance, relaxing the avoid-threat system can result in relaxing other regions of the brain.

Vignette: Rosemary

> A lack of confidence in 'most things' was what brought Rosemary (aged forty-eight) to therapy. This 'I'm far from adequate' feeling was particularly persistent right through her education and beyond post-graduate study, through her professional doctorate and into her working life. 'More than forty years of lacking in confidence.' Gradually (as if there were a quicker way) the stories giving rise to this began to emerge: 'critical father', 'semi-critical mother', 'both academics', 'the absence of praise', 'grazing my knees in the ice skating rink in full view of everyone at the age of eight', and so on. Eventually, within the contemplative feel of therapy, we were both able to notice other experiences coming into the room that sat alongside the negative: 'the joy of skiing in the Dachstein, in the Austrian Alps, during my gap year', 'the good friends who encourage me in my writing', 'the pleasure of camping in wild places', and so on. One by one, over many months, these positive experiences came to the fore. One by one, Rosemary was able to cultivate the felt-sense embodied experience of these memories, by allowing them to 'live' inside her, while at the same time returning to the feeling quality of these memories at random times outside therapy. Then gradually we were both able to welcome the growth of confidence.

Effective therapy resources: the therapeutic dyad

Re-sourcing or resource-making in therapy sits within the facilitative environment provided by the therapeutic relationship especially when characterised by qualities like empathic attunement, resonance, 'relational depth' and 'moments of meeting'. The resourcing nature of the therapeutic relationship, in particular the distinctive quality of the empathically attuned relational field, will be considered in Chapter 7, but I touch upon it briefly here as the principal resourcing container and facilitator for transformation. Attunement is a deep and sustained resonance arising from the therapist's conscious and unconscious felt-sense alliance with clients. As Schore (2003: 33; my emphasis) points out, 'in order to create an optimal working alliance, the therapist must access, in a timely fashion, both her own subjective, unconscious, *intuitive*, implicit responses, as well as her objective conscious, rational, theory-based explicit knowledge in the work'. Here I take intuition to mean 'the subjective experience as associated with the use of knowledge gained through implicit learning' (Liberman cited in Schore, 2003: 38), perhaps through an embodied felt sense of something or gut feeling. This description of attunement is similar to the constituent elements of what Sue Wiggins and colleagues (2012: 151) term meeting at 'relational depth'. In particular, aspects associated with significant relational experiences such as 'love, connectedness and respect', as well as 'experiences of transcendence [which] appear to constitute a specific component of relational depth, labelled by informants as "spiritual" and "magical"', or the spiritual dimension. This suggests relational depth encounters can include experiences that go beyond everyday therapeutic encounters, thereby momentarily connecting to the resourcing whole. The therapeutic relationship defined by these qualities becomes a resourcing experience. As Schore (2003: 38; my emphasis) argues, such qualities 'can act as an interactive affect regulating context that optimises the growth of two "minds in the making", that is, increases in complexity in *both our patient's and the therapist's* continually developing unconscious right minds'. Here is an example of how resourcing is 'mostly', but not exclusively, for clients. Also this quality of relating strengthens right brain functions more than left brain functions, such as the limbic system and both the sympathetic and parasympathetic branches of the autonomic nervous system, as these are more connected to the right brain. Development of these brain areas results in an increased capacity to cope with stress, and deepens empathy, as well as increases clients' capacity to self-attune and offer self-empathy. However, it should also be remembered that therapy is a whole brain activity and not just a right brain one.

To return to our 'coinfluencing' theme from earlier, I follow Abram (2010: 272) in that 'it is only by turning our bodily attention toward *another* that we experience the convergence and reassembly of our separate senses into a dynamic unity', suggesting further that 'the sensing body is like an open circuit that completes itself only in things, in others, in the surrounding earth'; again serving integration. A fundamental pathway for resourcing is through relationship in its widest sense. Relationship-making is engagement with a consequential aim to make a positive difference to oneself as well as to the life of another. Thus, in effect, resourcing through relationship benefits both people in the encounter *via* a number of dimensions, especially through the quality of attuned resonance in the feeling and interpersonal dimensions. Schore (2003: 32) further reminds us of a crucial role resonance plays in the therapy when he writes:

> a state of resonance exists when the therapist's subjectivity is empathically attuned to the patient's inner state, one that may be unconscious to the patient, and this *resonance* then interactively amplifies, in both intensity and duration, the affective state *in both members of the dyad.*

Here, again, benefit is 'mostly' but not exclusively for clients. Processes of this kind are often viewed as 'moments of meeting' (Knox and Cooper, 2010) where both client and therapist are mutually attuned (Sander cited in Schore, 2003: 32), often unconsciously (Loewald cited in Schore, 2003: 32). Writing on deep empathy Tobin Hart (2000: 266) quotes Parker Palmer who describes the '*impulse toward deep contact* – to know and be known' which often leads to 'falling deeply into the scene' (p. 258).

While clients are the focus of resourcing in therapy, not the therapist, an outcome or consequence of therapy is that the therapist is also resourced (Chapter 9); therapy resources the whole in this mutually resourcing dynamic (Chapter 5).

Concluding thoughts

This chapter has provided an overview of integrative resource focused therapy. By widening the context within which we understand clients we become aware of the range of influences on the person; potentially both positive and negative. This overview of resource focus in therapies presents a picture of the range of resource focused practices and focus areas, and highlights how increased awareness of the dimensions of human experience and the brain's affect regulating systems can broaden the scope of resourcing in therapy. Resource focused practice supports the 'greening' of all regions of the brain *via* the eight dimensions of experience, helped by the cultivation of positive experiences, and an awareness of related brain functions and processes. The dimensions are pathways to strengthen brain/mind/body as integrated operating systems. Above all, the therapeutic relationship is the context within which resourcing occurs; where two people come together with the intent on 'mostly' resourcing the one.

References

Abram, D. (2010) *Becoming Animal: An Earthly Cosmology*, New York: Pantheon Books.

Adams, W. W. (2010) 'Nature's Participatory Psyche: A Study of Consciousness in the Shared Earth Community', *Humanistic Psychologist*, 38(1): 15–39.

Amiras, M. Z. (2008) 'Experience Beyond Belief: The "Strangeness Curve" and Integral Transformative Practice', *Social Analysis*, 52(1): 127–143.

Ando, O. (2009) 'Psychotherapy and Buddhism: A Psychological Consideration of Key Points of Contact', in *Self and No-Self: Continuing the Dialogue Between Buddhism and Psychotherapy*, D. Mathers, M. E. Miller and O. Ando (eds), London: Routledge, pp. 8–18.

Bjorklund, P. (2000) 'Assessing Ego Strength: Spinning Straw into Gold', *Perspectives in Psychiatric Care*, 36(1): 14–23.

Bowland, S., Edmond, T. and Fallot, R. (2012) 'Evaluation of a Spiritually Focused Intervention with Older Trauma Survivors', *Social Work*, 57(1): 73–82.

Chang, J. and Nylund, D. (2013) 'Narrative and Solution-Focused Therapies: A Twenty-Year Retrospective', *Journal of Systemic Therapies*, 32(2): 72–88.

Connors, M. E. (2010) 'Symptom-Focused Dynamic Psychotherapy', *Journal of Psychotherapy Integration*, 20(1): 37–45.

Corrigall, J. and Wilkinson, H. (eds) (2003) *Revolutionary Connections: Psychotherapy and Neuroscience*, London: Karnac.

de Shazer, S. (2007) *More Than Miracles: The State of the Art of Solution-Focused Brief Therapy*, London: Routledge.

Diegelmann, C. and Isermann, M. (2006) 'Resource-Focused Psychotherapy for Cancer Patients', *Psycho-Oncology*, 15(2): 9–20.

Dornelas, E., Ferrand, J., Stepnowski, R., Barbagallo, J. and McCullough, L. (2010) 'A Pilot Study of Affect-Focused Psychotherapy for Antepartum Depression', *Journal of Psychotherapy Integration*, 20(4): 364–382.

Ferrer, J. N. (2000) 'Transpersonal Knowing: A Participatory Approach to Transpersonal Phenomena', in *Transpersonal Knowing: Exploring the Horizon of Consciousness*, T. Hart, P. L. Neilson and K. Puhakka, (eds), New York: SUNY, pp. 213–252.

Ferrer, J. N. (2002) *Revisioning Transpersonal Theory: A Participatory Approach to Human Spirituality*, New York: SUNY.

Ferrer, J. N. (2003) 'Integral Transformative Practice: A Participatory Perspective', *Journal of Transpersonal Psychology*, 35(1): 21–42.

Ferrer, J. N. (2014) 'Transpersonal Psychology, Science, and the Supernatural', *The Journal of Transpersonal Psychology*, 46(2): 152–186.

Ferrer, J. N., Albareda, R. V. and Romero, M. T. (2004) 'Embodied Participation in Mystery', *ReVision*, 27(1): 10–17.

Ferrer, J. N., Romero, M. T. and Albareda, R. V. (2005) 'Integral Transformative Education', *Journal of Transformative Education*, 3(4): 306–330.

Ferrer, J., Romero, M. and Albareda, R. (2006) 'The Four Seasons of Integral Education: A Participatory Proposal', *ReVision*, 29(2): 11–23.

Fields, R. D. (2013) 'Changes in Brain Structure During Learning: Fact or Artifact? Reply to Thomas and Baker', *NeuroImage*, 73 (June): 260–264.

Flückiger, C. and Grosse Holtforth, M. (2008) 'Focusing the Therapist's Attention on the Patient's Strengths: A Preliminary Study to Foster a Mechanism of Change in Outpatient Psychotherapy', *Journal of Clinical Psychology*, 64(7): 876–890.

Flückiger, C., Wusten, G., Zinbarg, R. E. and Wampold, B. E. (2010) *Resource Activation: Using Clients' Own Strengths in Psychotherapy and Counselling*, Gottingen, Germany: Hogrefe Publishing.

Flückiger, C., Zinbarg, R., Znoj, H. and Ackert, M. (2014) 'Resource Activation in Generalized Anxiety – An Observer-Based Microprocess Analysis of Patients' In-Session Outcomes', *Psychotherapy*, 51(4): 535–545.

Friedman, H. L. (2013) 'Transpersonal Self-Expansiveness as a Scientific Construct', in *The Wiley-Backwell Handbook of Transpersonal Psychology*, H. L. Friedman and G. Hartelius (eds), New York: Wiley-Blackwell, pp. 203–222.

Garcia-Romeu, A. P. and Tart, C. T. (2013) 'Altered States of Consciousness and Transpersonal Psychology', in *The Wiley-Backwell Handbook of Transpersonal Psychology*, H. L. Friedman and G. Hartelius (eds), New York: Wiley-Blackwell, pp. 121–140.

Gendlin, E. T. (1969) 'Focusing', *Psychotherapy: Theory, Research and Practice*, 6(1): 4–15.

Gendlin, E. T. (1981 [1978]) *Focusing*, New York: Bantam Books.

Germer, C. K., Siegel, R. D. and Fulton, P. R. (2013) *Mindfulness and Psychotherapy*, New York: Guilford Press.

Gilbert, P. (2009) *The Compassionate Mind*, London: Constable.

Gilbert, P. (2010) *Compassion Focused Therapy*, London: Routledge.

Goldstein, W. (1993) 'Psychotherapy with the Borderline Patient: An Introduction', *American Journal of Psychotherapy*, 47(2): 172–183.

Grand, D. (2013) *Brainspotting: The Revolutionary New Therapy for Rapid and Effect Change*, Louisville, CO: Sounds True.

Green, C. S. and Bavelier, D. D. (2008) 'Exercising Your Brain: A Review of Human Brain Plasticity and Training-Induced Learning', *Psychology and Aging*, 23(4): 692–701.

Greenberg, L. (2014) 'The Therapeutic Relationship in Emotion-Focused Therapy', *Psychotherapy*, 51(3): 350–357.

Grof, S. (2012) 'Revision and Re-Enchantment of Psychology: Legacy of Half a Century of Consciousness Research', *Journal of Transpersonal Psychology*, 44(2): 137–163.

Hagger, M. S., Wood, C. and Stiff, C. (2010) 'Ego Depletion and the Strength Model of Self-Control: A Meta-Analysis', *Psychological Bulletin*, 136(4): 495–525.

Hanson, R. (2009) *Buddha's Brain: The Practical Neuroscience of Happiness, Love and Wisdom*, Oakland, CA: New Harbinger.

Hanson, R. (2013) *Hardwiring Happiness: The Practical Science of Reshaping Your Brain – and Your Life*, London: Rider.

Hart, T. (2000) 'Deep Empathy', in *Transpersonal Knowing: Exploring the Horizon of Consciousness*, T. Hart, P. L. Neilson and L. Puhakka (eds), New York: SUNY, pp. 253–270.

Hayes, S. C., Strosahl, K. C. and Wilson, K. G. (2011 [2003]) *Acceptance and Commitment Therapy: The Process and Practice of Mindful Change*, London: Guilford Press.

Hebb, D. O. (2009 [1949]) *The Organisation of Behaviour: A Neuropsychology Theory*, New York: Taylor & Francis.

Heller, L. and LaPierre, A. (2012) *Healing Developmental Trauma: How Early Trauma Affects Self-Regulation, Self-Image, and the Capacity for Relationship*, Berkeley, CA: North Atlantic Books.

Holden, C. (1979) 'Paul MacLean and the Triune Brain', *Science*, 204(4397): 1066–1068.

Jung, C. G. (1981 [1959]) *Aion: Researches into the Phenomenology of the Self*, Collected Works 9/2, London: Routledge.

Kleim, J. and Jones, T. (2008) 'Principles of Experience-Dependent Neural Plasticity: Implications for Rehabilitation after Brain Damage', *Journal of Speech, Language and Hearing Research*, 51(1): S225–S239.

Knox, R. and Cooper, M. (2010) 'Relationship Qualities That Are Associated with Moments of Relational Depth: The Client's Perspective', *Person-Centered and Experiential Psychotherapies*, 9(3): 236–256.

Larsen, D. and Stege, R. (2010a) 'Hope-Focused Practices During Early Psychotherapy Sessions. Part I: Implicit Approaches', *Journal of Psychotherapy Integration*, 20(3): 271–292.

Larsen, D. and Stege, R. (2010b) 'Hope-Focused Practices During Early Psychotherapy Sessions. Part II: Explicit Approaches', *Journal of Psychotherapy Integration*, 20(3): 293–311.

Leeds, A. M. (2009) 'Resources in EMDR and Other Trauma-Focused Psychotherapy: A Review', *Journal of EMDR Practice and Research*, 3(3): 152–160.

Leonard, G. and Murphy, M. (1995) *The Life We Are Given*, New York: Jeremy Tarcher/Putnam.

Levin, D. M. (1985) *The Body's Recollection of Being: Phenomenological Psychology and the Deconstruction of Nihlism*, London: Routledge.

Levine, P. (1997) *Waking the Tiger: Healing Trauma – The Innate Capacity to Transform Overwhelming Experiences*, Berkeley, CA: North Atlantic Books.

Levine, P. (2010) *In an Unspoken Voice: How the Body Releases Trauma and Restores Goodness*, Berkeley, CA: North Atlantic Books.

Levy Berg, A., Sandell, R. and Sandahl, C. (2009) 'Affect-Focused Body Psychotherapy in Patients with Generalized Anxiety Disorder: Evaluation of an Integrative Method', *Journal of Psychotherapy Integration*, 19(1): 67–85.

Lovden, M., Wenger, E., Martensson, J., Lindenberger, U. and Backman, L. (2013) 'Structural Brain Plasticity in Adult Learning and Development', *Neuroscience & Biobehavioral Reviews*, 37(9): 2296–2310.

Luskin, F. (2004) 'Transformative Practices for Integrating Mind-Body-Spirit', *The Journal of Alternative and Complementary Medicine*, 10(1): 15–23.

May, A. (2011) 'Experience-Dependent Structural Plasticity in the Adult Human Brain', *Trends in Cognitive Sciences*, 15(10): 47–48.

Mollon, P. (2008) *Psychoanalytic Energy Psychotherapy*, London: Karnac.

Murphy, M. (1992) *The Future of the Body: Explorations into the Further Evolution of Human Nature*, Los Angeles, CA: Tarcher/Putnam.

Neff, K. D. (2008) 'Self-Compassion: Moving Beyond the Pitfalls of a Separate Self-Concept', in *Transcending Self-Interest: Psychological Explorations of the Quiet Ego*, L. Bauer and H. A. Wayment (eds), Washington DC: APA, pp. 95–106.

Ogden, P., Minton, K. and Pain, C. (2006) *Trauma and the Body: A Sensorimotor Approach to Psychotherapy*, London: W. W. Norton.

Ogden, P. and Fisher, J. (2013) *Body as Resource: A Therapist's Manual for Sensorimotor Psychotherapy*, London: Karnac.

Palmer, G. and Hastings, A. (2013) 'Exploring the Nature of Exceptional Human Experiences: Recognising, Understanding, and Appreciation EHEs', in *The Wiley-Blackwell Handbook of Transpersonal Psychology*, H. L. Friedman and G. Hartelius (eds), New York: Wiley-Blackwell, pp. 333–351.

Pollak, S. M., Pedulla, T. and Siegel, R. D. (2014) *Sitting Together: Essential Skills for Mindfulness-Based Psychotherapy*, London: Guilford Press.

Rappaport, L. (2008) *Focusing-Orientated Art Therapy: Accessing the Body's Wisdom and Creative Intelligence*, Philadelphia, PA: Jessica Kingsley.

Ray, W. A. and Keeney, B. (1993) *Resource Focused Therapy*, London: Karnac.

Riordan, R. and Kahnweiler, W. (1995) 'Job Focused Resources for Psychotherapists and Their Patients', *Psychotherapy: Theory, Research, Practice, Training*, 32(3): 467–475.

Rothschild, B. (2000) *The Body Remembers: The Psychophysiology of Trauma and Trauma Treatment*, New York: W. W. Norton.

Rowan, J. (2005 [1993]) *The Transpersonal: Spirituality in Psychotherapy and Counselling*, London and New York: Routledge.

Rubin, S. S. (1986) 'Ego-Focused Psychotherapy: A Psychodynamic Framework for a Technical Eclecticism', *Psychotherapy: Theory, Research, Practice, Training*, 23(3): 385–389.

Scaer, R. (2014 [2001]) *The Body Bears the Burden: Trauma, Dissociation, and Disease*, New York and London: Routledge.

Schore, A. N. (2003) 'The Seventh Annual John Bowlby Memorial Lecture', in *Revolutionary Connections: Psychotherapy and Neuroscience*, J. Corrigall and H. Wilkinson (eds), London: Karnac, pp. 7–52.

Sills, F. (2009) *Being and Becoming: Psychodynamics, Buddhism, and the Origins of Selfhood*, Berkeley, CA: North Atlantic Books.

Turnbull, A. N. (2003) 'Emotion, False Beliefs, and the Neurobiology of Intuition', in *Revolutionary Connections*, L. Corrigall and H. Wilkinson (eds), London: Karnac, pp. 135–162.

van der Kolk, B. (2014) *The Body Keeps the Score: Mind, Brain and Body in the Transformation of Trauma*, London: Penguin.

Walsh, R. and Vaughan, F. (eds) (1993) *Paths Beyond Ego: The Transpersonal Vision*, Los Angeles, CA: Tarcher/Perfigee.

Wiggins, S., Elliott, R. and Cooper, M. (2012) 'The Prevalence and Characteristics of Relational Depth Events in Psychotherapy', *Psychotherapy Research*, 22(2): 139–158.

Wilber, K. (2000) 'Integral Transformative Practice: In this World or Out of it?', *What is Enlightenment?*, 18 (Fall/Fall/Winter): 34–39, 126–127, 130–131.

Williams, M., Teasdale, J., Segal, Z. and Kabat-Zinn, J. (2007) *The Mindful Way Through Depression: Freeing Yourself from Chronic Unhappiness*, London: Guilford.

Witkiewitz, K., Lustyk, M. and Bowen, S. (2013) 'Retraining the Addicted Brain: A Review of Hypothesized Neurobiological Mechanisms of Mindfulness-Based Relapse Prevention', *Psychology of Addictive Behaviors*, 27(2): 351–365.

Woollett, K. and Maguire, E. (2011) 'Acquiring "The Knowledge" of London's Layout Drives Structural Brain Changes', *Current Biology*, 21(24): 2109–2114.

Yeomans, F. E., Levy, K. N. and Caligor, E. (2013) 'Transference-Focused Psychotherapy', *Psychotherapy*, 50(3): 449–453.

Chapter 2

The origins of resourcing

Cultivating resilience

Most of us are fortunate to be primed from birth (if not before) to engage fully in life. We are born with innate strengths and aptitudes, capacities and qualities which support growth in all areas of living and experiencing for the duration of a lifetime. Many of these resources arise out of our genetic disposition and personality temperament (Hutchinson, Stuart and Pretorius, 2010). Other resources may take time to cultivate. Rick Hanson (2013: 6) suggests that 'On average, about a third of a person's strengths are innate, built into his or her genetically based temperament, talents, mood, and personality. The other two-thirds are developed. *You get them by growing them.*' These strengths might include possible innate capacities like empathy and concern for others (Winnicott, 1965: 73–82; Aults, 2012), resilience (Wu et al., 2013), as well as learned optimism (believing that good things will happen to you in the future), openness to experience, and the ability to perceive, use and regulate emotions (de Terte, Stephens and Huddleston, 2014). It is also likely that our capacity for resourcefulness is largely developed in our early relational experiences of a hopefully nurturing and supportive environment (Rutten et al., 2013), and during childhood and adolescence (Wray-Lake and Syvertsen, 2011) as the brain/mind continues to develop and change to enable, for instance, 'planning, multi-tasking, inhibiting inappropriate behaviour; and social understanding, including perspective-taking and self-awareness' (Blakemore, 2007: 87), with the nervous systems and body growing as a resourceful whole, burgeoning with potentials and possibilities.

Taking resilience as an example of a resource or strength, we find a number of contributory factors to this capacity. Here resilience is taken to mean the ability of an individual to recover, bounce back or revive from adversity (Leipold and Greve, 2009) as well as to maintain psychological and physical well-being following a traumatic event (Bonanno, 2004). Gang Wu and colleagues (2013) provide a literature review on resilience summarising a number of factors which contribute to this ability. These include innate *genetic factors* as well as changes to genetic expression (epigenetics) brought about, for instance, by early adversity during significant periods of development, such as childhood abuse. Therefore, genetic factors may determine the degree of resilience, and epigenetic factors may positively or negatively alter this (Peedicayil, Grayson and Avramopoulos, 2014). Likewise, *developmental factors*, arising from the influence of the developmental environment on resilience, potentially affect the degree of control that a person has over a stressful event. For example, less control may lead to learnt helplessness and increased vulnerability, whereas more control may lead to heightened resilience. *Psychological factors* contributing to resilience include a tendency towards optimism and the ability to cultivate other positive feelings, to replace negative thoughts with positive ones, and to regulate difficult emotions and situations by learning to overcome rather than avoid these. Other psychological factors include the capacity to seek and access support already present, to offer concern towards others, to cultivate mindfulness (i.e., to acknowledge and notice the content of awareness in the present moment, rather than become this), and to use humour appropriately. John Berger (1997) has written extensively on the value of humour (among many functions) as a way to help relieve suffering by lightening it. Wu and colleagues (2013) also highlight studies on the importance of holding a sense of meaning and purpose, including spiritual or religious commitment, as valuable contributors to resilience. Studies have also shown that resilience reduces or minimises the negative impact of life challenges, including anxiety, depression and traumatic events. This finding is supported by other research which indicates that resilience provides a protective buffer against negative events in daily life and strengthens individuals' capacity to deal with potential threats (Hu, Zhang and Wang, 2015). However, as we have seen, it is likely that this depends on the intensity of a negative experience, the availability of support (Robertson and Cooper, 2013), as well as genetic (Russo et al., 2012; Rutten et al., 2013) and personality factors such as the capacity for experiencing positive emotions (Hanson, 2013: 6) during the course of a lifetime.

Resources like resilience, therefore, are both innate relatively stable traits and capacities (*nature*) which can be cultivated, developed and grown (*nurture*). We might also say that the development and maintenance of a resource is dependent upon a coinfluencing combination of *internal* (e.g., genetic predisposition, personality temperament, capacity for experiencing positive emotions) and *external* (e.g., family context, social environment) factors (see also Chapter 5).

Strengthening core capacities: self-regulation and self-awareness

Resourcing is also both stage relevant, being largely determined by the requirements and demands of each developmental stage, and also accumulative across stages of development. Self-regulation, in particular, is fundamental across stages of development as the pivotal capacity in the 'process of managing and changing oneself' (Baumeister and Vonasch, 2015: 4). It is a primary resource which enables a person to manage inner conflicts and responses, and thereby increase inner buoyancy in life situations, especially in meeting life challenges. As Roy Baumeister and John Tierney (2011: 112) put it, self-regulation is 'the capacity to override one response (and substitute another)'. For instance, we regulate our thoughts (e.g., in paying attention), emotions and moods (e.g., when increasing positive feelings and decreasing negative ones), impulses (e.g., in resisting temptation or delaying gratification), and performance (e.g., in persistence and perseverance).

Typically, the emergence or origins of affect regulation and then self-regulation lie in qualitative early life experiences within the 'facilitative environment' (Donald Winnicott) of the mother's orbit, as well as within the wider sensitive parental/caregiver field (e.g., father, other family members), and this capacity remains relatively stable throughout life. The full accomplishment of this innate capacity is largely dependent on our early years experience, and is also susceptible to influence from genetic and dietary factors in, for instance, the reduction in glucose (to blood, body, brain). It is also noted that it is the attuned and nurturing 'facilitative environment' which first enables affect regulation. However, with the emergence of a sense of self, affect regulation gives rise to self-regulation, having hopefully learnt to regulate affect on our own. This is a subtle differentiation but nonetheless worth acknowledging in our discussion on self-regulation. Incapacity and compromise in this area may indicate emotional or early relational trauma (Chapter 8) and make it difficult to self-regulate 'intense emotions, including shame, rage, disgust, panic, terror, hopelessness, despair, excitement and elation' (Schore in Sieff, 2015: 113); a rigid contraction of tolerable emotional range. Difficulties in the ability to self-regulate also often arise from other inner conflicts (Baumeister and Vonasch, 2015: 4), namely, through self-doubt, rumination, and unmanageable strong negative feelings and impulses. However, the capacity for self-regulation begun early in life may increase and become more sophisticated later in life through, for example, self-regulatory practices like mindfulness and meditation.

Self-awareness (i.e., the ability to be self-reflective) is intrinsically linked to self-regulation, and in many ways underpins the ability to self-regulate in that we can see with an 'inner eye' what requires regulating. It is the ability to notice inner processes by acknowledging and allowing the coming and going of feelings, thoughts and bodily sensations, and giving meaning to some of these. This reflectiveness requires a spacious attitude to be fully effective, so that there is a wide, non-judgemental, window of opportunity to view 'things' from different perspectives. For example, learning to step back from whatever arises in awareness (e.g., thought, feeling or sensation) in the present moment, by witnessing this content, rather than *becoming* it, is integral to increasing self-awareness. This capacity increases by continually stepping back (not disconnecting) into a soft compassionate observer position, while at the same time bringing attention to the breath as the locus or seat of self-awareness. Increasing such self-awareness can be a lengthy process but it is often developed through being in therapy.

The fluctuating power of the will

Considering further the relationship between self-awareness and self-regulation, Roy Baumeister and Andrew Vonasch (2015: 4) argue that 'anything that reduces self-awareness will weaken self-regulation, because it compromises the monitoring process'. This includes strong emotions (e.g., anger, sadness or fear), inner conflicts (e.g., impulsive desires or procrastination), or environmental distractions (e.g., temptations). However, willpower or self-control is perhaps the strongest innate motivating energetic resource which, when used wisely, can re-establish self-regulation. On this point, Baumeister and Tierney (2011) have forcefully argued that willpower is perhaps the 'greatest human strength'. For there must be the strength of will to build a resource and keep it going while it simultaneously 'sinks' into or becomes a part of our identity. Unwise use of the will includes employing the left brain will to prop up dissociations and keep emotions, especially when they are 'deeply embodied', mostly out of awareness, as is the tendency in cognitive therapy, thereby bypassing the therapeutic issue (Schore, in Sieff, 2015: 134).

Baumeister and Tierney (2011) suggest that willpower is a *limited resource* energy that when exerted gets depleted. Drawing upon a number of studies, they argue that like a muscle, the will becomes tired when used, particularly towards the end of the day, and especially if the day has been stressful or demanding. They refer to studies which reveal that 'Willpower is tied to glucose', in the same way as self-regulation. That is, willpower increases and decreases with the rise and fall of glucose levels, so for instance, depleted glucose leads to opting for effortless decisions, while decision-making itself depletes (glucose) energy leading to poor decision making. Drawing a link to difficulties with self-regulating, these authors further observe that successful people struggle less with temptations and crises because less of their limited will energy is diverted in other directions. However, it is reassuring to know that because self-regulation and other self-control abilities utilise the same energy resource, willpower can also recover after exercise.

On the other hand, this *limited resource theory* has been challenged by Veronika Job and colleagues (2015) in their *unlimited resource theory*. Their theory maintains that the *belief* in a limited resource theory has an undermining power over self-regulation, especially when demands are high; whereas they argue convincingly that the power of a *belief* in the unlimited resource theory can improve performance, and actually increase the goal-orientated focus to keep going and the ability to self-regulate. Examples of this include focusing the will with the use of strong intentions, as well as belief in the ability to remove or avoid temptations or distractions. It appears from these studies that the will is a fluctuating power or energy, its strength depending on a range of factors, including belief. If then a belief is able to influence the potency of a resource like willpower, it is likely that the focused use of imagination can also re-create and build up the experience of the resource.

My view is that more than through belief, a resource is strengthened by cultivating an *experience* of it: *a resource is an experience.* We become aware of an increase or depletion of it through energetic experience, for instance, in the lack of motivation, in an inability to self-regulate, in a temporary loss of will or self-control, in the lack of self-awareness, or in the decrease in concentration. We know the presence or absence of a resource by our bodily felt experience in the present moment. When we take the fact of the neuroplasticity of the brain into account, which makes it subject to change through the use of the mind (the activity of the brain), we come to realise the alterable nature of the brain/mind/body systems as a whole. But while persistently held thoughts certainly influence the brain, it is likely that the consequence of bodily felt experiences are more ubiquitous. This is because the brain is *experience dependent*, that is, experience changes the brain which then alters the mind, which then alters the brain, and so on. Given this fact, if we can activate an experience of something (e.g., strength, endurance, gratitude, etc.) through strongly imagining it with feeling (akin to Carl Jung's 'active imagination'), thus generating a bodily felt experience of the strength, then we can experience an increase of that resource.

Imagination and imagery as resource

Although the imaginative faculty is active early on in life, there is no consensus amongst theorists of infant cognition whether imagination is active at birth. However, Michael Washburn (1995 [1987]: 6) points out that this faculty is one of the 'primary features' of the pre-egoic or body-ego stage of development, present at this life stage as 'a creative but crude cognitive life conducted primarily in the medium of images'. Therefore, we might say that imagination is thinking without language and is largely an activity of the right brain hemisphere given that the origin of ego consciousness is principally in the right hemisphere (McGilchrist, 2009: 127).

From its rudimentary beginnings the faculty of imagination eventually enables forays into life situations, whether that situation is presently lived or not, as well as into the life perspective of another person through the imaginative process of empathy. Recent studies confirm that even in the absence of something, imagination activates body responses as if the imagined object or situation were actually present (Laeng and Sulutvedt, 2014: 196; cf. 'safe place' exercises when working with trauma in Chapter 8). Undoubtedly imagination cultivates the expansion of experience; including experiences of limitation. For while imagination is worthy of development in its own right, it is often neglected as a dimension of experience (Chapter 4), and as a resource, and unwittingly deployed to limit our lives by imaginary worries, anxieties or fears. In order to avoid this, the use of imagination requires encouragement from an early age so that it becomes an essential part of us in conducting our lives and helping to create positive experiences. Indeed, to imagine strengths and capacities is often a first step toward embodying these, and one of our most powerful resources in enabling a full embodied life (embodied imagery, Appendix). Without its limitless capacity we can become like a rudderless boat going wherever the tide takes us.

Vignette: Martin

It was the absence of life direction and accompanying sense of feeling lost which brought Martin (aged forty-nine) to therapy, prompted by a dream in which he was *building partitions, like cells or tombs, in a watery crypt. There were fifty tombs to complete so that the whole took the shape of a honeycomb in which Martin would become permanently entombed. There was a female figure lying in one of the cells. The overwhelming feeling was fear.* During exploration of this dream Martin sought 'respectful permission' from the female figure to merge with her through active imagination, so that he could see himself and his life situation from her perspective. Immediately he began to cry. 'It's as if she is my intuition' he said. 'She's telling me to put my trust in her. This "sweet wisdom" within me knows what my next step in life is.' At that moment a shaft of light synchronistically lit up the consulting room. Since getting married Martin longed to build a house for his family, with a smallholding to cultivate and keep *bees*, but fear got in the way. Now, it was as if the dream, and the light through the window, was nudging him in this direction. The months in therapy following this dream supported Martin to discern the resources necessary for him to embody more this breakthrough moment. The number 'fifty' and the fact that he was nearing fifty did not escape him either.

Working with dreams in this way draws upon Jung's 'active imagination', that is, imagination with feeling (e.g., Hannah, 1981), and the work of Robert Bosnak (1996) and Eugene Gendlin (1986) to fully engage with the aspects of the dream image and symbolism as an embodied meaning-making process.

Resourcing in the context of Michael Washburn's developmental perspective

Writing on imagination invites us to consider further the resourcing depths of the psyche; the resourcing Ground of Being. To this end, it is to acknowledgement of the valuable contribution to the field of human development made by Washburn that I now turn. Washburn's account of human development draws upon psychoanalytic, Jungian and transpersonal perspectives, thereby providing a comprehensive framework for my discussion, and puts resourcing in its deepest context. His holistic way of thinking is also sympathetic to my understanding of the dimensions of experiencing, especially regarding the origins of resourcing.

Beginning, then, with his triphasic structure of human development, Washburn (1994, 1995 [1987], 2003) argues that there are three dynamic developmental stages. These are: the 'preegoic or body ego stage' (from womb to the beginning of middle childhood or roughly to the resolution of the Oedipus complex), the 'egoic or mental ego stage' (from the beginning of middle childhood through to adulthood), and the 'transegoic or integration stage' (from about midlife onwards). Within this structure the origins of resourcing lie in what Washburn refers to as the 'Dynamic Ground', positing that this 'Ground is the seat of the nonegoic pole of the psyche and source of psychic energy'; the Ground is energetic and magnetic power (Washburn, 1995 [1987]: 122; see energetic, Chapter 4), from which ego consciousness differentiates. In this sense the view is that the psyche consists of two basic poles: the egoic and the nonegoic. It is the Ground which is active at the beginning of life, and the ego of the newborn 'is only an incipient ego, an ego just beginning to emerge from the Dynamic Ground' (Washburn, 2003: 40). Accordingly, the Ground is 'an energizer for all psychic processes and systems and is not itself reducible to or exclusively expressive of any particular process or system' (Washburn, 1995 [1987]: 121). The power of the Ground, then, is as an impartial enabler of brain/mind/body processes and functions, capacities and potentials, strengths and attributes.

During the 'preegoic or body ego stage' of development the newborn is an 'unbounded bodily self', knowing no distinction between itself and other; 'an incipient ego with a centre but no circumference' (Washburn, 2003: 150), being fundamentally open to everything inner or outer: 'At the outset of life we are *radically open* and, consequently, receptive not only to a wide range of external stimuli but also to a wide range of energies, impulses, feelings, and images rising up from the Dynamic Ground within' (Washburn, 2003: 41; my emphasis). Everything serves as a resource for living, developing and growing, in relation to the earthly context of our embodied lives.

This tendency to be 'radically open' to the potentials from the Ground gradually reduces, to allow for ego-emergence as the 'executive agency of consciousness' (Washburn, 1995 [1987]: 6). The Ground quietens and becomes submerged (through being repressed) to give way to the formation of identity, which is the task of the 'egoic or mental ego stage' of development. Becoming particularly pressing during adolescence, this stage involves a necessary commitment to an 'identity project' (i.e., through being in a relationship, and in a job or career, as well as in roles and lifestyles). Washburn (1994: 153) describes this as 'a type of involvement with self that is open to critical and confirming responses of others', as well as 'a form of self-assertion that submits to norms and limits', and 'an endeavour that aims at an [ego] ideal goal that, although never completely attainable, is nonetheless in touch with realistic possibility (i.e., the goal of perfectly achieving one's chosen identity)'.

For most people the developmental journey peaks at this stage of development, but for others (though perhaps this is rare) the 'transegoic or integration stage of development' brings about an adjustment of values to give priority to the reopening of the nonegoic pole, and the underlying potentials of the Dynamic Ground. This is not a U-turn to an earlier developmental stage, but a spiralling return to the attracting energy of the Ground; a furtherance or deepening of the person. This fundamental change is precipitated by being drawn increasingly to the depths. Carl Jung's (2009) *Red Book* is a remarkable testament of surrender to the gravitational pull of such depths in which he engages in imaginal dialogue with inner figures through the use of active imagination. Washburn (1999: 133) describes this return as 'restorative' in that it leads beyond the stage of ordinary ego development toward the goal of whole-psyche integration, where the two poles of the psyche (egoic and nonegoic) come together 'to achieve a higher integration' (Washburn, 1999: 134). In this sense the path of return is not to the same point of departure as for ego emergence and formation, though the foundation in the Dynamic Ground is the same. Realignment with the nonegoic core is with the increased insight, awareness and capacity brought about through the individual life journey. This widening of awareness and expansion of consciousness is also an *expansion of experience*, which enables the reframing of identity within the context of a whole psyche-integrative perspective. Ego is not primitively innocent as at the beginning of its journey, but is now developmentally different 'by the widest possible margin' (Washburn, 2003: 169). However, Washburn (1994: 25) further points out that 'the ego's openness to the nonegoic core is not only a receptivity but also a vulnerability' in that it opens to the mysterious, frightening, fascinating and awesome power of the Ground; what Rudolf Otto (1968) refers to as *mysterium tremendum et fascinans*. It can become an important therapeutic goal for the therapist qualified in recognising the signs of spiritual awakening and emergence, to enable clients to deepen their capacity for developing this spiritual dimension (spiritual, Chapter 4). This inevitably means supporting clients to find ways of coming into relationship with their vulnerability with an attitude of self-compassion, whilst also being discerningly open to the resources which will mature the spiritual dimension.

The term 'nonegoic core' refers to the inner depth of our being. This core is often viewed as the source of experience itself, the core from which conscious awareness (ego) arises, the energetic centre of consciousness within, the seemingly limitless aspect of consciousness. This core is qualitatively and functionally different from the reasoning and evaluating centre of ordinary consciousness, ego. For instance, if 'ego' is a metaphor for ordinary consciousness, then 'core self', 'inner self', 'higher self', 'nonegoic core', 'soul' are metaphors for this magnetic core of deep consciousness (see also Chapter 5). It is as if there is an energetic centre deep within, the absolute core of our being, from whence innate resources rise up. At times we may feel this centre as a guiding factor in life, with imagery and intuition as its language.

In this sense, the depth of being is often thought of as a well of innate wisdom residing in the body/mind/brain. This bodily felt sense of knowing is sometimes viewed as the authentic, true or unconditioned 'voice' of the individual. Gendlin (1996), for instance, developer of Focusing Orientated Psychotherapy, referred to this as that which arises when we pay particular attention or bring our focus to what is happening on the inside of our body, especially in the torso area. Awareness of these depths is thought to rise up from the non-cognitive or pre-cognitive parts of the brain, and may even be viewed as spiritual in nature, in the sense that these experiences connect us to something more than or beyond our ordinary egoic selves. Nelson (2012: 258), for instance, in writing on the spiritual brain notes: 'We have strong indications that much of our spirituality arises from arousal, limbic, and reward systems that evolved long before structures made the brain capable of language and reasoning.' Therefore, to turn our attention to the bodily felt-sense communications from the nonegoic pole (in the nonegoic/egoic dyadic polarity), and subsequently the underlying and pervading Dynamic Ground, is to enable access to almost limitless resourcefulness.

The quality of this paying attention is not dissimilar to insight meditation or mindfulness (or other forms of meditation and contemplation), in that we can focus our curiosity and interest on what is arising in our bodily felt awareness in the present moment. We might say that this self-empathic deep listening is a way of tuning into and taking note of brain/mind/body's resources. Therapies which give priority to resourcing in this way largely engage clients at the feeling, interpersonal, energetic, imaginal and spiritual dimensions of being. Within these modalities questions like 'What got/gets you through?' and 'What enabled/enables you?' are invitations for clients to listen carefully to what is resourcing them, especially when followed by 'listen to your body, not your thinking', or 'listen to your feeling-body, not your reasoning'.

We derive resources from a limitless range of stimuli. These are simultaneously available from within us, and from 'out there', in the multiple experiences of life circumstances and situations. However, prior to this, perhaps resourcing first occurs *in utero* through the nutrients and oxygen brought to the foetus by way of the healthy functioning of the mother's placenta, and the watery warmth of her womb. Therefore, placental development is fundamental to the survival of the foetus. From this biological perspective we find that the predominant cell type that forms considerable parts of the placenta is called 'trophoblast'. This comes from the Greek words 'terphein' meaning 'to feed' and 'blastos' meaning 'germinator'. So, the placenta is the essential nutrient provider and enabler of growth, not only for the foetus but also for the infant and subsequent life stages. Furthermore, Washburn (1994: 20) asserts that this *in utero* phase of life is 'nonegoic' (the deep unconscious, deep psyche or deep core of the psyche) and consists of a range of potentials including, 'energy, dynamism', 'instinctual drives and predispositions', 'affect, emotion', 'the imaginal, autosymbolic, process', and 'collective memories, complexes, or archetypes'. For example, emotive potentials give rise to potent spontaneous body-based feelings. And the autosymbolic imagination projects 'images upon

genetically selected stimuli as they appear within the field of perception'
(Washburn, 2003: 41). Washburn (2003: 35) again points out that 'With the
possible exception of the imagination and archetypal processes depended
thereon [e.g., collective memories, complexes or archetypes], all [or most]
nonegoic potentials are active from birth, plying the newborn with a profusion of
primitive but powerful experiences', with some potentials likely to be active *in
utero* (Washburn, 2003: 38). The point here is that it is probable that alongside
nutrients and oxygen these potentials are the beginnings of resources; capacities,
strengths, attributes and abilities to enable life to be resourcefully lived from
the outset. Related to this resourcing is the nature of breath itself.

The resourcing nature of breath

Meditation teacher since the 1960s, Joseph Goldstein (2013: 50) reminds us
that the breath is the one always present and available factor throughout life.
It is the remedy to distractions, preoccupations, discursive and dispersive
thoughts, and may even be a stabilising factor at time of death. To learn to
bring our attention habitually to the breath takes interest away from the often
overly distracting activity of the mind thereby stilling the mind and relaxing
the body. Within the meditation traditions focus on breath also allows other
types of information to come into awareness, for instance, body sensations and
feelings. By gently taking our attention away from our thoughts and other
phenomena to our breath, we establish a witnessing or observing position in
relation to these sources of information. Breath grounds us in the present
moment from where we can increasingly observe the activity and processes of
the mind/body as a whole. As the eminent Buddhist monk Thich Nhat Hanh
(1991: 15) writes: 'Body is the bridge which connects life to consciousness,
which unites your body with your thoughts. Whenever your mind becomes
scattered, use your breath as the means to take hold of your mind again.' In
this sense, allowing the body to find an alert, upright posture while also
returning to the anchor of the breath as a point of stability enables us to
notice more of the activity of the brain/mind/body, and thereby develop
insight into the processes of these and become increasingly less identified with
their content; which is one source of distress. Cultivating a habit of bringing
attention to the breath in this way also helps to increase concentration.

Breath is one of our basic resources, the dependable 'object' to keep
returning to when times are joyful or difficult, and the constant factor that sees
us through everything; as long as we are breathing we are alright. Sometimes,
when times are challenging, dependability of the breath is the one thing that
reassures. We consciously breathe in the freshness of the summer air just after
the rain, or draw in the forest air fragrant with pine and the mossy earth, and
the purging saltiness of sea air. Or we might notice how our breathing makes
more space around us. Interestingly, since 2015 there is a journal dedicated to
all aspects of breath science: *Journal of Breath Research*.

While the breath may well be a resource to many, Sue Pollak and colleagues (2014) remind us that for those with dissociative tendencies who struggle with anxiety, or have a trauma history, this is not so straightforward. Under these circumstances the body is often considered to be unsafe, and focusing attention on the body and the breath can activate overwhelming levels of anxiety. One of the tasks of resource focused therapy is to enable clients to re-establish breath as a stable and reliable resource, a point of reference from which to regulate thoughts and feelings.

Vignette: Jennifer

> Alongside reflective enquiry into the origins of Jennifer's (aged thirty-five) anxiety and activating circumstances, our aim together was to help her manage this troublesome feeling by bringing her awareness, first, to where the anxiety was located in her body and, second, to invite her to gently breathe into that area (Gibson, 2008) while at the same time noticing the experience of this and noting any simultaneously arising thoughts. Regulating anxiety in this way, while being mindful of the felt-sense experience, brought up memories of witnessing her mother's anxiety when her father was often late home from work in the winter months, driving those dark country lanes: 'What if ...?' As Jennifer grew up she absorbed her mother's anticipatory anxiety without fully understanding the reasons why, and it was not until years later that she began to realise this. During the months of therapy Jennifer was increasingly able to practise breathing in this way, while at the same time imagine soothing the anxiety with her breath, and notice it come and go. By paying attention to the transient experience of anxiety whenever it arose, Jennifer was gradually able to identify less with this, while at the same time acknowledge the attentiveness of her mother's concern.

Intentional and unintentional resourcing

Resources are both experiences of intentionally cultivated capacities, qualities, attributes and abilities, as well as unintentionally resourcing experiences. Intentionally enabled and activated resources include the capacity to self-regulate, to exercise self-control, to feel concern towards self and others, to activate resilience, to increase confidence, to find strength in feeling vulnerable, to cultivate a general bias towards optimism, and so on. These are either innate or learnt, or a combination of both. Most therapists are particularly accomplished at enabling clients to develop intentional capacity in the thinking, emotional, interpersonal and behavioural dimensions. But many of the other dimensions are not taken fully into account (e.g., imaginal, energetic, physical, spiritual).

Resourcing the dimensions also occurs randomly or unintentionally through ordinary living. Take for instance the experience of joy arising from a beautiful morning in late spring as you open the curtains to the day, or the delight of a letter bringing you good news, or the pleasure arising through a chance encounter of an old friend, or the unexpected thrill from an evening at the theatre, or the restful feeling of being at one with everything on hearing the evocative conversations of geese in the autumn sky and seeing their pattern of direction, and thousands of other unexpected resourcing experiences. These events are often the unacknowledged facilitators of resourcing. Interestingly, some of the most deeply resourcing experiences take place while alone in nature, and facilitate deepening of the spiritual dimension; this is possibly because there is a greater feeling of connection with our surroundings, when the mind is also less distracted and more focused on the experience of being in nature.

However, many people do not consider these events as resources, let alone pause long enough to acknowledge their resourcing impact. There are lasting benefits to be gained if we absorb the experience and dwell on it for a few minutes while at the same time noticing the influence (often subtle) of this on mind/body. We might, for instance, identify experiences like peace, rest, belonging or serenity.

A key role of the resource focused therapist is to draw clients' attention to their reports of such resourcing experiences, and to reflect on the embodied felt sense of these: 'Just notice that. Notice how this experience wants to embed itself in your brain/mind/body', or 'allow this experience to absorb you; breathe it in'. Also, engaging the imagination to facilitate the fullest resourcing experiences, perhaps through the use of guided or embodied imagery (see Appendix), helps to strengthen the potency of these resources.

This book proposes that it is not only the ego process that requires resourcing to increase strengths and capacities, but also the dimensions of experiencing as experience pathways in their own right (i.e., thinking, emotional, physical/ body/somatic, behavioural, imaginal, energetic, interpersonal, spiritual). Even the 'soul' itself. This supports the widening and expansion of awareness itself, beyond ego process, strength and functioning. These experience pathways grow, mature, flourish, and are replenished by developing aptitudes and abilities which correspond to these. For instance, self-regulation corresponds mostly to the thinking and emotional dimensions. The practice of self-compassion strengthens the emotional dimension. Exercise strengthens the physical dimension. Community activities strengthen the behavioural dimension. Then, by virtue of the interrelating and reciprocal brain/mind/body whole, growth in one dimension influences other dimensions.

The resourcing nature of relationship

It is generally agreed that the aptitude to self-resource originates primarily in and through being in relationship with others, most crucially an affirmative primary or significant other, particularly during early years' development. The corollary of the accumulative experience, verbal and non-verbal, of this early relational bond or attachment with a sensitive primary caregiver often lasts a whole lifetime, and can determine the degree of our resourcefulness. Such

secure attachment is 'a basic biological need, wired into the species as fundamental as is nest-building behaviour in a bird' (Mitchell, 1993: 22), and enables
the achievement of 'social competence, trust, a strong sense of self, and resilience
against stress' (Huebner and Thomas, 1995: 112), and may 'influence intellectual
and motor development' (p. 115). It may also help us to 'reframe situations as
less emotional and less likely to suppress emotional expression' (Wu et al.,
2013: 6), as well as relate to 'higher cognitive reappraisal and resilience' contributing to well-being (Karreman and Vingerhoets, 2012: 821). Whereas
insecure attachment is more likely to lead to psychopathology (Huebner and
Thomas, 1995: 112), and diminished well-being as a result of less application
of cognitive reappraisal (Wu et al., 2013: 6).

And the origins of resourcing are also to be found in our relationship to our
surroundings or place, be it our immediate environment, the space we inhabit,
our 'nest', the area in which we live with views of cityscape, landscape and
seascape. Place is the sum total experience of where we feel we belong: and
where we put our roots. Accounts of the resourcing nature of place are to be
found in every genre of literature, from poetry to prose, as well as in painting,
music, and so on, and are testimony to our embodied connection to or disconnection from place. Arguably our identity arises as much out of relationship
with place as it does from our attachment to people. For place is where we feel
a sense of belonging or dispossession; place brings meaning or meaninglessness.
Whatever our relationship with place, it is invariably a point of reference for
memories, be they of pleasure, loss, safety, love or identity (Morgan, 2010).
Interestingly, there is growing research interest in 'place attachment', and scope
for enquiry into the processes of attachment to place (Lewicka, 2011: 224).
Perhaps such enquiries will take into account those variables which contribute
to what I want to call 'place resource'.

Therefore, it is useful to enquire about clients' relationship with place as a
significant part of their relational history, with questions like 'How did/does
your relationship with [the name of the place] resource or support you?' or
'What is it about [the name of the place] that influences you?' or 'What was
difficult for you about living in [the name of the place]?' Sometimes, it is a
person's relationship with place that helps them through a difficult time. Our
consulting rooms are full of stories about gardens and wilder settings as some
of the 'safest' spaces (Angela, Chapter 8).

Within the context of resourcing, attachment, then, is understood as consisting of a number of components within a unified facilitating whole, where
each part plays a significant role in enabling or disabling the development of
resource capacities. Many of these points will be taken up in later chapters.

Concluding thoughts

Gathering together consideration of the above themes on the origins of
resourcing, we find that resources are potentially simultaneously available

from both inner and outer realities; initially for the infant there is no difference between these, being at the same time immersed in nonegoic processes and in symbiotic union with its 'facilitating environment' (Winnicott, 1965) which includes the primary facilitator of mother or caregiver. The infant is radically open to this wide range of experiences. As Washburn (1994: 38) puts it, the infant's resourcing experience 'includes not only externally derived stimuli but also a wide variety of indigenous contents, contents that emerge from the non-egoic core of the psyche', in which the infant is initially absorbed or 'originally embedded' (Washburn, 1995 [1987]: 48). Washburn (1994: 49) describes this embedded state as a 'condition of dynamic plenitude' where the infant is unreservedly fulfilled and content. The embodied psyche is a powerful self-resourcing system. Rooted in the Dynamic Ground, life enhancing resources are available from deep within the evolving brain/mind/body systems, and also from the unlimited depth of the Dynamic Ground itself, which includes and transcends the resourcefulness of the primary care giving relationship. To put it another way, resources are potentially concurrently available from intra-personal, interpersonal and transpersonal sources. As David Michael Levin (1985: 9) observes, we are caught up in a 'web of ontical relationships with a multitude of beings' with roots in Being, the Dynamic Ground or Ground. Our resourcing, then, is not separate from or independent of this relational web, but arises out of our being in relationship with the whole. Everything is profoundly interwoven together in a dynamic resourcing whole.

Just as the power of the Ground subsides to allow for the development of ego identity, we find ourselves gradually and mostly separating from our primary resourcing influences. We eventually come to view ourselves as an autonomous centre of resourcing, either with a sense of being well-resourced, not resourced enough, or somewhere in between. Strengths, capacities, aptitudes and abilities are for the most part taken to be either established, in the process of being established, or lacking. We have either learnt or not learnt how to resource ourselves, or how to recognise and value the resources we have. On the whole we are always open, even radically so, for ongoing resourcing.

Radical openness to resourceful experiences means that cultivating these enables resources to grow. This is a key theme throughout this book. Another key theme is that resource focused therapy is most effective when more dimensions are taken into account as this helps to embed the resource on different experience levels. For instance, while capacities and abilities like self-awareness and self-regulation can be increased through developing the thinking, feeling and physical dimensions, these can be further enhanced through the experi-ence of being in therapy; through the healing nature of the therapeutic relationship particularly when characterised by deep and sustained attune-ment (feeling and interpersonal). These capacities can also be developed through the cultivation of embodied mindfulness in some mindfulness-based psychotherapies (thinking, feeling, physical, imaginal, energetic, interpersonal and spiritual). However, the mistake we sometimes make is in thinking that we are self-sufficient, independent brain/mind/body systems. Sometimes we are taught that 'reaching out is wrong', and the push towards separation and independence is construed as 'self-sufficiency is right'; but where our early resource providers are harmful or damaging, then self-sufficiency is certainly wise, but only up to a point. We sometimes forget that resourcing is an ongoing process at intrapersonal, interpersonal and transpersonal levels. The dimensions are continually 'seeking' to widen into the fullness of 'their' potentials as we cannot necessarily live a satisfactory life within the confines of one dimension alone; certainly not a fully integrated life. We are brain/mind/body systems in relation to other brain/mind/body systems, in the context of the 'brain/mind/body Earth systems'. Everything requires resourcing, including the Earth itself. We are part of a unified resourcing whole.

Therefore, the dimensions are like connecting pathways to the 'universe'; supply routes to wholeness. Each dimension is unique with its own developmental needs and often its own language (e.g., the imaginal). And development in one dimension influences other dimensions, but this is not a substitute for the development of each dimension in its own unique right. As part of a resourcing and self-resourcing whole, we resource the whole by giving something back; for resourcing is not only about receiving. This view has implications beyond the scope of this book, to include consideration of the complex nature of resource seeking that impacts other parts of the whole, for example, in the exploitation of others and the environment. But the point here is that resourcing is a dynamic process in relation to the resource 'seeking' of others (including other species), and that the brain/mind/body systems require resourcing within the context of this bigger picture.

References

Aults, C. (2012) 'Origins and Functionality of Empathy', *Psychology Journal*, 9(12): 46–55.

Baumeister, R. F. and Tierney, J. (2011) *Willpower: Discovering our Greatest Human Strength*, New York: The Penguin Press.

Baumeister, R. F. and Vonasch, A. J. (2015) 'Uses of Self-Regulation to Facilitate and Restrain Addictive Behaviour', *Addictive Behaviours*, 44 (May): 3–8.

Berger, P. L. (1997) *Redeeming Laughter: The Comic Dimension of Human Experience*, New York: Walter de Gruyter.

Blakemore, S. (2007) 'Brain Development During Adolescence', *Education Review*, 20(1): 82–90.

Bonanno, G. A. (2004) 'Loss, Trauma, and Human Resilience: Have We Under-Estimated the Human Capacity to Thrive After Extremely Aversive Events?', *The American Psychologist*, 59(1): 20–28.

Bosnak, B. (1996) *Tracks in the Wilderness of Dreaming: Exploring Interior Landscape Through Practical Dreamwork*, New York: Delacorte Press.

de Terte, I., Stephens, C. and Huddleston, L. (2014) 'Stress and Health', *Journal of the International Society for the Investigation of Stress*, 30(5): 416–424.

Gendlin, E. T. (1986) *Let Your Body Interpret Your Dreams*. Wilmette, IL: Chiron Publications.

Gendlin, E. T. (1996) *Focusing-Orientated Psychotherapy: A Manual of the Experiential Method*, London: Guilford Press.

Gibson, R. (2008) *My Body, My Earth: The Practice of Somatic Archaeology*, New York: iUniverse.

Goldstein, J. (2013) *Mindfulness: A Practical Guide to Awakening*, Boulder, CO: Sounds True.

Hanh, T. N. (1991) *The Miracle of Mindfulness* (trans. M. Ho), New York: Rider.

Hannah, B. (1981) *Encounters with Soul: Active Imagination as Developed by C. G. Jung*, Santa Monica, CA: Sigo Press.

Hanson, R. (2013) *Hardwiring Happiness: The Practical Science of Reshaping Your Brain – and Your Life*, London: Rider.

Hu, T., Zhang, D. and Wang, J. (2015) 'A Meta-Analysis of the Trait Resilience and Mental Health', *Personality and Individual Differences*, 7(6): 18–27.

Huebner, R. A. and Thomas, K. R. (1995) 'The Relationship Between Attachment, Psychopathology, and Childhood Disability', *Rehabilitation Psychology*, 40(2): 111–124.

Hutchinson, A. K., Stuart, A. D. and Pretorius, H. G. (2010) 'Biological Contributions to Well-Being: The Relationships Amongst Temperament, Character Strengths and Resilience', *South African Journal of Industrial Psychology*, 36(2): 1–10.

Job, V., Walton, G. M., Bernecker, K. and Dweck, C. S. (2015) 'Implicit Theories About Willpower Predict Self-Regulation and Grades in Everyday Life', *Journal of Personality and Social Psychology*, 108(4): 637–647.

Jung, C. G. (2009) *The Red Book (Liber Novus)* (trans. S. Shamdasani, J. Peck and M. Kyburz), London: W. W. Norton.

Karreman, A. and Vingerhoets, J. J. M. (2012) 'Attachment and Well-Being: The Mediating Role of Emotion Regulation and Resilience', *Personality and Individual Differences*, 53(7): 821–826.

Laeng, B. and Sulutvedt, U. (2014) 'The Eye Pupil Adjusts to Imaginary Light', *Psychological Science*, 25(1): 188–197.

Leipold, B. and Greve, W. (2009) 'Resilience: A Conceptual Bridge Between Coping and Development', *European Psychologist*, 14(1): 40–50.

Levin, D. M. (1985) *The Body's Recollection of Being: Phenomenological Psychology and the Deconstruction of Nihilism*, New York: Routledge.

Lewicka, M. (2011) 'On the Varieties of People's Relationships with Places: Hummon's Typology Revisited', *Environment and Behaviour*, 43(5): 676–709.

McGilchrist, I. (2009) *The Master and His Emissary: The Divided Brain and the Making of the Western World*, New Haven and London: Yale University Press.

Mitchell, S. (1993) *Hope and Dread in Psychoanalysis*, New York: Basic Books.

Morgan, P. (2010) 'Towards a Developmental Theory of Place Attachment', *Journal of Environmental Psychology*, 30(1): 11–22.

Nelson, K. (2012) *The Spiritual Doorway in the Brain: A Neurologist's Search for the God Experience*, London: Plume.

Otto, R. (1968) *The Idea of the Holy* (trans. J. W. Harvey), New York: Galaxy.

Peedicayil, J., Grayson, D. R. and Avramopoulos, D. (eds) (2014) *Epigenetics in Psychiatry*, San Diego, CA: Elsevier.

Pollak, S., Pedulla, T. and Siegel, R. (2014) *Sitting Together: Essential Skills for Mindfulness-Based Psychotherapy*, New York: The Guilford Press.

Robertson, I. and Cooper, C. L. (2013) 'Resilience', *Stress and Health: Journal of the International Society for the Investigation of Stress*, 29(3): 175–176.

Russo, S. J., Murrough, J. W., Han, M., Charney, D. S. and Nestler, E. J. (2012) 'Neurobiology of Resilience', *Nature Neuroscience*, 15(11): 1475–1484.

Rutten, B., Hammels, M., Geschwind, N., Menne-Lothmann, C., Pishva, E., Schruers, K., van den Hove, D. C., Kenis, G., van Os, J. and Wichers, M. (2013) 'Resilience in Mental Health: Linking Psychological and Neurobiological Perspectives', [Online] *Acta Psychiatrica Scandinavica*, 128(1): 3–20.

Sieff, D. F. (2015) *Understanding and Healing Emotional Trauma: Conversations with Pioneering Clinicians and Researchers*, London and New York: Routledge.

Washburn, M. (1995 [1987]) *The Ego and the Dynamic Ground: A Transpersonal Theory of Human Development*, New York: SUNY.

Washburn, M. (1994) *Transpersonal Psychology in Psychoanalytic Perspective*, New York: SUNY.

Washburn, M. (1999) 'Embodied Spirituality in a Sacred World', *The Humanistic Psychologist*, 27(2): 133–172. Reprinted by permission of Division 32, Society for Humanistic Psychology (http://www.apadivisions.org/division-32).

Washburn, M. (2003) *Embodied Spirituality in a Sacred World*, New York: SUNY.

Winnicott, D. W. (1965) *The Maturational Process and the Facilitating Environment: Studies in the Theory of Emotional Development*, London: Hogarth.

Wray-Lake, L. and Syvertsen, A. K. (2011) 'The Developmental Roots of Social Responsibility in Childhood and Adolescence', *New Directions for Child and Adolescent Development*, 134 (Winter): 11–25.

Wu, G., Feder, A., Cohen, H., Kim, J. J., Calderon, S., Charney, D. S. and Mathe, A. A. (2013) 'Understanding Resilience', *Frontiers in Behavioural Neuroscience*, 15(7): 1–15.

Chapter 3

Resourcing of emotional systems

The focus areas for resourcing in therapy were weighted traditionally on inner or intrapersonal processes such as developing egoic-capacity or functioning (e.g., self-regulation, self-esteem), deepening insight and understanding, as well as increasing interpersonal strengths (e.g., fostering secure relationships). While these remain the core resourcing areas, within the past few decades and certainly since the 'age of the brain', resourcing in therapy has been turning its attention to neuroscience for insight and understanding about brain functions and processes, and also to psychology (e.g., evolutionary psychology) as well as other disciplines. Allan Schore (2012: 4) further notes that 'this *paradigm shift from behaviour, to cognition, to [right brain] bodily based emotion* has acted as an integrating force for forging stronger connections between disciplines of psychology, social neuroscience and psychiatry, all of which are now focusing on affective phenomena.' These disciplines help increase the effectiveness of the therapeutic benefits for clients at least in terms of: a right hemisphere focus in therapy (Schore, 2014); self-regulation of brain/mind systems (e.g., Hanson, 2009, 2013); the primacy of emotion (e.g., Siegel, 2001; Gainotti, 2012); the process and experience of the therapist's presence (e.g., Geller and Greenberg, 2012) in the present moment (e.g., Stern, 2004a, 2004b); and in other innovative ways of healing the brain/mind and resourcing emotional systems. These areas are the focus of this chapter with reference to a single case: Colin.

First, it is worth putting this in the context of two brain integration pathways: bottom-up–top-down, and left brain, right brain. By integration I mean the ways in which functionally unique components come to be gathered into a functional whole (Siegel, 2001: 70). Non-integration, in contrast, alludes to 'functional isolation' 'between, or within, hemispheres', such as in dissociation (Siegel, 2001: 83).

Bottom-up–top-down loop

The bottom-up–top-down loop is a circuitry pathway of brain integration which loops 'from the top of our head down into the depths of the brain and back again' (Cozolino, 2010 [2002]: 27), and includes understanding from

Paul MacLean's (1990) 'triune brain' theory. Louis Cozolino (2010 [2002]: 27) notes that the term 'Top-down integration includes the ability of the cortex to process, inhibit, and organize the reflexes, impulses, and emotions generated by the brainstem and limbic system', and therefore 'refers to how the cognitive structures of the brain impact the emotional and instinctive systems of the body' (Heller and LaPierre, 2012: 16). The term bottom-up 'refers to how regulation in the nervous system impacts cognitions' (p. 16). Familiar top-down therapies include Cognitive Behavioural Therapy (CBT), Mindfulness-Based Cognitive Behavioural Therapy (MBCT) and Paul Gilbert's (2010) Compassion Focused Therapy (CFT), while bottom-up therapies include the range of body psychotherapies, such as Body Psychotherapy, Transpersonal Psychotherapy and Core Process Psychotherapy, as well as trauma therapies such as Peter Levine's (1997) Somatic Experiencing (SE) and Pat Ogden and colleagues' (2006) Sensorimotor Psychotherapy. However, most therapies sit somewhere on the bottom-up and top-down loop, while also facilitating left brain (cognitive) and right brain (embodied-emotion-experience) integration. Therapies like CBT and some analytic therapies are more left brain focused, largely depending on the practitioner's capacity for (brain/mind/body) integrative practice. Therapist engagement with clients at right brain depth may only be possible if they themselves engage with their own right brain as 'the patient's unconscious right brain can develop only as far as the therapist's right brain can take them', that is, the therapist is able to tolerate felt-sense embodied activation of their own wounds when these arise in the therapeutic relationship (Schore in Sieff, 2015: 131).

Left brain, right brain

Iain McGilchrist furthers our understanding of the left right brain integration pathways in a profoundly influential discussion on these uniquely different processing hemispheres. He notes that 'the relationship between them is no more symmetrical than that of the chambers of the heart – in fact, less so; more like that of the artist to the critic, or a king to his counsellor' (2009: 13) He writes that in evolutionary terms, the cognitive, focused, purposeful, categorising, verbalising, naming left hemisphere, arises out of the emotion dominant, embodied 'primacy of the right hemisphere' (p. 176), and that 'the most fundamental difference between the hemispheres lies in the type of attention they give to the world' (p. 4). He explains this as follows:

> The right hemisphere underwrites breadth and flexibility of attention, where the left hemisphere brings to bear focused attention. This has the related consequence that the right hemisphere sees things whole, and in their context, where the left hemisphere sees things abstracted from context, and broken into parts, from which it then reconstructs a 'whole': something very different.
>
> (pp. 27–28)

Moreover, 'the right hemisphere pays attention to the Other, whatever it is that exists apart from ourselves, with which it sees itself in profound relation. It is deeply attracted to, and given life by, relationship, the betweenness, that exists with this Other', while 'the left hemisphere is ultimately disconnected from the Other' (p. 93) including spirituality. This may account for findings that spiritual experiences sometimes arise out of significant empathic therapeutic encounters given their right hemisphere locus (e.g., Wiggins, Elliot and Cooper, 2012). In seeing things whole, the right hemisphere has 'primacy of wholeness' as well as 'primacy of experience' (McGilchrist, 2009: 179), and is the 'primary mediator of experience' (p. 227) in the sense of being the deliverer (to the left hemisphere) of new experiences. Since, 'Emotion and the body are at the irreducible core of experience' (p. 185) the right hemisphere also has 'primacy of affect' (p. 184). This means that the right hemisphere is connected to body, sensation, and the limbic and brainstem functions; for example, stress, anxiety and fear arise from activation of the right cortical and subcortical structures.

It is not surprising, therefore, that Schore (2016: 473) asserts that:

> The patient–therapist relationship acts as a growth promoting environment that supports the experience-dependent maturation of the right brain, especially those areas that have connections with the subcortical limbic structures that mediate emotional arousal. Structural change, an outcome of long-term psychological treatment, specifically involves the rewiring of the connections of the right frontolimbic cortex and the consequent replacement of toxic with more benign internal representations of self. These events allow for the emergence of a system that can efficiently mediate psychobiological transitions between various internal states.

This endorses the accepted view that 'psychotherapy changes brain function and structure' (Glass quoted in Schore, 2012: 10), through the process of brain neuroplasticity (Siegel, 2001; Scaer, 2014 [2001]) which enables momentary *states* in therapy to become in time stable *traits* (Hanson and Mendius, 2009) based on the neuroscientific principles of *neurons that fire together, wire together* and *use it or lose it* (Chapter 1). In describing the brain as 'experience-dependent', Daniel Siegel (2001: 72) notes, it is important to make the distinction between 'experience-dependent' and 'experience-expectancy'. Growth relies on the expectancy of new experiences, whereas the maintenance and strengthening of the existing brain structure is dependent on familiar experiences, which can also lead to growth. This is a subtle but nevertheless important distinction. We can strengthen what already is by *using* it, or cultivate growth of the new by metaphorically leaning towards this (even if in the imagination) in expectation and openness.

Moreover, given that 'the right hemisphere is the primary seat of emotional arousal and the processing of novel information' as well as 'nonverbal, unconscious, holistic, and subjective emotional processing' and 'stress regulation, intersubjectivity, humour, empathy, compassion, morality, and creativity' (Schore, 2012: 7), it is likely that therapeutic communications are largely right brain to right brain in the client–therapist relationship (Schore, 2014), since right brain communications reconnect us to the whole. Meanwhile, as Cozolino (2010 [2002]: 308) points out, 'the right hemisphere constantly provides information to the left, but while we are awake, the left hemisphere may or may not allow this input into consciousness'. This is significant for therapists working with dreams and the deep imagination (imaginal, Chapter 4).

While I acknowledge that therapy is a whole brain activity, it is important to understand (Cozolino, 2010 [2002]: 28) that '*Left–right* or *right–left integration* involves abilities that require the input of both the left and right cerebral cortex and lateralised limbic regions for optimal functioning.' For instance, 'Left–right integration allows us to put feelings to words, consider feelings in conscious awareness, and balance the positive and negative affective biases of the left and right hemispheres.' To describe feelings is a prime illustration of left–right hemisphere integration, as is to acknowledge moments of felt incongruence where left hemisphere narrative is out of alignment with right hemisphere communications (e.g., non-verbal communications and emotions).

Vignette: Colin

> Loss of direction in life, an inability to discern his way forward, fear of not living the life that was 'right' for him, and feeling trapped by his successes, were the presenting concerns that brought Colin (aged forty) to therapy. Alongside his pervasive feeling of 'flatness', during the first few months of therapy Colin began to notice and acknowledge other feelings that were at the edges of his awareness, in particular dissatisfaction, regret, sadness and fear, as well as the feeling content of metaphors like 'an empty boat going nowhere' and 'running on an empty tank'. Exploration of these feelings and feeling-metaphors enabled Colin to build a bridge between his thinking and felt-sense experience of himself, especially through his naming of them. The breakthrough came when Colin brought a dream in which he was *sitting in the role of therapist opposite a young man in his early twenties who had lost his father. Then the lights in the room began to flicker alarmingly, and Colin said 'it's alright, your father is here now' and spoke to the young man about the feelings that his deceased father wanted to convey.* On waking, Colin felt 'waves of grief' and awareness that the young man was a part of himself and lost without his 'feeling compass' to guide him. It was as if this 'young man' part of him was coming back to life. Working together with the dream in felt-sense depth (Gendlin, 1986) brought other feelings and insights to the surface. These included transference feelings (the therapist was the enabling father Colin never knew), grief from not knowing his father, who left when he was born, fear of loosening ties to his present life comforts, but also courage to be more of the person he wanted to be.

Overview of evolutionary psychology and affect regulating systems

I return to consider the bottom-up–top-down loop. Despite its relative simplicity, MacLean's (1990) 'triune brain' theory maintains that the structure and function of the brain reflect our evolutionary history, and is as good as any point of departure. His theory describes three affect regulating systems (functions and processes) that correlate to three regions of the brain and which are taken up by evolutionary psychology and rooted in biology and psychology (e.g., Buss, 1999; Gilbert, Bailey and McGuire, 2000). They also form the foundation for Paul Gilbert's (2010) tripartite model of affect regulation in his Compassion Focused Therapy (CFT), and Rick Hanson's (2013) Positive Neuroplasticity Training (PNT). However, Ryle (2005: 386) warns against a tendency in evolutionary psychology for 'offering a reductive account of human development, behaviour and experience which cannot provide an accurate basis for psychotherapy'. Despite this observation, the following insights from evolutionary psychology do, however, usefully sit alongside those from the ongoing dialogue between neuroscience and psychotherapy, especially as neuroscience increasingly focuses on affect, affect regulation, motivation, consciousness, trauma, dreams, and other processes. At the same time, neuroimaging–psychotherapy studies are seeing the effects of psychotherapy on the brain, for instance, with clients suffering from obsessive-compulsive disorder (OCD), major depression, a range of phobias and post-traumatic stress disorder (PTSD) (Peres and Nasello, 2008). Beginning, then, from a bottom-up consideration of regions of the brain and their affect regulating systems, these are as follows:

1   The threat regulating system or safety seeking system correlates to the earliest part of brain, the brainstem, also known as the reptilian brain. The key function of this system is to avoid threats and seek safety. This system regulates key processes such as heart rate, eye movement, breathing, body temperature and balance; the processes which monitor safety, both outer and inner.

2   The resource or achievement seeking regulating system, or more accurately the 'curiosity-interest-expectancy' system (Turnbull, 2003: 141), correlates to the mid-brain, or paleo-mammalian brain which contains the limbic system. This part of the brain is a core centre for emotions and hence often referred to as the emotional brain, and is the seat of conscious and unconscious value judgements as well as the storehouse of behaviour and agreeable or disagreeable experiences.

3   The attachment seeking system is embedded in the left and right hemispheres of the neocortex, or neo-mammalian brain. The affect regulating system for these parts of the brain gravitates towards fulfilling, nurturing and establishing secure connections with others.

The systems relating to these regions of the brain operate as a coinfluencing, interpenetrating whole so that negative or positive activation in one region directly affects other regions. For instance, a conflict in a personal relationship that temporarily undermines relationship security (in the neocortex or neo-mammalian brain) and might activate feelings of threat (in the brain stem or reptilian brain) and feelings of upset (in the emotional brain or paleo-mammalian brain) might arise out of feared and anticipated loss of a loving relationship. Conversely, a feeling that life is good on the whole reduces negative activation in these areas and increases positive experiences. Crucially, these 'three layers continue to evolve along with the emergence of ever more complex vertical [bottom-up–top-down] and horizontal [left–right] neural networks' (Cozolino, 2010 [2002]: 6–7) to process the increasing demands of modern living and more complex sensory, emotional and cognitive participation.

Such awareness of the function of the emotional systems in the triune brain enables the therapist to support clients in the therapeutic relationship more effectively, together with the educative aspect of therapy in (at least) the following ways:

a   increasing clients' awareness of when affect regulating systems become negatively activated, recognising what activates these, and knowing how to relax these systems through self-regulation practices (e.g., mindfulness, cultivating positive experience) or through regulation brought about by the sensitively attuned empathic relationship. Hanson (2013) argues that learning to respond to activations, reactive responses or metaphorical 'reddening' of brain/mind regions by soothing, relaxing or metaphorically 'greening' these from within that region, is more effective than resourcing from other regions. In this sense, resourcing is most effective from *within* regions, rather than *across* regions. He suggests, for instance, that 'greening' of threat activation occurs through cultivating positive experiences of peace, rest or a felt sense that 'everything is alright now' (thereby responding within the self-protect system), rather than by cultivating lasting experiences of accomplishment (responses from the seeking system);

b   enabling therapeutic exploration of negative activations, including the felt-sense meaning of these, particularly in relation to trauma (Chapter 8);

c   being aware of the 'negativity bias' of the brain to lean towards rumination (see below) through the educative role of therapy (Chapter 6);

d   increasing the capacity to cultivate positive experiences as an important part of self-regulation;

e   recognising more fully the transformative impact of the therapeutic relationship (Chapter 7).

To offer clients therapeutic support and exploration in these ways helps them grow in confidence and progressively become more able to regulate these systems outside therapy, as the following consideration of the affect regulating systems further illustrates.

Cultivating experiences of safety

While the tendency of the brain/mind is towards safety, even in the tangible absence of threat, we are frequently on alert for the possibility of it. Cozolino (2010 [2002]: 253) notes 'It is an unfortunate twist of evolutionary fate that the amygdala is mature before birth while the systems that inhibit it take years to develop. This leaves us vulnerable to overwhelming fear with little or no ability to protect ourselves', other than through our primary caregivers' capacity to regulate. This ancient brain/mind system is sometimes referred to as the 'threat and self-protect system' (Gilbert, 2009: 23). Gilbert (2010: 44) notes that when this system is activated, 'attention, thinking and reasoning, behaving, emotions and motives, and images and fantasies, can be threat focused, with each aspect of our minds orientated to the goal of detection and safety'. The effect of this system, then, is fight/flight/freeze/submit, or as Gilbert (2009: 23) puts it 'to activate us to run or fight, or inhibiting us so that we freeze, submit or simply stop doing things', and activates self-protective responses like fear, anxiety, frustration, anger, rage, as well as disgust and contempt. But as Stephen Porges (2011) points out, this avoid-threat system is in fact two defensive systems; the fight/flight mobilisation of behaviours system, and the 'shutting down, fainting, and dissociating' or immobilisation of behaviours system. In such ways our understanding of the brain/mind continues to advance, as does our conception of its functions and processes.

'Negativity bias' of the brain

Gilbert (2009: 23) reminds us that 'the brain gives more priority to dealing with threats than to pleasurable things'. This prioritisation towards attending to threat has given rise to the 'negativity bias' of the brain hypothesis, which authors Paul Rozin and Edward Royzman (2001: 298) argue is 'based on both innate predispositions and experience, in animals and humans, to give greater weight to negative entities (e.g., events, objects, personal traits)' and that 'negativity bias is a pervasive and consequential feature of human existence'. Bias toward the negative often features in our active waking daily lives, as well as in anxiety dreams and nightmares, and is embedded in our genes through millions of years of evolution, often hampering our innate capacity to self-resource and self-regulate. Similar to Rozin and Royzman's hypothesis on the pervasiveness of this bias and its consequential tendency, Roy Baumeister and colleagues (2001: 323) suggest that 'bad is stronger than good'. This means that negatively weighted events such as loss of friendship or negative criticism often have a greater impact on the individual than positively weighted events of the same type, such as gain of friendship and receipt of praise. These authors say we are evolutionarily adaptive for bad to be stronger than good, and argue that 'throughout our evolutionary history, organisms that were better attuned to bad things would have been more likely to survive threats and, consequently, would have increased the probability of passing along their genes' (p. 325). For instance, while the failure to notice a positive opportunity may disappoint, failure to notice negative events may give rise to regret, or worse, lead to death. Therefore, our default 'negativity bias' can help ensure survival. Yet the potency of this bias must take temperament, background and upbringing into account as the bias influence differs with everyone. Despite this, there is a strong probability that we will encounter more favourable than unfavourable events during the course of a lifetime. Hanson (2009, 2013) has also drawn upon these ideas and applied them to his Positive Neuroplasticity Training (PNT), and his reverse emphasis on *good is stronger than bad*. Like Hanson, one of the aims of resource focused therapy is to help clients to tilt this bias more toward its positive polarity in ways I shall describe in subsequent chapters.

Cultivating experiences of achievement

Playfulness, curiosity, interest and exploration are key aspects of the achievement-seeking regulating system. Described in different ways, the distinctiveness of this system is perhaps most comprehensively encapsulated by Jaak Panksepp (1998: 145) as the 'foraging/exploration/investigation/curiosity/interest/expectancy/SEEKING' system or the 'curiosity-interest-expectancy' (Panksepp quoted in Turnbull, 2003: 141). It may also be referred to simply as the 'seeking' system or 'reward' system, or the 'incentive and resource-seeking, drive-excitement system' (Gilbert, 2010: 47). The primary orientation within this system is towards going and getting, expecting and achieving. As Gilbert (2009: 23) notes:

> The function of this system is to give us positive feelings that guide, motivate and encourage us to seek out resources that we (and those we love and care about) will need to survive and prosper. We're motivated by and find pleasure in seeking out, consuming and achieving nice things (e.g., food, sex, comforts, friendships, status, recognition).

This system also guides us towards important life goals, and is the seat of 'motivation, energy, desires'. Conversely, over-stimulation leads to increasing consumerism, and to frustration, disappointment, anxiety and anger when desires are not met. Given the interpenetration of systems, failure in the 'seeking' system potentially activates experiences of threat.

Regulating this system may involve cultivating qualities like patience, gratitude (Emmons and Stern, 2013), a capacity to let go, to see the value in consuming less, and to find humble satisfaction in limitation. Significantly, the contemplative traditions invariably emphasise learning to diminish cravings and abandon desire for achievements and seek instead the liberation that simplicity of life brings. As Hanson notes, practices that cultivate and engender positive feeling states, such as gratitude, can stimulate the brain's dopamine reward which alerts and enhances the processes of the mind.

Colin sometimes found himself bemoaning his lack of achievement and sinking further into feelings of hopelessness for the future. Greater awareness of his inner life, and the strength of his 'negativity bias', brought him to face his difficulties more directly, and to be able to value what brought him to his present crisis at this particular 'crossroads' of his life. His experience of these positives opened up a more balanced view of his world and helped him to know that life was satisfactory on the whole, that there was wisdom in limitation which need not be construed as 'failure' or diminishing the quality of his life. At the same time, he felt that his relationships were good and that a hint of something new was presenting itself.

Cultivating experiences of contentment in relationships

The 'soothing, contentment and the safeness system' (Gilbert, 2010: 48) is embedded in the right and left hemispheres of the neocortex, and gravitates towards fulfilling nurturing, accepting, safe and secure experiences in relationships. Conversely, 'reddening' of this system gives rise to a tendency to disconnect or withdraw, especially when connection or intimacy feels threatening. Disconnection or isolation is qualitatively different from the pursuit of solitude, which is mostly experienced as something secure, positive and chosen. But disconnection from others cloaks disconnection from a part of ourselves, namely those parts longing for satisfying connections with others, given that we become mostly ourselves in and through relationship. 'Reddening' of this affect regulating system may also give rise to the difficult experiences of self-criticism and shame (e.g., Gilbert, 2010) which often come from not feeling deserving or worthy enough.

Emotion as a fundamental process in right brain dominant therapy

Resourcing clients in the affect regulation systems enables healing at neurobiological depths. Within the wider aim of left–right brain integration, which includes affect regulation, it is 'emotion [that] is integrative in that it is the process that connects other processes to each other' (Siegel, 2001: 82). Daniel Siegel (1999) brings the perspective of interpersonal neurobiology (meaning: inter/between-and-personal), and the concept of 'embodied brain', or brain, as the way through which 'energy and information flow within us' (Baldini et al., 2014: 219) and between persons, and is regulated by the fundamental process of emotion (Siegel, 2001: 81). From this viewpoint Siegel notes that, contrary to some opinions, 'emotion is *not* limited to some specifically designated circuits of the brain', but is 'an integrative process throughout the brain' (p. 81), though acknowledging the wide ranging influence of limbic regions in the right hemisphere on most areas of the brain and brain functions. This is a key point to stress, that emotion not only emanates from the right brain (through the limbic system) but, according to Siegel, emotion is a whole brain process. Interpersonal communication positively impacts the brain/mind/body, and the communication of emotion is core to this (p. 80), facilitating profound integration *between* others and *personally* within the brain (p. 89). This communication of emotion is also a type of 'resonance' arising from the experience of integration, both joining and integrating minds, and is fundamental to well-being and resilience (p. 90).

The mind, Siegel continues, has a profound capacity to go beyond its body, and make compassionate connections with others (p. 87), with which the right hemisphere 'sees itself in profound relation' (McGilchrist, 2009: 93; cf. Abram, 2010). We are participatory coinfluencing beings in the sense that our 'self-organisation' (Baldini et al., 2014: 219) regulates this flow of energy and information both *personally* and *between*. Siegel (2001) also notes that integration occurs when this dynamic interpersonal 'system' is flexible, adaptable and stable. Conversely, non-integration is when this harmony gives rise to fragmentation, distancing or over-connecting. Mind is a process which arises out of this participatory understanding. Within this view, Siegel's concept of 'mindsight' refers to the ability to discern, influence and regulate 'the mind's energy and information flow, both in oneself and in relationships', through verbal and non-verbal communications, and cultivating present moment awareness *personally* and *between* in a type of feeling-resonance.

In psychotherapy, right hemisphere bidirectional communications largely enable this sense of 'feeling-resonance' which occurs non-verbally at personal depth creating a type of map or neurobiological imprint of the other's mind in both persons (Siegel, 2001: 84). When this 'feeling-resonance' presence is cultivated, the therapist is open and receptive to all communications from clients, especially when supported by compassionate and mindfulness attitudes. The therapist simultaneously offers the same to themselves, perhaps by pausing to notice the breath as nature's way of coming into the resourcefulness of the present moment.

Gradually, by coming into relationship with the 'forgotten language' of bodily felt-sense experience, Colin felt a widening of identity. The 'empty boat' was beginning to move, to turn itself toward a possible new, more fulfilling direction. As if preparing for a voyage, he began reading David Whyte's (2002 [2001]: 61) *The Unknown Sea*, and considering its theme of 'inhabitation' of one's 'genius' or spirit. He became drawn to the idea of being unutterably oneself, and 'inhabit[ing] [his] life fully, just as we find it, and in that inhabitation, let everything ripen to the next stage of the conversation'. In such ways Colin found himself appreciating far more the fertility of the present moment, and felt this deepening in his relationships outside therapy too.

Coming into the present moment as core effective practice

Affirmative findings suggest that 'paying attention to the present moment with openness and acceptance changes the structure of the brain' (Cahn and Polich quoted in Geller and Greenberg, 2012: 163). Therapeutic presence is the embodied experience of being openly and discerningly alert in the present moment to clients' process as well as our own, and to the felt-sense in-between quality of the participatory process. For it is this felt-sense experience from which therapeutic responses emanate. As Shari Geller and Leslie Greenberg (2012: 94) note:

> This dance of attending to self, other, and between is what the process of presence is about. It is what we [therapists] *do*, when we are present, to facilitate a deepening of relational connection and self-awareness regardless of the particular theoretical vehicle we align with. We [the authors] distinguish between the process of presence and the experience of presence. The experience of presence is the 'being' state, what it feels like to be fully present (...). The process of presence is what we do when we allow the experience of presence to guide the therapy process.

Daniel Stern (2004a: 367) continues on this theme and notes that 'present moments' are Kairos moments (from Greek meaning: timely moment). These are 'critical moments' in therapy where something breaks through to bring about lasting change, moment by moment: 'the propitious moment or the moment of something coming into being' (Stern, 2004b: xv). Timeless moments breaking through the 'fiction' of time. From a transpersonal perspective, Kairos experiences are 'vertical' breakthroughs into the horizontal, linear or chronological clock-time (Chronos is the Greek god who personifies linear time). In psychotherapy these are moments of profound connection and breakthrough.

From this perspective of something unfolding, moment by moment, Stern (2004a: 268) notes that the primary goal of psychotherapy is finding a balance between mutual understanding of verbal and non-verbal, explicit and implicit, subjective communications or 'intersubjectivity'. He notes further that these communications are '*relational moves* to adjust or regulate the "intersubjective field"', and comprise the full range of empathic communications, including gestures, postures, stillness, verbalisations, and from '*relational move* by *relational move*', step by step, sometimes spontaneously so. This inevitably results in 'many mismatches, derailments, misunderstandings, and indeterminacies' or 'mistakes' which require 'repair'. Therefore, in many ways Stern (2004a: 269) sees therapy as a dynamic progress, move by move, through attunement, misattunement and repair, punctuated by Kairos moments or 'now moments' pulling the therapist into the present moment in an authentic verbal or non-verbal 'moment of meeting' felt-sense experience. Stern writes (2004a: 219–220):

A therapy session (or any intimate dialogue) is made up of a series of present moments that are driven forward by the desire for intersubjective contact and an enlargement of the shared intersubjective field. Inter-subjectivity is a primary motive in this movement. As the dyad moves along, linking together present moments, a new way of-being-with-the-other may arise at any step along the way. These new experiences enter into awareness but need not enter consciousness all the time. They add to the domain of implicit knowing. This kind of change occurs at the local level. These moments, each lasting only several seconds, accumulate and probably account for the majority of incremental therapeutic change that is slow, progressive, and silent.

Attentiveness to the present moment is the expression of presence. We might also view 'present moments' as resourcing moments in their potential to facilitate brain/mind transformation. The focus here is on felt-sense experience. Recalling that the brain is both experience-dependent and 'experience-expectant' (Siegel), it is experience that is always transformative. Throughout his writing Stern (2004a: 221) emphasises the importance of experience rather than meaning because, he asserts 'the content of language and narrative is an abstracted experience' and is 'once-removed from direct experience'. This is reminiscent of McGilchrist's (2009: 28) earlier point that 'the left hemisphere sees things abstracted from context, and broken into parts', which is different from the whole perspective of the right hemisphere. By giving primary importance to experience, Stern makes an interesting point when he asserts how lasting brain/mind transformation can occur when therapy allows memories of wounding to be felt in the present moment, so that they can in some way be overwritten by a new experience. He notes that 'If past experiences are to be changed, they must be rewritten or replaced by a new temporal experience occurring in the same time framework. The rewiring must also be lived through with its own temporal dynamics.' Rewriting or over-writing is only possible for 'the explicit past, not the implicit experienced past' (2004b: 221). In this sense, it is only by allowing past experiences to be felt explicitly in the present moment, that is, to be *in* the emotion rather than consciously reflecting on it, that the rewriting or rewiring or change of these can take effect. Inter-estingly, Stern (p. 41) considers that the present moment extends on average between three to four seconds, but probably not more than ten seconds, and is 'our primary subjective reality' (p. 8); that we may refer to these moments of meeting as transient experiences of consciousness. As Siegel (2001: 75) remarks, 'Core consciousness is a "here-and-now" experience of focused attention', suggesting that in these moments we are most susceptible to lasting transformation.

Moreover, from a neurobiological perspective, mirror neurons (which help us understand the actions of others and imitate what we see) sit alongside motor neurons (the commutator of information from nerves to body) and only fire in a person who is looking at another person. This allows us to experience something of them, *as if* them. Therefore, 'the mirror neuron system may take us far into understanding (at the neural level) contagion, resonance, empathy, sympathy, identification, and intersubjectivity' (Stern, 2004b: 79). This is significant in many ways for the therapist, not least because it furthers our understanding of the process of resourcing in therapy and enables us to fine-tune our effectiveness, by using the present moment for resource-making opportunities.

As Colin cultivated the 'art' of being in the present moment, he came to see that the 'boat voyage' was to himself, and to deepen the life he was already living rather than to prioritise feeding his entrepreneurial spirit. His true 'genius' was in learning to come into relationship with himself, to listen more to his felt-sense as the core of his being. It was as if he was seeking this missing part of himself by *doing more* rather than by *being more*. Instead of taking him *further out* of life, his loss of direction found him journeying *further in*. Therapy with Colin continues.

Resourcing emotional systems in trauma therapies

The resourcing of complex processes will be considered more fully in the penultimate chapter. Meanwhile I consider briefly here ways in which the group of trauma-focused therapies resource emotional systems. First, trauma modalities are grounded in their understanding of bottom-up–top-down and right–left brain/mind/body systems. They focus on embodied felt-sense experience within the resourcing and emotion regulating environment of the empathic relationship as the baseline for practice in order to process trauma memories (here defined as more than ordinary negative experience). These therapies also draw upon a range of interventions to enable clients to self-regulate emotions and understand the symptoms of trauma when working through difficult processes. These may include meditation and mindfulness practices, breathing exercises, education (Chapter 6) and the use of imagery (Chapter 4). For instance, meditation practices like Transcendental Meditation (Scaer, 2014 [2001]: 178) and mindfulness (Bernstein, Tanay and Vujanovic, 2011) may help to moderate stress responses by concentrating attention on the present moment, rather than on the trauma memory. Within this contemplative framework, breathing exercises are sometimes useful to help clients manage their anxiety when activation occurs (Leeds, 2009; Gibson, 2008). Apprising clients of the effects of trauma is an educative aspect of therapy which helps normalise the experience, reduce rumination and self-blame, and increase self-compassion. Imagery also helps to increase self-compassion and feelings of safety, as with the generation of compassionate images in Compassion Focused Therapy (Gilbert, 2010), and the use of the 'safe place' exercise (SPE) in Eye Movement Desensitization and Reprocessing (EMDR) (Leeds, 2009). However, Frank Corrigan and Alastair Hull (2015: 81) note that while 'The "safe place" is used in the preparation for EMDR to provide an imaginal resource for stabilisation if processing becomes too distressing', alternative 'calm or peaceful imagery' is offered to clients who struggle with the idea of 'safe'. They point out that this, too, can be challenging 'as the lowering of vigilance may trigger switching to protective ego states' or activate traumatic memories; however, '*Safety resources that do not extend below the cortex are unlikely to have the required depth when processing becomes difficult*', and they suggest instead that finding a sense of safety in the body is preferable (p. 82; my emphasis). Therefore, imagery is not necessarily resourcing unless it is embodied (embodied imagery, Appendix). This is why, alongside versions of mindfulness practice, emphasis is laid on resourcing clients through embodied felt-sense *experiences*, as in the grounding practices in Peter Levine's (1997) Somatic Experiencing, Babette Rothschild's (2006) Somatic Trauma Therapy, and Lisa Schwarz's (2016) Comprehensive Resource Model. However, locating 'safety' in the body is not always possible, especially if the body was the subject of trauma, for example, in sexual abuse. Above all, as we have considered, the therapist's attunement in the therapeutic relationship is perhaps the most significant resourcing factor for clients.

Concluding thoughts

The neuroplasticity of the brain and its influence on therapy is mostly acknowledged amongst therapists across traditions. Sharon Begley (quoted in Greenfield, 2014: 64) also reminds us that 'the brain remakes itself throughout life, in response to outside stimuli to its environment and to experience'. If the brain is constantly remaking itself, then experience is a primary factor in this, especially given that the brain is both experience-dependent and experience-expectant. This is most significant in the cultivation of positive experiences, which is the focus of resourcing. More specifically, it is the learning of something new which appears significant, as new felt-sense experiences are brought into awareness and enable the transformation in the brain/mind/body systems, even if these are felt expectations of an experience. Thinking alone is not enough, neither is bringing thoughts into awareness. It is the sensitive facilitation of the embodied felt-sense experience, as it comes into awareness, that is important; whether this is via bottom-up–top-down (vertical) integration, or right–left (horizontal) brain integration, or both. In the considerately empathic therapeutic relationship particular emphasis will be given to the right brain to right brain focus, when clients experience the therapist as a compassionate, open, receptive and alert presence in the present moment.

It is now evident that 'changes in conscious cognition alone, without changes in emotion processing, are *limited*' (Schore, 2012: 5 my emphasis), thereby challenging some applications of CBT, especially where clients 'present with a history of relational trauma and thereby a deficit in affect regulation' (p. 5). Despite CBT's status as the ubiquitous default therapy for depression, it seems probable that it is 'more effective with only lower levels of depression' (p. 200) than with more complex depressive processes. On this point, Peter Fonagy and colleagues' (2015) Tavistock Adult Depression Study (TADS) found significant benefits in offering long-term psychoanalytic psychotherapy, with its implied right hemisphere focus, for treatment-resistant depression. Therapists are therefore adopting an increasing view that 'more so than the cognitive mechanisms of interpretation and insight, relational-affective processes between patient and therapist are at the core of the change mechanism' (Schore, 2012: 6). This paradigm shift may well emphasise the 'ascendance' (p. 11) of relational modalities of therapy over preference to CBT.

Fundamentally, then, in 'the age of the brain', where transformative primaries include experience and emotion, and in-depth right brain communication, 'psychotherapy is not the "talking" cure but the "communicating" cure' (Schore, 2014: 391), and as Bessel van der Kolk (2014: 86) puts it, 'communication is the royal road to regulation'.

References

Abram, D. (2010) *Becoming Animal: An Earthly Cosmology*, New York: Pantheon Books.

Baldini, L. L., Parker, S. C., Nelson, B. W. and Siegel, D. J. (2014) 'The Clinician as Neuroarchitect: The Importance of Mindfulness and Presence in Clinical Practice', *Clinical Social Work Journal*, 42(3): 218–227.

Baumeister, R., Bratslavsky, E., Finkenauer, C. and Vohs, K. (2001) 'Bad is Stronger Than Good', *Review of General Psychology*, 5(4): 323–370.

Bernstein, A., Tanay, G. and Vujanovic, A. A. (2011) 'Concurrent Relations Between Mindful Attention and Awareness and Psychopathology Among Trauma-Exposed Adults: Preliminary Evidence of Transdiagnostic Resilience', *Journal of Cognitive Psychotherapy*, 25(2): 99–113.

Buss, D. M. (1999) *Evolutionary Psychology: The New Science of the Mind*, Boston, MA: Allyn & Bacon.

Corrigan, F. M. and Hull, A. M. (2015) 'Recognition of the Neurobiological Insults Imposed by Complex Trauma and the Implications for Psychotherapeutic Interventions', *BJPsych Bulletin*, 39(2): 79–86.

Cozolino, L. (2010 [2002]) *The Neuroscience of Psychotherapy: Healing the Social Brain*, New York: W. W. Norton.

Emmons, R. A., and Stern, R. (2013) 'Gratitude as a Psychotherapeutic Intervention', *Journal of Clinical Psychology: In Session*, 69(8): 846–855.

Fonagy, P., Rost, F., Carlyle, J-A., Mcpherson, S., Thomas, R., Pasco Fearon, R. M., Goldberg, D. and Taylor, D. (2015) 'Pragmatic Randomised Controlled Trial of Long-Term Psychoanalytic Psychotherapy for Treatment-Resistant Depression: The Tavistock Adult Depression Study (TADS)', *World Psychiatry*, 14(3): 312–321.

Gainotti, G. (2012) 'Unconscious Processing of Emotions and the Right Hemisphere', *Neuropsychologia*, 50(2): 205–218.

Geller, S. M. and Greenberg, L. S. (2012) *Therapeutic Presence: A Mindful Approach to Effective Therapy*, Washington, DC: APA Publications.

Gendlin, E. T. (1986) *Let Your Body Interpret Your Dreams*, Wilmette, IL: Chiron Publications.

Gibson, R. (2008) *My Body, My Earth: The Practice of Somatic Archaeology*, New York: iUniverse.

Gilbert, P. (2009) *The Compassionate Mind*, London: Constable.

Gilbert, P. (2010) *Compassion Focused Therapy*, London: Routledge.

Gilbert, P., Bailey, K. G. and McGuire, M. T. (2000) 'Evolutionary Psychotherapy: Principles and Outline', in *Genes on the Couch: Explorations in Evolutionary Psychology*, P. Gilbert and K. G. Bailey (eds), Hove: Brunner-Routledge, pp. 3–27.

Greenfield, S. (2014) *Mind Change: How 21st Century Technology is Leaving its Mark on the Brain*, London: Random House.

Hanson, R. (2013) *Hardwiring Happiness: The Practical Science of Reshaping Your Brain – and Your Life*, London: Rider.

Hanson, R. and Mendius, R. (2009) *Buddha's Brain: The Practical Neuroscience of Happiness, Love and Wisdom*, Oakland, CA: New Harbinger Publications.

Heller, L. and LaPierre, A. (2012) *Healing Developmental Trauma: How Early Trauma Affects Self-Regulation, Self-Image, and the Capacity for Relationship*, Berkeley, CA: North Atlantic Books.

Leeds, A. M. (2009) 'Resources in EMDR and Other Trauma-Focused Psychotherapy: Review', *Journal of EMDR Practice and Research*, 3(3): 152–160.

Levine, P. (1997) *Waking the Tiger: Healing Trauma*, Berkeley, CA: North Atlantic Books.

MacLean, P. D. (1990) *The Triune Brain in Evolution: Role in Paleocerebral Functions*, New York: Springer.

McGilchrist, I. (2009) *The Master and His Emissary: The Divided Brain and the Making of the Western World*, New Haven and London: Yale University Press.

Ogden, P., Minton, K. and Pain, C. (2006) *Trauma and the Body: A Sensorimotor Approach to Psychotherapy*, New York: W. W. Norton.

Panksepp, J. (1998) *Affective Neuroscience: The Foundations of Human and Animal Emotions*, New York: Oxford University Press.

Panksepp, J. and Watt, D. (2011) 'What is Basic about Basic Emotions? Lasting Lessons from Affective Neuroscience', *Emotion Review*, 3(4): 1–10.

Peres, J. and Nasello, A. G. (2008) 'Psychotherapy and Neuroscience: Towards Closer Integration', *International Journal of Psychology*, 43(6): 943–957.

Porges, S. W. (2011) *The Polyvagal Theory: Neurophysiological Foundations of Emotions, Attachment, Communication, and Self-Regulation*, New York: W. W. Norton.

Rothschild, B. (2006) 'Controlling Empathic Imagery', *Self & Society*, 33(6): 15–21.

Rozin, P. and Royzman, E. B. (2001) 'Negativity Bias, Negativity Dominance, and Contagion', *Personality and Social Psychology Review*, 5(4): 296–320.

Ryle, A. (2005) 'The Relevance of Evolutionary Psychology for Psychotherapy', *British Journal of Psychotherapy*, 21(3): 375–388.

Scaer, R. (2014 [2001]) *The Body Bears the Burden: Trauma, Dissociation, and Disease*, New York and London: Routledge.

Schore, A. N. (2012) *The Science of the Art of Psychotherapy*, New York and London: W. W. Norton.

Schore, A. N. (2014) 'The Right Brain is Dominant in Psychotherapy', *Psychotherapy*, 51(3): 388–397.

Schore, A. N. (2016) *Affect Regulation and the Origin of the Self: The Neurobiology of Emotional Development*, New York: Routledge.

Schwarz, L., Corrigan, F., Hull, A. and Raju, R. (2016) *The Comprehensive Resource Model: Effective Therapeutic Techniques for the Healing of Complex Trauma*, London: Routledge.

Sieff, D. F. (2015) *Understanding and Healing Emotional Trauma: Conversations with Pioneering Clinicians and Researchers*, London and New York: Routledge.

Siegel, D. (1999) *The Developing Mind: How Relationships and the Brain Interact to Shape Who We Are*, New York: Guilford.

Siegel, D. J. (2001) 'Toward an Interpersonal Neurobiology of the Developing Mind: Attachment Relationships, Mindsight, and Neural Integration', *Infant Mental Health Journal*, 22(1–2): 67–94.

Stern, D. N. (2004a) 'The Present Moment as a Critical Moment', *Negotiation Journal*, 20(2): 365–372.

Stern, D. N. (2004b) *The Present Moment in Psychotherapy and Everyday Life*, New York: W. W. Norton.

Turnbull, A. N. (2003) 'Emotion, False Beliefs, and the Neurobiology of Intuition', in *Revolutionary Connections*, J. Corrigall and H. Wilkinson (eds), London: Karnac, pp. 135–162.

Van der Kolk, B. (2014) *The Body Keeps the Score: Mind, Brain and Body in the Transformation of Trauma*, London: Penguin.

Wiggins, S., Elliott, R. and Cooper, M. (2012) 'The Prevalence and Characteristics of Relational Depth Events in Psychotherapy', *Psychotherapy Research*, 22(2): 139–158.

Whyte, D. (2002 [2001]) *Crossing the Unknown Sea: Working and the Shaping of Identity*, London: Penguin.

Chapter 4

Dimensions of experiencing

Defining dimensions

Resource focused therapy recognises a number of distinct, though intrinsically interdependent, dimensions or modalities constituent to being human, in and through which we express ourselves, experience life, and connect with the world and everything in it, on it and above it, including the other-than-human and more-than-human worlds. As David Michael Levin (1985: 97) writes, 'the transformative process reverberates through many dimensions', and 'we are finite openings-for-Being localised as bodies within the field of Being as a whole.' In my view, these dimensions include: thinking (or mental, cognitive), feeling (or emotion or affect), physical (or body or sensation), imaginal, energetic, behavioural, interpersonal and spiritual. The Jungian influence here is obvious (i.e., Carl Jung's four functions: thinking, feeling, sensation and intuition), but the present framework is preferred as it often appears that intuition occurs across the dimensions rather than as a separate dimension. Within this view intuition is understood as characteristic of each dimension; if you like, it is the dimension's connate and accumulative wisdom. So, there is thinking intuition, feeling intuition, imaginal intuition, intuition of the body, and so on; this understanding is similar to that of Eligio Stephen Gallegos (1991).

Further, the maturity of these dimensions relies on our responsiveness to, and engagement with the world. To put it another way, the comprehensive enablement and individuation of these modalities is only possible through our being in relationship with our environment. We cannot individuate on our own, and only do so in and through relationship with external factors. What is more, I suggest that this multimodal actualising process is largely participatory, in that its fulfilment relies on the experiences arising out of the interaction with the other and outer 'reality' as a whole.

My views here are particularly inspired by the work of Jorge Ferrer (2000, 2002) and his participatory consciousness paradigm in transpersonal psychology and spiritual studies. He puts forward the view that spiritual experiences arise out of a cocreative participatory process, where experiences occur as 'events' or 'participatory events' following a participatory enactment with the other, rather than an experience arising only from 'me'. By relating this theory to areas in addition to spirituality, we locate the development of a range of dimensions within a participatory framework. Specifically, we come to view significant aspects of our development as inseparable from the development of the whole. So, for instance, I suggest the realisation of the emotional, behavioural, interpersonal, imaginal, energetic and spiritual dimensions, in particular, are largely reliant on the responsiveness from the other. This other or these others, through *their* reaching out, are also in the process of becoming fully and uniquely themselves in relation to others. This is a cocreative participatory process in which the becoming of one is dependent on the other, so that the experience of becoming and the expansion and development of the dimensions is not individually or singularly achieved. Rather, achievement arises out of encounters with the other, giving rise to an experience brought about by an 'event' created by both in the encounter. Extending the application of the participatory consciousness paradigm to other dimensions in this way also implies that this other can be an animal, person, presence or even a work of art, as we are potentially enabled by everything around us (Wilson, 2011), just as the garden gate grants us freedom, or the solitary cry of the curlew in winter stirs the imagination.

Another fundamental point made in this chapter is the idea of a dimension having *its own right*, its own developmental path, or its own potential (albeit often unlived) in some way *decided* or *directed* by the distinctive nature of that dimension. To view each dimension as a 'person' with its own unique developmental needs and dimension specific language may be a useful way of considering this. Each dimension is a unique mode of expression, of experiencing, of processing information within the brain/mind/body systems. This means that the need of a dimension can *only* be known by *that* dimension rather than by another dimension. In other words, the need is to 'feel' what you 'feel' rather than to 'think' what you 'feel', or to 'sense' the need of the 'body' rather than to merely 'think' what might be good for the body, or to discern the needs of the interpersonal, behavioural, imaginal or spiritual dimensions rather than to decide from a left brain thinking bias. As Ferrer (2011: 24) points out, '*human dimensions cannot mature autonomously*', but require 'spaces in which [to] mature according to their own developmental principles and dynamics, not according to the ones the mind considers most adequate'. For instance, people sometimes find themselves pulling away from an interpersonal opportunity (e.g., joining or engaging in something) because of a strong thinking judgement (often self-critical), despite feeling the interpersonal pull. Obvious in many ways, I am bringing a spotlight to each of these dimensions in the belief that separating the parts from the whole enables viewing these in their distinctiveness. However, crucially, my view is that development of the dimensions is a cocreative, participatory, coinfluencing process between the dimensions and with 'reality out there', and that this enterprise brings about the fullest integration of a person; the dimensions coming together like a dance of maturity in the dance of life; this is integration. This chapter, then, surveys the field and suggests ways to strengthen clients in these dimensions, within therapy and in their lives in general. The chapter will also consider research into increasing capacity in these dimensions, and examine the effect of developing specific dimensions on other dimensions; the coinfluencing participatory whole.

It is of course unlikely that a person will consider the full scope of these modalities or dimensions as vehicles for experiencing and expressing, but will mostly identify with either feeling or thinking, or conflate the dimensions into an undifferentiated whole. It is also probable that a person will often take for granted the development of most of these dimensions, or may not consider these as *parts with potentials*, and as such worthy to be separately developed. And it is perhaps rarer still that a person may view a dimension as deserving development *in its own right*. Unless, of course, it is left brain thinking which, arguably, is overly regarded in Western culture and is generally life-defining (and life-limiting) to the detriment of such other dimensions as feeling, imaginal or spirituality.

Resourcing via the physical dimension

The physical dimension refers to our bodily felt sensate experience which includes the way our breath sustains us (Chapter 2), and how through our movement and posture we shape and carry our bodies, as well as the myriad forms of bodily information which enable our participatory life; we might refer to this as 'body intelligence' (BQ) or 'physical intelligence' (PQ). While it is not easy to separate body from feeling, affect or emotion, it helps to bracket temporarily the feeling and energetic dimensions to highlight the body. In relation to the thinking dimension, we seldom allow left brain thinking, often taken for granted and driven by the will, to become companion to a somatic way of being with its own deeply embedded right brain intelligence. Iain McGilchrist (2009: 67) informs that the right and left brain hemispheres view the body in different ways. The right hemisphere 'is responsible for our sense of the body as something we "live", something that is part of our identity'; the point of connection with our surroundings. Conversely, for the left hemisphere, 'the body is something from which we are relatively detached, a thing in the world, like other things' (p. 67), an object, or it views identity 'as an assemblage of parts' (p. 439) without reference to the whole (i.e., other dimensions). Following his thesis that Western culture is largely left brain dominant, we may argue that most Westerners tend to be somewhat dissociated from their bodies; not wholly embodied, lived in, grounded or present; and perhaps, he suggests, even suffering from 'The left hemisphere's assault on our embodied nature' (p. 440) through a life lived from the myopia of a left brain bias. This disconnection from our bodies is one source of alienation from the whole.

The physical dimension in the modalities

Comprehensive integration of the body is to be found in the body psychotherapies; for example, some Gestalt therapy, Focusing Orientated Psychotherapy (Eugene Gendlin), many mindfulness-based therapies (e.g., transpersonal psychotherapies, Buddhist orientated psychotherapies), and some Jungians. Body is the main mode of listening to the client in these therapies, as the therapist listens to the client's body with their body. In this sense, conjointly with the interpersonal, feeling and energetic dimensions, the physical dimension is the vehicle for attunement in the therapeutic relationship, within which the client's body communicates its narrative, the content of what it is holding (e.g., joys, trauma), its 'truth', and what it has absorbed from other sources (e.g., the joy of others, the therapist and perhaps the cry of Earth's body). We are not always aware of what it might be from others that we have embodied. As I have indicated earlier, by 'others' I not only mean person, place and culture, but everything that might take refuge in our bodies: not only genetic potentials passed on from our ancestors, but also experiences drawn from whatever is within range of our senses, be this in our own daily lives or through the media. Everything enters into our bodies through the gateways of our senses.

The physical dimension in working through trauma

The more informed we are from neurobiology of the profound interplay between brain, body and mind, especially as this relates to experiences of trauma, and in particular how traumatic events are processed and held in the body, it becomes imperative to integrate this learning into therapy. Somatic focused therapies (e.g., Peter Levine's Somatic Experiencing), in different ways, give primacy to the body with a specific focus on resolving trauma (Angela, Chapter 8). Here somatic intelligence is a guiding factor in the therapeutic process and relationship (Chapter 7). Again, the maxim is: 'Allow your body to lead the way'.

Physical symptom as symbol

The 'language' of the right hemisphere is that of image, metaphor and symbol (see imaginal, below), therefore meanings are often implicit, layered and somewhat veiled. From this perspective, body symptoms (e.g., blushing, tears, sighing, twinges) and some somatic illnesses (e.g., dysmorphia, anorexia nervosa, chronic fatigue syndrome) may contain information or meanings other than the apparently obvious. These meanings are perhaps mostly discernible through entering into embodied imagination as a way of listening to body's wisdom, for example, Carl Jung's 'active imagination' (e.g., Hannah, 1981) or Gendlin's (1996) 'focusing'; arguably associated with mostly right hemisphere orientated activities, with 'one foot' in the unconscious. We may indeed recall how Georg

Groddeck (1977: 116), often considered the founder of psychosomatic medicine and writing in the early twentieth century, identified that:

> The unconscious (…) reveals itself in every gesture, in the twitching of the forehead, the beating of the heart, yet also in the quiet warning of a uric-acid diathesis [i.e., gout], a sensitive sympathicus [i.e., sensitive nerves], the phthisic behaviour [i.e., consumptive symptoms], and finally in the insistent voice of illness too.

Naturally, viewing everything symbolically is as reductive as viewing everything literally, and it is always wise to seek medical advice.

The physical dimension, then, is its own 'person'. It is not an appendage of the mind; rather the mind evolves out of the body. As therapists, we may want to remain intently contiguous to what is *ready to unfold*, develop or emerge, rather than *impose* a method or practice (e.g., mindfulness or other therapeutic interventions). For by so doing we potentially bypass areas that require reparation or development. The physical dimension must 'enter a process of healing, maturation, and germination according to [its] own developmental principles', which allows the body, rather than the mind, to discern what is 'more natural and vital for its optimum development' (Ferrer, 2003: 27). The physical dimension is regularly the most neglected.

Resourcing via the feeling dimension

There seems to be no consensus in the literature what the concepts 'feeling' and 'emotion' mean, especially their nature, and so their consideration is complex. However, a reasonable premise for now is that emotion is an activity in the body which gives rise to feeling. As Antonio Damasio (2001: 781) states: 'The main target of the emotional responses is the body', or as McGilchrist (2009: 66) indicates, 'Emotion is inseparable from the body in which it is felt', and feelings are the 'direct consequences of emotions' (Damasio, 2001: 781). The span of development in this dimension includes our felt propensity to engage with life and our surroundings. As McGilchrist (2009: 66) identifies, emotion is our point of entry for this engagement through, for instance, empathic connection and concern for others. Emotions are our 'inner compass' of evaluation, determining what we turn towards and how, and feelings are our more conscious knowing of this. Each one of us navigates by a different 'compass' and its innate intelligence has immense potential, even if this is mostly unlived.

Emotional intelligence

Riding on the assumption that 'intelligences' are innate across the dimensions, we first consider a description of 'emotional intelligence' (EQ) and its nuances, following Daniel Goleman's (1996) popularising of the term.

Perceiving emotions: this is a knowing of one's emotions and feelings with a basic capacity for being aware of them as they arise in the present moment, and includes the ability to precisely recognise and express emotions, which helps to differentiate between hospitable and hostile situations (Schneider, Lyons and Khazon, 2013).

Focused self-regulation: this is the ability to activate, utilise or influence emotions to support thinking, and includes 'altering emotion to redirect cognitive processes, obtain new perspectives, and enhance problem-solving or creativity' (p. 909). This may also include cultivating the capacity to '*change emotion with emotion*' (Greenberg, 2004: 10), rather than with thinking, thereby enabling the dimension to transform itself. However, it is likely that mental fatigue weakens emotion regulation (Grillon et al., 2015), which again highlights the participatory nature of the dimensions.

Emotional comprehension: this capacity enables the 'understand[ing] of emotional information, the manner in which they combine, and their causes and consequences' (Schneider, Lyons and Khazon, 2013: 909).

Emotional authority: this 'includes the ability to be open to feelings and modulate them to facilitate growth, even during duress' (p. 909). However, while they accurately highlight the participatory nature of the dimensions by referring to the role of emotion in assisting cognitive processes, Tamera Schneider and colleagues (2013: 909) seem to diminish the dynamic nature of the feeling dimension by limiting it to a 'set of four emotional skills' and insisting on a hierarchical attainment of these.

The wide-reaching capacity of emotional intelligence also includes the way in which empathic responding and expressions of concern are possible. I begin with Levin's (1985: 148) sentiment that 'the fulfilment of our capacity for becoming fully human depends upon, and calls for, *a body of feeling whose gestures are gestures of love* – of caring, of solicitude, of compassion, of loving kindness.' These 'gestures' arise out of bringing a particular attention to what matters; as if rising up from the wellspring of our collective humanity. Therefore, more than a cognitive function, the 'ontological status of [attention] is something prior to functions and even to things' (McGilchrist, 2009: 28). These 'gestures' are principally right hemisphere functions, and convey a sense of responsiveness, connection and affinity. McGilchrist (2009: 29) writes:

> Attention, however, intrinsically is a *way in which*, not a thing: it is intrinsically a relationship, not a brute fact. It is a 'howness', a something between, an aspect of consciousness itself, not a 'whatness', a thing in itself, an object of consciousness. It brings into the world and, with it, depending on its nature, a set of values.

The feeling dimension, as with other dimensions, invites its own specific maturing to enable its fullest capacity, and is defined at its most developed expression by a range of self-decided virtues or values. These may include, as we have seen above, love and passion (desire of the heart, not the ego), loving kindness, loving presence, compassion and self-compassion, trust in one's own 'truth finding' process; and the following felt 'gestures' and virtues: honesty, patience, gentleness, warmth, peace, appreciation of beauty, joy, openness and receptiveness characterised by a sense of allowing in the spirit of acceptance (e.g., of your inner self-guidance, and vulnerability), self-enquiry, generosity, strength and equanimity, capacity to let go (of expectations, of over-identification with the content of awareness), a sense of humour, a capacity for entering into stillness (while perhaps allowing something 'greater' to move), optimism, contentment, a sense of curiosity and wonderment, discernment and responsiveness (e.g., of your growing edges), commitment (loyalty, fidelity), courage, integrity to inform intentions, humility, a sense of empowerment, resourcefulness, enthusiasm in life, as well as a sense of gratitude and appreciation.

Gratitude as a therapeutic intervention

Take 'gratitude' for instance. Robert Emmons and Robert Stern's (2013: 848) study on 'gratitude as a psychotherapeutic intervention' suggests that its benefits are highly correlated to well-being, more so than optimism, hope or compassion. They argue that grateful people experience more positive emotions (e.g., joy, love) and that 'gratitude as a discipline protects us from the destructive impulses of envy, resentment, greed, and bitterness'. They also point out that grateful people even cope more effectively with ordinary stress, are more resilient to trauma related stress, make more rapid recovery from illness, and benefit from stronger physical health. 'Taken together, these results indicate that gratitude is incompatible with negative emotions and pathological conditions and that it may even offer protection against psychiatric disorders' (p. 848). Of course, these positive emotions and feelings contend with those of loneliness, despair, worthlessness, isolation, grief, fear, guilt, shame, and so on, as important sources of information that require responsive attention in the feeling dimension. These authors recognise gratitude is not always easy to cultivate.

Resilience revisited

Despite this, studies suggest that 'positive emotions protect psychological health by undoing or buffering against the effects of stress' and help protect against susceptibility toward depression (Rutten et al., 2013: 12). Findings also indicate that positive emotions correspond strongly to a sense of meaning and purpose in life (p. 13), while meditation and mindfulness-based approaches, such as loving-kindness meditation (Pali: *metta bhavana*) may not only foster a greater sense of self-awareness, but also support the increase of positive emotions like resilience.

This resilience (see also Chapter 2) has been found to enable 'people to maintain their mental health and well-being when faced with adversity – not necessarily only when recovering from trauma', and to remain effective in the implementation of life tasks and goals (Robertson and Cooper, 2013: 175). Therapists may help clients increase resilience through, for example: exploring concerns about achieving wished for goals, including related themes of confidence and self-doubt; setting realistic and achievable mutually agreed goals; reviewing and reminding clients of their capacities in overcoming previous challenges; and supporting them to find ways of engaging in life. Ultimately, we enable clients to find grounding in their own 'inner compass', comprising values, attitudes, beliefs and principles both existent and emergent. With this intention we help them to explore fully their emotional and feeling nature, and to anchor their identity in what feels maximally authentic. While therapists across the modalities will aim to enable this, Gendlin's 'focusing' offers an established method of achieving this.

Eugene Gendlin's 'focusing'

Focusing was developed in the 1960s by Gendlin (1969) and based on research conducted at the University of Chicago in which he found that people who were able to pay particular attention to their bodily felt-sense benefited most from therapy, describing this introspective process as self-guiding wisdom. He called these 'pre-verbal and pre-conceptual' experiences (Gendlin, 1969: 8) moments of knowing or 'felt meaning' (Gendlin, 1969: 7) which give rise to new meanings and new perspectives on life's situations. This 'felt sense' and 'felt meaning' is similar to Carl Jung's concept of 'active imagination' which is an unfolding process of knowing through bodily-felt imagination, rather than cognition; or, in other words, an intuitive-sensate-imaginal-feeling, which is fundamentally a right brain rather than left brain process. Gendlin (1981 [1969]: 9) maintained that paying specific attention to emerging bodily felt sense experiences or images in this way, rather than thoughts, enables a person to live from greater depth. Following development of his basic method of self-enquiry (Gendlin, 1969) he incorporated the use of imagery (Gendlin and Olsen, 1970; cf. embodied imagery, Appendix), and later dreams (Gendlin, 1986), and continued to develop focusing into the 1990s (Gendlin, 1996). My use of the term 'embodied felt-sense' in this book combines both Jung's and Gendlin's understanding of this right brain process. Focusing is taken up and adapted by many and is a core method in some psychotherapy practices (e.g., Transpersonal Psychotherapy, Core Process Psychotherapy, Person-Centred Therapy and Art Psychotherapy). It has also been applied to some areas of psychoanalysis to bring attention to implicit dimensions of experience, that is, experience 'which is in some sense known, but not yet available to reflective thought or verbalisation' (Preston, 2008: 348). Studies have also considered the contribution of focusing to psychotherapy in a number of areas, including to reduce anxiety (Elliot, 2013), process trauma in Art Psychotherapy (Rappaport, 2010), explore the continuum of dissociative states (Krycka, 2010), and integrate spiritual and religious experiences (Hinterkopf, 2005; Leijssen, 2008).

The feeling dimension is further, and perhaps essentially, cultivated in the feeling environment of the therapeutic relationship (Chapter 7), where the therapist empathically engages with clients' conscious and unconscious emotional and feeling processes. The emollient quality of the therapeutic relationship heals at an emotional and feeling level, which is the level where clients often remember their bodily felt experience of abandonment, vulnerability, fear, of being lost, and so on. Indeed, if we are cut off from feeling, or if feeling appears unavailable to us, then we are truly lost. Naturally resourcing the feeling dimension takes time, and increasing our amplitude and experience within this dimension is often a painful, yet liberating, process.

Resourcing via the thinking dimension

Our discussion of the thinking dimension follows on from our earlier consideration of brain/mind processes (Chapters 1 and 2). To recapitulate, first, there are three main self-regulating systems in the brain. These are the avoiding threat regulating system; the 'curiosity-interest-expectancy' system (Turnbull, 2003: 141); and the attachment seeking system. Second, Paul Rozin and Edward Royzman (2001) hypothesise that the brain/mind system tilts towards a 'negativity bias' which can obstruct our innate capacity to self-resource and self-regulate. Also, a similar hypothesis from Roy Baumeister and colleagues (2001) posits that we are evolutionarily adaptive for 'bad' to be stronger than 'good'. According to this view, while it is likely that we will encounter more 'good' than 'bad' things in life, we are more susceptible to attuning to 'bad' things as our well-being may depend on this. At the same time, thinking is a whole brain function. However, over the centuries, priority has been given to logic over experience, allowing the left hemisphere to increase in dominance, particularly when we use thinking to attempt to create 'stasis, certainty, fixity' where there is none (McGilchrist, 2009: 428). For instance, we may find ourselves scanning for such stability with regard to safety, satisfaction and security in the face of possible threat or uncertainty in these areas, even when everything is alright (for example, when our evaluation of current safety is determined by past trauma), and battle with the 'negativity bias' of the brain/mind.

The restrictiveness of self-doubt

Repeated failed attempts to establish such 'stasis, certainty, fixity', where there is none, may lead to a spiralling into self-doubt with its distinctive judgemental, vacillating temperament. This is a frequently occurring theme in therapy and is expressed as a concern to get things 'right' or make the 'right' decision. With this comes a feeling of deficiency or paralysis; forgetting that often there is no 'right' but only what *feels* preferable from a number of options; sometimes only marginally so. Most of the time there is no 'right', but only consequences or outcomes of decisions, and mostly nothing quite matching those arising from 'negativity bias' concerns. Even so, self-doubt often leads to resistance to leaning into life's possibilities for fear of making a mistake. Although it is unable to navigate fully through life with the resources provided by thought alone, left hemisphere thinking often discounts *feeling*, or felt-sense, in making decisions, and does not value enough experiences of uncertainty. On the other hand, self-doubt is a leveller of ego-inflation, a companion to humility, providing it does not tip the balance toward ego-deflation. As an antidote to this self-doubt and negativity, in finding the 'right' thing or potential to follow through, and ruminating about safety, satisfaction and security, and in the unfavourable tilting of the 'negativity bias', the thinking dimension can be resourced by strengthening a range of capacities (Alice, Chapter 5). These include the following.

Cultivating optimism

Optimism is the tendency to expect 'good' things to happen in life. Relatively stable over time, this trait is either innate or learnt and has a 'genetic component' (Carver, Scheier and Segerstrom, 2010: 887). Studies into optimism indicate that this trait may activate cognitive resources, like resilience, by expanding the ability to cope in the face of stressful life events, and increase persistence in the face of life challenges, as well as develop confidence. Optimism also benefits the interpersonal dimension in helping form relationships (Carver, Scheier and Segerstrom, 2010). Like all resources, optimism is a felt experience and not only a thought, and can be stimulated in a number of ways (e.g., Hanson's Positive Neuroplasticity Training (PNT) in Chapter 6). However, Charles Carver and colleagues (2010: 886) caution 'that it can be unwise to simply substitute an unquestioning optimism for an existing doubt' as there are occasions when self-doubt is useful, for instance, when there is a strong drive towards perfection. We may also caution against an overly confident use of 'positive psychology' in general, as it can give rise to a subtle (or not so subtle) devaluing of certain feelings as negative, and therefore unwanted. My suggestion is that it is more useful to view phenomena (e.g., feelings, thoughts, sensations) as information worthy of compassionate enquiry, while gently encouraging or easing into areas which enhance the quality of life.

Cultivating mindfulness and self-compassion

On the contrary, to resist the view that phenomena are either positive or negative, and to allow an experience to simply 'be there', without taking sides or wanting to change it through cultivating 'non-interfering awareness' (Goldstein, 2013: 14), is at the heart of mindfulness. This is a *paying attention* with receptivity, in the present moment, to the content of awareness from the perspective of an impartial yet compassionate witness. This is more than just another left hemisphere thinking function, but a capacity to pay attention which 'is prior to functions and even things' (McGilchrist, 2009: 28). It is like the qualitative experience of resting in awareness itself without 'doing' anything. In this sense, paying attention is an embodied felt experience imbued with stillness; a cultivation of a sense of presence in the present moment; or consciousness noticing itself, and is perhaps most fully enabled through the practice of contemplation or meditation.

One of the benefits of mindfulness is that it reduces over-identification with the content of awareness which is one of the causes of psychological stress or suffering. It does this by adopting an attitude of loosening or letting go of pushing or pulling, wanting or not wanting, and grasping or rejecting. So if we do not become the object of attention (whether it be thought, feeling, sensation or image), while at the same time allow the object of attention to simply 'be there', we become a compassionate witness to our experience in the present moment. There are a growing number of publications on the integration of mindfulness in therapy, and its related practice of self-compassion or self-kindness, which incorporate and enhance mindfulness by increasing openness to our suffering (e.g., Germer, Siegel and Fulton, 2013; Pollak, Pedualla and Siegel, 2014). This body of literature supports the mindfulness-based therapist to facilitate further an increase in clients' self-awareness and reduce over-identification with the content of their awareness.

The benefits of self-compassion or self-kindness purport to revise clients' view of themselves and their relationship to negative self-evaluations. This is largely because 'self-compassion is *not* based on self-evaluations or set standards' (Neff, 2004: 3), but on acceptance, in the sense of allowing rather than agreeing. Studies on the benefits of self-compassion include a reduction in the following psychological areas: in feelings of shame and self-criticism (e.g., Neff, 2003; Gilbert, 2009; Kelly, Zuroff and Shapira, 2009); in avoidance strategies following exposure to trauma (e.g., Thompson and Waltz, 2008); and in 'neurotic perfectionism, depression, anxiety, rumination and thought suppression, as well as greater life satisfaction, social connectedness and emotional intelligence' (Neff, 2003: 240; cf. Kelly, Zuroff and Shapira, 2009; Raes, 2010). Moreover, self-compassion is also inversely associated with eating disorders, depression and anxiety (Longe et al., 2010) in reducing the self-critical part of these conditions. Also, self-compassion does not give rise to self-inflation or self-deflation in the way that 'high' or 'low' self-esteem can (Neff, 2004). On this point I agree with Neff (2008) that self-compassion is preferable to self-esteem since the former is judgement free and achieves all the benefits of healthy self-esteem (e.g., confidence, increased self-worth and strength) while also embracing qualities inherent in compassion such as kindness, warmth, tenderness, acceptance and empathic understanding.

Finally, Kristin Neff's (2009: 213) research has found that 'self-compassion [is] associated with more noncontingent and stable feelings of self-worth over time, while also offering stronger protection against social comparison, public self-consciousness, self-rumination, anger and closed-mindedness'.

Strengthening the 'two' wills

Following on from our previous section, I suggest that mindfulness, con-templation, meditation and self-compassion deepen our nesting into a right hemisphere 'disposition towards the world', in so far as these practices foster qualities and attitudes of connecting to the whole, openness, spaciousness, care and letting go of a tendency to control. Borrowing the phrase 'disposition towards the world' from McGilchrist (2009: 171) helps us to look more closely at the idea of 'will'.

McGilchrist (p. 171) points out that our 'disposition towards the world' is bipolar, in that the will of the left hemisphere is about increased 'use' and 'control' (e.g., self-control or willpower), while the will of the right hemisphere is about concern, 'care' and expansiveness, for 'Its will relates to a desire or longing towards something, something that lies beyond itself, towards the Other' (p. 171) (my view is that this also relates to the spiritual dimension which we will come to later). It therefore seems there are 'two' wills: what I am calling the right-brain-will and the left-brain-will.

Even though it is predominantly a right brain activity (Schore, 2014), therapy arguably gives more attention to strengthening the left-brain-will, by increasing self-control, self-motivation, and reducing ego-depletion, often to the neglect of the right-brain-will (Chapter 2). Conversely, the right-brain-will helps to increase spaciousness, openness, and to allow the experience and the cultivation of self-care as some mindfulness-based therapies encourage. An integrative (of the person) approach to therapy would clearly want to resource development of the 'two' wills. However, 'doing' therapy invariably focuses on managing stress or anger, and puts more emphasis on rationality than reasonableness (rooted in feeling), the pursuit of material things, and the impossible search of happiness. However, in these ways therapy risks being out of relationship with the body, which 'holds in itself the disposition of both hemispheres towards the world' (McGilchrist, 2009: 172), and with the bodies of others (interpersonal). It is important to keep both left and right hemisphere thinking in balance, rather than to increase the dominance of the left. I believe that resource focused therapy takes into account the whole and anchors this in the life of the body in relationship to another body, namely the therapist.

Finally, up to now, with the possible exception of Mindfulness-Based Cognitive Therapy (MBCT) (Kabat-Zinn et al., 2013 [2012]) and the Emotion-Focused Cognitive Behavioural Therapies (ECBT) (e.g., Thoma and Mckay, 2014), there is a tendency within some areas of the mental health professions to prioritise left hemisphere thinking as the focus of treatment, usually in the form of CBT, which has not easily taken into account the therapeutic benefits gained from other modalities, and which is mostly technique driven. So, for example, in relation to this, Carver and colleagues (2010: 886) offer, in my view, a typical example of these tendencies in stating that 'The most straightforward way to talk about turning a pessimist into an optimist is a set of techniques known collectively as cognitive-behavioural therapies.' This emphasis on 'straightforward', and 'turning' through use of 'techniques' is devaluing of an experience and its meaning, and undermining of the complex nature of personhood. In a convincing article challenging the dominance of so called 'evidence-based therapy', Jonathan Shedler (2015: 47) asks 'where is the evidence for evidence based therapy?' He argues that in CBT 'treatment may be prescribed in a way that leaves little room for understanding of the patient' (p. 47), and focuses primarily on resolving negative cognitive distortions, and targets beliefs and teaches skills to decrease negative automatic thoughts. Many clients may benefit from these interventions (e.g., those with anxiety or some forms of depression), but contrary to popular perception the evidence to support this is not totally convincing. Shedler (2015: 55) found from his surveys that 'evidence-based' therapies fail to demonstrate greater effectiveness than other therapies, and makes a plea to therapists to challenge declarations of treatment benefits by requesting and then examining the reported evidence. Frank Corrigan and Alastair Hull (2015: 79) offer a similar challenge in writing on the treatment of trauma, arguing that CBT is 'over-optimistic' in its assertions of effectiveness. It is also a key component of scientific research that results are repeatable, yet it appears that many studies in cognitive psychology fail repetition (Staples, 2015). To summarise, thinking is a whole brain function, and not just of the left hemisphere. We cannot come to wholeness by placing emphasis on one part of the brain alone, or one part of a dimension alone, even if the benefits gained from resourcing capacities in these areas filter from one part of the brain and from one dimension to another.

Resourcing via the imaginal dimension

Jung wrote (1981 [1921]: 63) 'The debt we owe to the play [i.e., fantasy] of imagination is incalculable.' Indeed, everything arises first in imagination. Whether we are aware of it or not our imagination is unceasing, going wherever we rest our attention. In this way it helps us access the experience of familiar resources (e.g., 'patience is one of my strengths'), rekindle remembered resources (e.g., 'my capacity for perseverance brought me through that difficult time') and anticipate future resources (e.g., 'trusting the loving support of my partner will enable my next step in life'). We also know, for example, that by bringing our attention to either positive or negative thoughts, the embodied felt experience of these thoughts occurs now, in the present moment, even as we ruminate about the past or worry about the future; whatever we focus our attention on creates the experience in the now. We can take advantage of this fact by drawing upon our imagination to embellish the experience of a resource to increase its positive benefit. We can, for instance, recall a strength or capacity (e.g., enthusiasm for life, gratitude or appreciation, joy, self-acceptance, contentment) while at the same time imagine the quality of that strength as a bodily felt experience in the moment, which allows the capacity to be fully present now.

Mary Warnock (1976: 133) suggests that the faculty of imagination enables the joining together of experiences by association, thereby creating a coherence or wholeness of something so, for example, our perception of the fullness of a tree includes the many aspects that remain hidden. Imagination fills in the gaps. We may deduce from this that imagination is the capacity to help create possibilities in life by first paving the way through considering the potential whole. If something can be first imagined then it can exist, if not in life itself, then certainly in the arts and in other ways. It also reinforces the feeling of concern for others, empathy and compassion. On the other hand, imagination can help create an expansive life experience, but it can also establish a narrow airless space with little scope. Both possibilities are the fruit of imagination; felt experience follows the content of imagination. *An experience grows where imagination goes.*

As a faculty, imagination is perhaps our most potent resource, especially if we allow images to engage us 'actively' rather than 'passively' watch them. Following Jung, 'active imagination' is imagination with feeling; an *experience* rather than just a thought. Experiences by definition bring together the brain/mind/body dimensions, particularly the physical, energetic, feeling, thinking, imaginal and spiritual. As we have seen, experiences, more than thoughts, bring about lasting changes in the brain/mind/body.

The nocturnal expression of imagination is dreaming. In fact, dreams are a powerful form of imagination, often taking on the felt experience of waking life. Renowned examples of inspiration gained from night dreams include Albert Einstein, Carl Jung, Edgar Allan Poe, and countless others. Dreams also resource meaning-making and decision-making in life, and enable the processing of difficult emotional experiences, including trauma, as is particularly demonstrated in the work of Donald Kalsched (1996, 2013).

Daydreams, on the other hand, far from being lapses of attention, can be a way for the brain to achieve an 'at rest' state. Felicity Callard (2014) rightly points out that daydreaming is also 'invaluable for important psychological attributes such as creativity, happiness and planning our future'. This is largely because daydreaming can engage imagination to consider new possibilities. Gaston Bachelard (1994 [1964]: 193) writes:

> Daydream undoubtedly feeds on all kinds of sights, but through a sort of natural inclination, it contemplates grandeur. And this contemplation produces an attitude that is so special, an inner state that is so unlike any other, that the daydream transports the dreamer outside the immediate world to a world that bears the mark of infinity.

However, the value of daydreaming also depends on its qualitative nature. Daydreaming on the absence of relationship, for example, can increase feelings of loneliness and so decrease feelings of life satisfaction (Mar, Mason and Litvack, 2012). The resource focused therapist will find ways of working with dreams as best fits their modality(ies), and may want to take into account the pioneering work of Gendlin, especially his (1986) *Let Your Body Interpret Your Dreams* which sets out a comprehensive approach to body-based dreamwork.

Another powerful resource is imagery. Though strongly aligned with imagination, imagery is sometimes viewed as a separate concept, and refers to the ability to produce representations of things previously experienced, perhaps even innate or genetically rooted (Agnati et al., 2013), rather than novel imaginings. The therapeutic use of guided imagery is widespread; from its extensive use in Jungian Psychotherapy, Transpersonal Psychotherapy and Art Psychotherapy, to its incorporation in CBT and the trauma-focused therapies.

Therefore, images can emerge during wakefulness, sleeping or in such liminal spaces as a reverie or hypnogogic state, trance or during active imagination. The imagination is also not limited to the thinking dimension but is present in all the dimensions as the primary language of the brain/mind/body and the language of the in-between, almost regardless with whom or what we are in relation, inner or outer. I suggest, too, that imagination is the language of consciousness, making communications possible with whatever we might call Other.

Resourcing via the energetic dimension

'Energy' is a term often used to describe a felt-sense experience of vitality, drive and libido, or 'energy that is instinctually organized or expressed' (Washburn, 1999: 170), such as sexual or erotic energy. This also includes Freud's understanding of energy as 'cell motility, particle, motion, and electric current' (quoted in Germine, 1998: 82), and the energy of the brain/mind/body systems as a whole. We may even say that energy is the movement of consciousness itself. At the same time, we often express the potency of this energy in everyday language by phrases like: 'lacking in energy', 'my energy is flat', 'my energy is buzzing', 'full/lots of energy' or 'lots of get-up-and-go', or more humorously as 'my get-up-and-go has just got-up-and-gone', and so on.

Energy in perspective of lifespan development

I find inspiration again from Michael Washburn's writings as he offers a comprehensive perspective on the organisation and expression of life energy at stages in lifespan development, through his use of rich language and imagery to describe the nature of the energetic dimension.

Washburn suggests that this energy rises up as a 'power' from the Ground or Dynamic Ground of our being. That is, energy as the movement of life itself is present in everything, and gives rise to life's potentials. Washburn (2003: 13) writes, 'The Dynamic Ground is the seat of the *nonegoic potentials*: energy – (...) the "power of the Ground" – the instincts, sources of affective response, and the creative, symbol-producing imagination.' That is, energy finds expression, and is organised, in and through potentials which spontaneously originate from the Ground. We may even say that these potentials are the dynamic life activity in the right brain itself from which the egoic processes arise, both embedded in a greater consciousness or 'power'. Putting it another way, we are 'radically open' (p. 41; see Chapter 2) to this energetic power, especially at the beginning of life. The ground of our being is embedded in the Ground of Being, and this is an energetic 'power'.

Briefly, Washburn (1999: 140) argues that 'power of the Ground is the enveloping "water" of the so-called oceanic experience, the state of blissful suspended animation prior to ego differentiation'. This 'water' is strongly active when the newborn is alert, but settles as an 'inner reservoir' when the newborn is resting or sleeping. In other words, life's limitless energy is fully available at the beginning of life; or to put it differently, we are in a right brain experience of non-separation, the source of egoic origin. In this state 'The power of the Ground (...) greatly intensifies and magnifies the world, rendering it superabundantly alive: fascinating, magical, miraculous' (p. 141). Moreover, the complete pervasiveness of this energy is active as a whole body experience, surging and quieting, rising and falling as a vast oceanic tide. The energetic power of this all-embracing Ground eventually subsides. Washburn views this 'primary repression' of energies as being partially 'put to sleep' (p. 148) to allow for the emergence and development of another part of consciousness: ego. That is to say, the Ground gives way like a tide going out (though still present) to the emergence of left brain egoic processes which press for expression; this is our coming to awareness from prior life in the depths.

The power of the Dynamic Ground potentially awakens later in life with the deepening of identity through the considered integration of repressed parts (typically through psychotherapy), and a more conscious openness to this power, especially through spiritual awakening. This awakening is fundamentally a receptiveness to the energetic power of the Ground which once again becomes consciously available. According to Washburn (2003: 164), the symptoms of awakening to this power in and through the body include, for example, 'Itching, tingling sensations, twitches, tremors, spasms, rushes of energy, hyperactivity, and even heightened sexual desire'. These symptoms are reportedly caused by body tissue and nerves laden with surplus energy. All this is a reminder that the energetic power of the Ground is a whole brain/mind/body experience.

Our bodies are also part of nature so that awakening to the power of the Ground is also an experience in relating to the numinous power and energy of the Earth as a whole, which, as Washburn (2003: 28) describes:

is now ready to erupt with numinous energy, energy that here manifests itself not only in direct epiphanies and through extraordinary people but also through objects, events, and places of special significance. Such objects (e.g., precious gems and metals, scriptures, relics), events (e.g., ritual actions, unusual natural occurrences), and places (e.g., hallowed or haunted grounds, sacred or eerie openings or enclosures) pulsate with an ineffable, spellbinding power.

This view of energy, then, takes the whole into account, understanding energy 'outside' as not so different from energy 'inside'; for we are part of one participatory whole. The foregoing is only a brief outline of the expression of energy within the context of lifespan development. However, I suggest that it is with this understanding of energy that we are able to recognise more fully the value of the energetic dimension in therapy. Regrettably, the consideration of energy, here, does not allow for an exploration of the concepts 'projection', 'numinous attractors', 'liminality' and Jung's 'participation mystique' (symbiotic experiences with nature). These, too, are experiences full of energy from the Ground (Wilson, 2011).

Energy psychology

Since the 1960s a family of therapies under the collective umbrella of energy psychology has emerged and evolves and continues to gather interest as an area for psychological enquiry and therapeutic practice. Most notable of this family of therapies are Roger Callahan's Thought Field Therapy (TFT), David Craig's Emotional Freedom Techniques (EFT) which evolved out of Thought Field Therapy, Tapas Acupuncture Technique (TAT), Asha Clinton's Advanced Integrative Therapy (AIT), and Phil Mollon's Psychoanalytic Energy Psychology (PEP). Although these therapies have found their way into psychotherapy as ancillary methods for working with a range of conditions (e.g, anxiety, trauma, phobias, depression), Asha Clinton and Phil Mollon have developed ways of comprehensively integrating energy psychology methods with psychotherapy. Mollon (2008: 21) informs us that these therapies activate the person's body energy fields underlying those troubled feeling states and thought processes which perpetuate and maintain distress, and negatively impact the nervous systems, thereby enabling 'rapid, deep, and gentle change.' These therapies work with meridian systems (acupuncture points or energy pathways which reportedly transport energy through the body); chakras (reported energy centres aligning the spine); the biofield (energy matrix or aura); and muscle testing (a system for diagnosing illness or treatment through testing muscle strength or weakness) which is usually deployed to receive biofeedback from the body in helping to regulate body functions and physiological processes, such as stress. These practices are often viewed as lacking in evidence (e.g., Bakker, 2013), yet there are an increasing number of studies which support their effectiveness in treating a range of conditions (e.g., Feinstein, 2008; Mollon, 2008).

It is widely regarded that energy psychology is not an alternative for psychotherapy, and that it cannot achieve the benefits gained by reflective examination of life in all its aspects, including the complex nature of values, beliefs and attitudes, and difficulties, dilemmas, problems, concerns and struggles which are part of ordinary living. It is then fair to say that people tend to settle for symptom relief without more deeply exploring the possible meaning and purpose of these, often because of a need for a quick 'fix'.

The resource focused therapist may usefully reflect on how they already recognise the energetic dimension in their practice, without necessarily integrating energy psychology methods. For instance, the 'voice' of the energetic dimension can be prioritised by asking clients 'Where does the energy want to move/go?' or 'Does the energy have an image?' or 'Where in your body do you hold the energy?' or 'Where does the energy feel blocked or trapped?' and 'Might there be an image for this?' These, and other questions, help to open up the dialogue with the energetic dimension and be guided by its 'voice'. Similarly, following the principle that an image is often energy 'wearing' a form, when working with dreams the therapist may ask 'what part of the dream carries the most energy?' then explore the related images. Certainly, by working with the imaginal, feeling or physical dimensions with an informed awareness of the energetic dimension as embedded within these, the therapist can holistically attune to clients and together discern what requires therapeutic attention.

Resourcing the energetic dimension

Finally, given that our theme is 'resourcing', perhaps the most known way to resource the energetic dimension is through diet. As Mark Germine (1998: 83) points out, 'The basic physiology of energy in the central nervous system is now known. Oxidation of food substances provides our source of energy as heat or calories.' Hanson (2011: 50) in writing about nourishing the brain informs us that not only is the brain two to three per cent of the total bodyweight, but requires at least twenty-five per cent of the energy from glucose in the blood, as well as healthy fats and other nutrients besides. He affirms that 'filling up your neural cupboard with good supplies will bring you more energy, resilience, and well-being'.

Resourcing via the behavioural dimension

Characteristic of this dimension is the capacity to be fully ourselves so that our core sense of identity is visible through our actions and achievements. This dimension is fundamentally about the embodiment and expression of this sense of self; it is about stepping into our authenticity. More than a decision, this is a process which develops and changes throughout a lifetime and is primarily the result of inner enquiry, perspicacity and evaluation of what is worth committing to, and revealing, through our behaviour: 'this is how I choose to live'. This, then, is fundamentally a moral dimension, where our actions are a declaration of consciously and unconsciously held values, attitudes and beliefs.

For most people there is no map, no prescribed way of how life 'should' be lived, not even a compass, but rather an (often vague, often subtle) evolving inner sense of what being 'fully myself' means. Hopefully through endeavouring to be ourselves, our life course brings a sense of coherence, cohesiveness and a life defined by integrity, but there is no guarantee. What is more, in the behavioural dimension our sense of authenticity grows within the context of the coinfluencing whole, which possibly also wants to become fully itself, even perhaps for the fox and the heron, and their habitats, as well as for human-kind. Authenticity and integrity emerge within the context of family, society, culture and heritage, which shape our sense of embeddedness, and contribute to the development of social and cultural intelligences. As John Beebe (1992: 32) puts it, 'Integrity implies an ecological sense of the harmony and inter-dependence of all the parts of the whole, a felt sense of the entirety of any situation.' This 'entirety' represents all aspects which contribute to and are affected by our becoming fully ourselves.

Values in therapy

An important focus in this dimension is supporting clients to differentiate their unique 'voice' from those of parents, and even ancestors. Peter Lomas states (1999: 7):

> The patient comes and the therapist listens with rigorous care and thought, looking especially for clues to experiences that are beyond the patient's conscious knowledge. He does not comment on the patient's moral condition or sermonize on what is right or wrong behaviour: he merely encourages him to find his own voice, and in order to help him to do this he pieces together, as best he can, the arguments, contradictions, distortions, evasions, and silences, and then constructs an account which is both coherent and commensurate with reality.

Different therapy modalities, and therapist integration of these, offer distinct versions of this, but the aim is the same: to enable clients to be fully themselves (Colin, Chapter 3). Invariably this means to explore considered obligations of all kinds; the 'oughts', 'shoulds' and 'musts' of life, as well as felt-discussion on areas of possible compromise. How far to depart from their status quo remains a question. The fact is we become mostly aware of our values in experiences of joy, contentment and other positive experiences, and in negative experiences like sadness, loss, disappointment or dissatisfaction with aspects of life, when our expectations or projections are either fulfilled or unfulfilled. We could say that the whole of life experience is a constant play of values; often watery and metamorphosing, though sometimes fixed or rigid. Scrutinising these experiences (to make them explicit) may help increase insight into the fabric on which we base our life. Our identity is in our values.

What of the benign influence of the therapist? The client is not immune, of course, from the values of the therapist, who is not morally neutral. To begin with, the therapist's modality is not value free. For instance, therapeutic modalities determine ways of being with clients (therapist behaviour), as well as theoretical frameworks to inform thinking about clients and the content of what they bring to therapy. Modalities also offer theoretical views on human nature (e.g., the meaning of fully functioning, healthy or authentic), theoretical ways of understanding the therapeutic relationship, methodological ways of intervening, and views on aetiology, treatment and the healing process itself (Owens, Springwood and Wilson, 2012). Psychotherapy also embraces the values of being trustworthy, respecting client autonomy, promoting client well-being (beneficence), avoiding harm (non-maleficence), embodying fairness and practising self-care. These are *professional values*.

Then there are the therapist's own *personal values*, conveyed verbally and non-verbally, and which are likely to include *professional values*. Take 'integrity', for instance; whether viewed as a virtue or not, it is likely that the cultivation and embodiment of this by the therapist influences the client to be likewise (Lomas, 1999: 57). Similarly with other values, all of which must certainly influence the assessment, process and outcome of therapy.

Studies of life satisfaction values

What then are the values to live one's life by? A preliminary study of Positive Psychology's Values in Action Inventory (VAI) of Strengths of an American sample, found that traits or strengths often strongly associated with the experience of life satisfaction or fulfilment were 'hope, zest, gratitude, love, and curiosity' (Park, Peterson and Seligman, 2004: 603). In contrast, 'modesty, and the [mental or] intellectual appreciation of beauty, creativity, judgment, and love of learning' were found to be weakly associated with life satisfaction (p. 603). Given that cultural variations are inevitable, VAI of Strengths studies were also conducted in other countries. The UK study found strongly associated strengths were 'open-mindedness, fairness, curiosity, and love of learning' (Linley, Maltby, Wood et al., 2007: 341), with gratitude, hope, humour and spirituality being weakly associated with life satisfaction. It is interesting to note that this represents almost a reversal of values from the American study, and that of the twenty-four VAI strengths, 'integrity' was in the eighth position in the UK and sixteenth in the American studies, while 'authenticity' and 'honesty' were listed as synonyms for 'integrity'.

While these strengths represent study samples, the focus of psychotherapy is on the clients and their inimitable set of values. Resourcing in the behavioural dimension, then, involves supporting the emergence and embodiment of these uniquely held values, and wherever possible enabling clients to distinguish these from those 'given' by life conditioning, dogma or indoctrination.

Resourcing via the interpersonal dimension

One feature of the integrated life is our capacity to turn in kinship towards the other. Washburn (1994: 296) argues that this progressive capacity for an 'other-centred, affirmative openness' is conveyed as an 'immediate caring for others' who are regarded as members of a large family, and where a sense of self–other dualism drops away. Psychotherapy fundamentally enables the deepest resourcing of the interpersonal dimension in the therapeutic relationship (Chapter 7). However, I believe that the deepening of this dimension also includes an openness of kinship to the more-than-human and other-than-human worlds and a radical moving away from single-species concern. I want to make a plea here that within this dimension 'personhood' is not limited to a single species but applies to trans-species. This is a return to our recurrent theme, in Chapter 1, of the interconnection within a coinfluencing whole of which we are a part: the part resources the whole; the whole resources the part. David Abram (2010: 254) notes:

> Only by entering into relation with others do we effect our own integration and coherence. Such others might be people, or they might be wetlands, or works of art, or snakes slithering through the stubbled grass.

Further:

> Incomplete on its own, the body is precisely our capacity for metamorphosis. Each being that we perceive enacts a subtle integration within us, even as it alters our prior organisation. The sensing body is like an open circuit that completes itself only in things, in others, in the surrounding earth.

This 'subtle integration' includes the way in which we often unconsciously absorb our environments, landscapes and all that inhabits these places, so that they become an intrinsic part of our felt-sense identity. It follows from this that loss of species and landscapes is also loss of the experience of these; and therefore a loss of identity. Although loss presents itself in psychotherapy in many ways, it is unlikely that many therapists are familiar with loss of nature experience as a significant aspect of loss.

For instance, practitioners who turn to the Diagnostic Statistical Manual of Mental Disorders (DSM) for understanding conditions will find that there is only one reference to our relation to nature, namely Seasonal Affective Disorder (SAD), brought about by the loss of sunlight in the winter months. But the fact is that nature-based loss is more complex than this. Written about widely in the growing literature on ecopsychology (e.g., Bernstein, 2005; Totton, 2011) it is enough to limit my discussion to loss in order to demonstrate the importance of holistic thinking in the interpersonal dimension. A further example is in Glenn Albrecht's (2006: 35) term 'solastalgia' which:

> describe[s] the pain or sickness caused by the loss of, or inability to derive solace from, the present state of one's home environment. Solastalgia exists when there is a recognition that the beloved place in which one resides is under assault (physical desolation).

That which impacts on the environment potentially impacts on the individual.

Integration in the interpersonal dimension, then, necessitates development of proactive concern of the dimension as a whole, not only a part(s) which is most familiar. To this end, therapists might take more notice of how clients orientate themselves in this dimension, and find ways to bring attention to this, especially during the initial assessment for therapy when they can be invited to comment on the following:

Positive experiences in nature.
What resources them in life (often this includes nature).
Provide a sense of where they feel safest in life (sometimes when there is a history of trauma safety is to be found in nature).
Express where they feel most themselves (quite often this is being in a nature setting).
Recount relational history with nature, including relationships with animals.
Describe the qualities of environments where clients spend a lot of time, and the impact of these, for example, an artificially lit office environment in front of a computer.
Describe any sustained injuries (physical traumas often happen outside).

Even minimal exploration of these areas can open up possibilities for resourcing. Meanwhile, there are a growing number of studies which validate the common sense benefits of connections with nature (e.g., Hug et al., 2009; Brymer, Cuddihy and Sharma-Brymer, 2010; Ryan et al., 2010).

Resourcing via the spiritual dimension

Although sometimes fraught with difficulty in the context of therapy, spirituality is one of the most resourcing areas of experience, and yet is often a neglected, undervalued and misunderstood dimension of life, and frequently viewed reductively as 'a resource for finding meaning and hope in suffering'

(Mohandas, 2008: 64). While in some ways this view may be true, the primary purpose of spirituality embraces a significantly wider scope. For the purpose of our present discussion, two interrelated themes are worth considering: spirituality as a developmental and participatory process, and spirituality as a wholing activity.

Spirituality as a developmental and participatory process

Available as a resource throughout life, it is likely that 'much of our spirituality arises from [the] arousal [of] limbic and reward systems [in the right brain] that evolved long before structure made the brain capable of language and reasoning', and that a wide spectrum of spiritual experiences, including 'mystical feelings', may predate language (Nelson, 2012: 258). We may also say that maturing spirituality consciously turns to deepen identity further and widen experience in relation to intimate encounters with life's Mystery. This may be understood as an embodied response to the gravitational pull of the nonegoic core and the potentials of the Dynamic Ground, from which the emerging ego pulled away in defining itself early in life (Washburn, 1994). Moreover, frameworks describing spiritual development across a lifetime include James Fowler (1981), Ken Wilber (2004), Michael Washburn, and Jane Loevinger (1976), as well as Jorge Ferrer's participatory (rather than developmental) perspective. This participatory perspective emphasises encounters with Other (e.g., person, presence, aspect of nature or work of art) as giving rise to an experience or 'event' which is cocreated with the Other, rather than self-originated through personal effort (Chapter 1). These and other writers are widely referred to in the literature on spirituality and transpersonal psychology (e.g., Roehlkepartain et al., 2006; Friedman et al., 2012).

Spirituality as a wholing activity

Spirituality is largely a right brain hemisphere activity concerned with connection, embodiment and wholeness, and often uses the language of metaphor, image and symbol, and orientates towards engagement with unconscious processes, for example, dreams, visions, intuitions and the deep imagination. McGilchrist (2009: 93) points out:

> the right hemisphere pays attention to the Other, whatever it is that exists apart from ourselves, with which it sees itself in profound relation. It is deeply attracted to, and given life by, the relationship, the betweenness, that exists with this Other.

This 'profound relation' bares no trace of differentiation from the Other, but experiences itself as an intrinsic part of the whole. He writes:

Then there is the *primacy of wholeness*: the right hemisphere deals with the world before separation, division, analysis has transformed it into something else, before the left hemisphere has *re*-presented it. It is not that the right hemisphere connects – because what it reveals was never separated; it does not synthesise – what was never broken down into parts; it does not integrate – what was never less than whole.

(p. 179)

If spirituality is, then, in some way about returning to wholeness, or wholing, we can say that spiritual practices facilitate left–right brain integration; or that the process and 'journey' toward wholeness is a return to living more from right brain potentials, and from what Washburn (1995 [1987]: 48) describes as our 'original embedment', but with a developed awareness of the egoic life. In support of this view, research indicates that contemplative practices like meditation appear to facilitate greater right brain connectivity (e.g., Mohandas, 2008; Luders et al., 2012).

Benefits of the spiritual dimension

Benefits to psychological well-being arising out of engaging in spiritual practices, especially meditation practices across traditions, include 'greater longevity, coping skills and health-related quality of life (even during terminal illness) and less anxiety, depression and suicide' (Mohandas, 2008: 64). Studies also suggest that 'Spiritual practices can have considerable antidepressant effects due to the associated increase in serotonin and dopamine' (Mohandas, 2008: 76). This association is particularly made in relation to meditation (e.g., Kjaer et al., 2002; Yu et al., 2011). Meditation may even '[offset] age-related cortical thinning', and 'promote neuroplasticity' (Mohandas, 2008: 77), thereby potentially indirectly facilitating benefits of practices across the dimensions. Also, Bart Rutten and colleagues (2013: 16) suggest that engaging in spiritual practices appears to increase resilience. They propose, for example, that prayer, unitive experiences with God or humanity, and experiencing meaning in life, positively impact on well-being because they facilitate strong positive internal experiences.

Resource focused therapy in the spiritual dimension

Therapeutic modalities which integrate the spiritual dimension are well known, and include transpersonal psychotherapies (e.g., Transpersonal Psychotherapy, Psychosynthesis), some mindfulness-based and Buddhist approaches (e.g., Core Process Psychotherapy), as well as many Jungians. Writing on spirituality as a resource in psychotherapy, Edward Shafranske and Len Sperry (2005) offer an evaluative comparison of perspectives drawing attention to the place of spirituality in therapy, arguably an enterprise begun by Brant Cortright (1997) and others.

Regardless of theoretical perspective, the resource focused therapist must be aware of the impact on clients of their spiritual orientation and/or a spiritual practice (as resources in this dimension). Meditation, contemplation, vision quests in wild places, or prayer are practices to both capacitate growth and promote opportunities for escape. Therefore, the therapist and therapeutic process may be helped by considering some of the psychological challenges of cultivating a spiritual life.

These include 'spiritual bypassing', ego-inflation and spiritual pride. John Welwood (2000: 12) coined the term 'spiritual bypassing' to highlight how many people use spirituality to bypass, sidestep or 'prematurely transcend' examining psychological issues (both conscious and unconscious), or engaging in developmental tasks like forming intimate relationships or finding meaningful employment. In this sense 'spirituality becomes just another way of rejecting one's experience', or circumventing life's demands and challenges (p. 207).

This ego-inflation or grandiosity can certainly be the most ubiquitous problem amongst spiritual aspirants believing that spiritual experiences are self-generated. Ferrer (2002: 22) refers to this tendency as 'intrasubjective reductionism', suggesting, instead, a letting go of the ownership of spiritual experiences as self-generated by emphasising encounters with Mystery as 'events' which *bring about* a subjective experience through the cocreative participative 'event' itself. That is, the encounter is participatory, and the ensuing knowing is transformative (p. 123). With this participatory perspective, spirituality is viewed as embodied rather than transcendent: 'Interpersonal cocreation affirms the importance of being rooted in *spirit within* (i.e., the immanent dimension of Mystery) and renders participatory spirituality essentially *embodied*' (Ferrer, 2011: 3). This focus on embodied spirituality is an invitation to remain grounded in the process.

Regarding spiritual pride, Washburn (1994: 218) describes this predilection as 'self-satisfaction in that which is supposed to surmount the self', which inveigles a sense of superiority in a person's 'good works and presumed spiritual advancement'. Again, pride often arises from falsely assuming that commitment to practices are measures of development, rather than demonstrations of commitment as an end in itself.

Whatever the tendency, the frequent underlying unexplored themes in the spiritual dimension are vulnerability, fragility and (Washburn, 1994: 219) 'ego hunger', often characterised by 'inner emptiness and lack of value', a 'covert sense of deficiency and need', demanding 'a special need for the recognition and praise of other people', and so on. Therapy may well consider whether these themes are obstructing authentic spirituality, and find ways of working through these.

Although therapy is not the same as spiritual direction or spiritual accompaniment, it can enable spiritual development, for example, by cultivating embodied mindfulness presence, and working with dreams. Therapy can also facilitate the complex nature of the psychological side of spirituality through exploring the above mentioned themes. Working sensitively with these processes, and also paying attention to emerging spiritual themes, potentially enables the spiritual dimension to become pathology free (Cortright, 1997: 214), and recognised as an intelligence (SQ) in its own right. Keeping a therapeutic eye on both 'sides' of the psycho-spiritual spectrum, 'ego' and 'soul', while working extensively with the psychological, allows for integration and development of the whole.

Concluding thoughts

The points worth emphasising in this overview of the eight dimensions are, first, that resourcing in one dimension positively influences other dimensions. However, to avoid lop-sided development, this is not a reason to focus only on developing existing strengths in a few dimensions. Second, a dimension is worthy of development in its own right, and is not reducible to the particularities of a single dimension. Third, resource focused therapists can increase their effectiveness by acknowledging existing client strengths while negotiating the cultivation of further strengths across the dimensions rather than a few. Integration is, in part, the result of this, given that integration is the maturation of parts coming together into a coherent whole. For instance, psychological maturation is different from spiritual maturation. Also, increasing strengths is similar to a practice or discipline which requires sustaining to reach long-term benefits. Fourth, we are part of a planet-wide coinfluencing whole which also requires resourcing. Holistic thinking is one of the cornerstones of resourcing.

References

Abram, D. (2010) *Becoming Animal: An Earthly Cosmology*, New York: Pantheon Books.
Agnati, L., Guidolin, D., Battistin, L., Pagnoni, G. and Fuxe, K. (2013) 'The Neurobiology of Imagination: Possible Role of Interaction-Dominant Dynamics and Default Mode Network', *Frontiers of Psychology*, 4(296): 1–17.
Albrecht, G. (2006) 'Solastalgia', *Alternatives Journal*, 32, (4/5): 34–36.
Bachelard, G. (1994 [1964]) *The Poetics of Space* (trans. M. Jolas), Boston, MA: Beacon Press.
Bakker, G. M. (2013) 'The Current Status of Energy Psychology: Extraordinary Claims with Less Than Ordinary Evidence', *Clinical Psychologist*, 17(3): 91–99.
Baumeister, R., Bratslavsky, E., Finkenauer, C. and Vohs, K. (2001) 'Bad is Stronger Than Good', *Review of General Psychology*, 5(4): 323–370.
Beebe, J. (1992) *Integrity in Depth*, College Station: Texas A&M University Press.
Bernstein, J. (2005) *Living in the Borderland: The Evolution of Consciousness and the Challenge of Healing Trauma*, London: Routledge.
Brymer, E., Cuddihy, T. F. and Sharma-Brymer, V. (2010) 'The Role of Nature-Based Experiences in the Development and Maintenance of Wellness', *Asia-Pacific Journal of Health, Sport and Physical Education*, 1(2): 21–27.

Callard, F. (2014) 'Don't Stop Daydreaming – It Sets Your Mind to Work', *The Guardian*, 27 March.

Carver, C. S., Scheier, M. F. and Segerstrom, S. C. (2010) 'Optimism', *Clinical Psychology Review*, 30(7): 879–889.

Corrigan, F. M. and Hull, A. M. (2015) 'Recognition of the Neurobiological Insults Imposed by Complex Trauma and the Implications for Psychotherapeutic Interventions', *BJPsych Bulletin*, 39(2): 79–86.

Cortright, B. (1997) *Psychotherapy and Spirit: Theory and Practice in Transpersonal Psychotherapy*, New York: SUNY.

Damasio, A. R. (2001) 'Fundamental Feelings', *Nature*, 413: 781.

Elliot, R. (2013) 'Person-Centered/Experiential Psychotherapy for Anxiety Difficulties: Theory, Research and Practice', *Person-Cantered and Experiential Psychotherapies*, 12(1): 16–32.

Emmons, R. and Stern, R. (2013) 'Gratitude as a Psychotherapeutic Intervention', *Journal of Clinical Psychology: In Session*, 69(8): 846–855.

Feinstein, D. (2008) 'Energy Psychology: A Review of the Preliminary Evidence', *Psychology Theory, Research, Practice, Training*, 45(2): 199–213.

Ferrer, J. N. (2000) 'Transpersonal Knowing: A Participatory Approach to Transpersonal Phenomena', in *Transpersonal Knowing: Exploring the Horizon of Consciousness*, T. Hart, P. L. Neilson and K. Puhakka, (eds), New York: SUNY, pp. 213–252.

Ferrer, J. N. (2002) *Revisioning Transpersonal Theory: A Participatory Vision of Human Spirituality*, New York: SUNY.

Ferrer, J. N. (2003) 'Integral Transformative Practice: A Participatory Perspective', *The Journal of Transpersonal Psychology*, 35(1): 21–42.

Ferrer, J. N. (2011) 'Participation, Metaphysics, and Enlightenment: Reflections on Ken Wilber's Recent Work', *Transpersonal Psychology Review*, 14(2): 3–24.

Fowler, J. W. (1981) *Stages of Faith: The Psychology of Human Development and the Quest for Meaning*, New York: Harper & Row.

Friedman, H., Krippner, S., Riebel, L. and Johnson, C. (2012) 'Models of Spiritual Development', in *The Oxford Handbook of Psychology and Spirituality*, L. J. Miller (ed.), Oxford: Oxford University Press, pp. 207–223.

Gallegos, E. S. (1991) *Animals of the Four Windows: Integrating Thinking, Sensing, Feeling and Imagery*, Santa Fe, NM: Moon Bear Press.

Gendlin, E. T. (1969) 'Focusing', *Psychotherapy: Theory, Research and Practice*, 6(1): 4–15.

Gendlin, E. T. (1981 [1969]) *Focusing*, New York: Bantam Books.

Gendlin, E. T. (1986) *Let Your Body Interpret Your Dreams*, Wilmette, IL: Chiron Publications.

Gendlin, E. T. (1996) *Focusing-Orientated Psychotherapy: A Manual of the Experiential Method*, London: Guilford Press.

Gendlin, E. T. and Olsen, L. (1970) 'The Use of Imagery in Experiential Focusing', *Psychotherapy: Theory, Research and Practice*, 7(4): 221–223.

Germer, C. K., Siegel, R. D. and Fulton, P. R. (2013) *Mindfulness and Psychotherapy*, New York and London: Guilford Press.

Germine, M. (1998) 'The Concept of Energy in Freud's Project for a Scientific Psychology', in *Neuroscience of the Mind on the Centennial of Freud's Project for a Scientific Psychology*, R. M. Bilder and F. F. Leftever (eds), *Annals of the New York Academy of Sciences*, 843: 80–90.

Gilbert, P. (2009) *The Compassionate Mind*, London: Constable.

Goleman, D. (1996) *Emotional Intelligence and Social Intelligence: The New Science of Human Relationships*, London: Bloomsbury.

Goldstein, J. (2013) *Mindfulness: A Practical Guide to Awakening*, Boulder, CO: Sounds True.

Greenberg, L. S. (2004) 'Emotion-Focused Therapy', *Clinical Psychology and Psychotherapy*, 11(1): 3–16.

Grillon, C., Quispe-Escudero, D., Mathur, A. and Ernst, M. (2015) 'Mental Fatigue Impairs Emotion Regulation', *Emotion*, 15(3): 383–389.

Groddeck, G. (1977) *The Meaning of Illness*, London: The Hogarth Press.

Hannah, B. (1981) *Encounters with Soul: Active Imagination as Developed by C. G. Jung*, Simi Valley, CA: Sigo Press.

Hanson, R. (2011) *Just One Thing: Developing a Buddha Brain One Simple Practice at a Time*, Oakland, CA: Harbinger.

Hinterkopf, E. (2005) 'The Experiential Focusing Approach', in *Spiritually Oriented Psychotherapy*, L. Sperry and E. P. Shafranske (eds), Washington, DC: APA, pp. 207–233.

Hug, S. M., Hartig, T. T., Hansmann, R. R., Seeland, K. K. and Hornung, R. R. (2009) 'Restorative Qualities of Indoor and Outdoor Exercise Settings as Predictors of Exercise Frequency,' *Health & Place*, 15(4): 971–980.

Jung, C. G. (1981 [1921]). *Psychological Types*. Collected Works 6. (trans. H. G. Baynes), London: Routledge.

Kabat-Zinn, J., Segal, Z. V., Williams, J. M. G. and Teasdale, J. D. (2013 [2012]) *Mindfulness-Based Cognitive Therapy for Depression*, New York and London: Guilford Press.

Kalsched, D. (1996) *The Inner World of Trauma: Archetypal Defenses of the Personal Spirit*, London: Routledge.

Kalsched, D. (2013) *Trauma and the Soul: A Psycho-Spiritual Approach to Human Development and its Interruption*, London: Routledge.

Kelly, A. C., Zuroff, D. C. and Shapira, L. B. (2009) 'Soothing Oneself and Resisting Self-Attacks: The Treatment of Two Intrapersonal Deficits in Depression Vulnerability', *Cognitive Therapy Research*, 33(3): 301–313.

Kjaer, T. W., Bertelsen, C., Piccini, P. Brooks, D. Alving, J. and Lou, H. C. (2002) 'Increased Dopamine Tone During Meditation-Induced Change of Consciousness', *Cognitive Brain Research*, 13(2): 255–259.

Krycka, K. C. (2010) 'Multiplicity: A First-Person Exploration of Dissociative Experiencing', *Person-Centred and Experiential Psychotherapies*, 9(2): 143–156.

Leijssen, M. (2008) 'Encountering the Sacred: Person-Centred Therapy as a Spiritual Practice', *Person-Centred and Experiential Psychotherapies*, 7(3): 218–225.

Levin, D. M. (1985) *The Body's Recollection of Being: Phenomenological Psychology and the Deconstruction of Nihilism*, New York: Routledge.

Linley, P. A., Maltby, J., Wood, A. M., Joseph, S., Harrington, S., Peterson, C., Park, N. and Seilgman, M. E. P. (2007) 'Character Strengths in the United Kingdom: The VIA Inventory of Strengths', *Personality and Individual Differences*, 43(2): 341–351.

Loevinger, J. (1976) *Ego Development*, San Francisco, CA: Jossey-Bass.

Lomas, P. (1999) *Doing Good? Psychotherapy Out of its Depth*, Oxford: Oxford University Press.

Longe, O., Maratos, F. S., Gilbert, P., Evans, G., Volker, F., Rockliff, H., Ripon, G. (2010) 'Having a Word with Yourself: Neural Correlates of Self-Criticism and Self-Reassurance', *NeuroImage*, 49(2): 1849–1856.

Luders, E., Kurth, F., Mayer, E. A., Toga, A. W., Narr, K. L. and Gaser, C. (2012) 'The Unique Brain Anatomy of Meditation Practitioners: Alterations in Cortical Gyrification', *Frontiers in Human Neuroscience*, 6(34): 1–9.

Mar, R. A., Mason, M. F. and Litvack, A. (2012) 'How Daydreaming Relates to Life Satisfaction, Loneliness, and Social Support: The Importance of Gender and Daydream Content', *Consciousness and Cognition: An International Journal*, 21(1): 401–407.

McGilchrist, I. (2009) *The Master and His Emissary: The Divided Brain and the Making of the Western World*, New Haven and London: Yale University Press.

Mohandas, E. (2008) 'Neurobiology of Spirituality', *Medicine, Mental Health, Science, Religions, and Well-being*, A. R. Singh, and S. A. Singh (eds), *Mens Sana Monographs*, 6(1): 63–80.

Mollon, P. (2008) *Psychoanalytic Energy Psychotherapy*, London: Karnac.

Neff, K. D. (2003) 'Self-Compassion: An Alternative Conceptualization of a Healthy Attitude', *Self and Identity*, 2(2): 85–101.

Neff, K. D. (2004) 'Self-Compassion and Psychological Well-Being in Constructivism', *The Human Sciences*, 9(2): 27–37.

Neff, K. D. (2008) 'Self-Compassion Versus Global Self-Esteem: Two Different Ways of Relating to Oneself', *Journal of Personality*, 77(1): 23–50.

Neff, K. D. (2009) 'The Role of Self-Compassion in Development: A Healthier Way to Relate to Oneself', *Human Development*, 52(4): 211–214.

Nelson, K. (2012) *The Spiritual Doorway in the Brain: A Neurologist's Search for the God Experience*, London: Plume.

Owens, P., Springwood, B. and Wilson, M. (2012) *Creative Ethical Practice in Counselling and Psychotherapy*, London: Sage.

Park, N.Peterson, C. and Seligman, M. E. P. (2004) 'Strengths of Character and Well-Being', *Journal of Social and Clinical Psychology*, 23(5): 603–619.

Pollak, S. M., Pedualla, T. and Siegel, R. D. (2014) *Sitting Together: Essential Skills for Mindfulness-Based Psychotherapy*, New York and London: Guilford Press.

Preston, L. (2008) 'The Edge of Awareness: Gendlin's Contribution to Explorations of Implicit Experience', *International Journal of Psychoanalytic Self Psychology*, 3(4): 347–369.

Raes, F. (2010) 'Rumination and Worry as Mediators of the Relationship Between Self-Compassion and Depression and Anxiety', *Personality and Individual Differences*, 48(6): 757–761.

Rappaport, L. (2010) 'Focusing-Oriented Art Therapy: Working with Trauma', *Person-Centred and Experiential Psychotherapies*, 9(2): 128–142.

Robertson, I. and Cooper, C. L. (2013) 'Resilience', *Stress and Health: Journal of the International Society of the Investigation of Stress*, 29(3): 175–176.

Roehlkepartain, E. C., King, P. E., Wagener, L. and Benson, P. L. (eds) (2006) *The Handbook of Spiritual Development in Childhood and Adolescence*, Thousand Oaks, CA: Sage.

Rozin, P. and Royzman, E. B. (2001) 'Negativity Bias, Negativity Dominance, and Contagion', *Personality and Social Psychology Review*, 5(4): 296–320.

Rutten, B., Hammels, C., Geschwind, N., Menne-Iothmann, C., Pishva, E., Schruers, K., Den Hove, D., Kenis, G., Os, J. and Wichers, M. (2013) 'Resilience in Mental

Health: Linking Psychological and Neurobiological Perspectives', *Acta Psychiatrica Scandinavica* [Serial online], 128(1): 3–20.

Ryan, R. M., Weinstein, N., Bernstein, J., Brown, K. W., Mistretta, L. and Gagne, M. (2010) 'Vitalizing Effects of Being Outdoors in Nature', *Journal of Environmental Psychology*, 30(2): 159–168.

Schneider, T., Lyons, J. B. and Khazon, S. (2013) 'Emotional Intelligence and Resilience', *Personality and Individual Differences*, 55(8): 909–914.

Schore, A. (2014) 'The Right Brain is Dominant in Psychotherapy,' *Psychotherapy*, 51(3): 388–397.

Shafranske, E. and Sperry, L. (eds) (2005) 'Addressing the Spiritual Dimension in Psychotherapy: Introduction and Overview', in *Spiritually Orientated Psychotherapy*, Washington, DC: APA, pp. 11–29.

Shedler, J. (2015) 'Where is the Evidence for "Evidence-Based" Therapy?', *The Journal of Psychological Therapies in Primary Care*, 4 (May): 47–59.

Staples, I. (2015) 'Study Delivers Bleak Verdict on Validity of Psychology Experiment Results', *The Guardian*, 27 August.

Thoma, N. C. and Mckay, D. (2014) *Working with Emotion in Cognitive-Behavioural Therapy*, New York and London: Guilford Press.

Thompson, B. L. and Waltz, J. (2008) 'Self-Compassion and PTSD Symptom Severity', *Journal of Traumatic Studies*, 21(6): 556–558.

Totton, N. (2011) *Wild Therapy: Undomesticating Inner and Outer Worlds*, Ross-on-Wye, UK: PCCS Books.

Turnbull, A. N. (2003) 'Emotion, False Beliefs, and the Neurobiology of Intuition', in *Revolutionary Connections*, J. Corrigall and H. Wilkinson (eds), London: Karnac, pp. 135–162.

Warnock, M. (1976) *Imagination*, London: Faber & Faber.

Washburn, M. (1995 [1987]) *The Ego and the Dynamic Ground: A Transpersonal Theory of Human Development*, New York: SUNY.

Washburn, M. (1994) *Transpersonal Psychology in Psychoanalytic Perspective*, New York: SUNY.

Washburn, M. (1999) 'Embodied Spirituality in a Sacred World', *The Humanistic Psychologist*, 27(2): 133–172.

Washburn, M. (2003) *Embodied Spirituality in a Sacred World*, New York: SUNY.

Welwood, J. (2000) *Toward a Psychology of Awakening: Buddhism, Psychotherapy, and the Path of Personal and Spiritual Transformation*, Boston, MA: Shambahala.

Wilber, K. (2004) *Integral Spirituality: A Startling New Role for Religion in the Modern and Postmodern World*, Boston, MA: Shambhala.

Wilson, M. (2011) 'Encounters with Nature as a Path of Self-Realisation: A Meaning-Making Framework', *Journal of Transpersonal Research*, 3(1): 11–29.

Yu, X., Fumoto, M., Nakatani, Y., Sekiyama, T., Kikuchi, H., Seki, Y., Sato-Suzuki, I. and Arita, H. (2011) 'Activation of the Anterior Prefrontal Cortex and Serotonergic System is Associated with Improvements in Mood and EEG Changes Induced by Zen Meditation Practice in Novices', *International Journal of Psychophysiology*, 80(2): 103–111.

Chapter 5

Integrative resource focus in therapy

Resourcing clients brings together our understanding of embodied brain/mind systems and processes (Chapter 3) with an understanding of the dimensions as modalities to increase core strength and capacity, and pathways to be developed in their own right (Chapter 4). That is, resourcing occurs horizontally (top-down–bottom-up in the brain/mind) and vertically (left–right brain/mind), and in the eight dimensions which can be divided into intrapersonal (thinking, feeling, physical, energetic, imaginal), interpersonal (interpersonal and behavioural), and transpersonal (spiritual) modalities. The resource focus also orientates towards either strengthening ego processes and functions (e.g., building confidence, increasing self-awareness and self-regulation), or developing core-self or 'soul' processes (e.g., embodying core values, deepening integrity, processing dreams, spiritual emergence), or both. Bringing these distinct areas together into a dynamic unified whole is partly what 'integrative' means. It also refers to combining therapeutic modalities, or aspects of these, to increase therapeutic effectiveness, although this is not our focus here. Within this view, the egoic part of the self-system orientates towards *contraction*, while the deeper nonegoic part, by definition, orientates towards *expansion*. But for a sense of wholeness and integration, both parts of the self-system require resourcing. This takes the therapeutic focus away from egoic processes alone to include facilitating the emergence of deeper aspects of self or 'soul'. Resources are, from this perspective, simultaneously inner/internal and outer/external, innate and developed over time, as well as intentionally/purposefully and unintentionally/inadvertently enabled, though the balance is unlikely to be equal.

We may say further that resources fall into at least three orientations or categories: *pseudo resources, protective resources*, and *growth facilitating* or *authentic resources*. These categories strengthen clients in different ways, and the first two assist clients in a self-protective defence, and therefore, as a life stance or orientation, lean more towards contraction than expansion. The nature of the conscious mind, or awareness, or ego, continues to contract and expand within its contracting bias. However, a tendency to over-contract may indicate difficulties which clients are unable to resolve on their own, when life events increase feelings of vulnerability and fear, and especially in the 'locked in' experiences of trauma (Chapter 8). The term 'resource' in relation to these three orientations is used to acknowledge their fundamental importance in serving a genuine purpose, but I am also highlighting the likelihood of hidden difficulties in relying and basing identity on pseudo and protective resources.

Pseudo resources increase functionality in many ways, yet avoid confronting the difficulties or issues camouflaged by the resource and sometimes create other complications. For example, to return to work too soon after a bereavement can resource clients' capacity to function and resume 'normality' (behavioural), and they may benefit from being with other people (interpersonal). However, their experience of loss may not be fully faced (emotional and thinking) and they may want to avoid painful reminders of the loss (interpersonal). Or, an overly driven client may not allow full recovery from exhaustion (physical, energetic and emotional) when seeming to cope by 'ploughing on' (thinking). Pseudo resources, then, provide ways of coping by side-stepping or ignoring difficulties.

Protective resources provide ways of coping by withdrawing and are present (with pseudo resources) where there is trauma (Chapter 8). In this instance they may be thought of as survival resources to keep clients 'safe'. A strong protective resource is drawn on, especially in terms of identity, when clients are seeking to further life possibilities and confront their limitations, and experience fear of rejection or failure as a boundary 'line' which is difficult to cross; especially if this is compounded by developmental trauma.

Growth-facilitating resources put more weight on expansion than contraction and, with it, the tendency for clients to embrace new opportunities and experiences that 'lean' into life and embrace life's difficulties rather than recoil or disengage from these. This receptive, open and spacious view of life enables identity to widen.

Most of the time, through the healing experience of therapy, the transition from contractive to expansive resources will naturally occur. However, if clients find it difficult to make this transition, the therapist may at some point want to discuss with them what purpose the pseudo or protective resources serve, and facilitate processing of any unresolved concerns. Sometimes contractive resourcing becomes a habit, and bringing awareness to this alone can release clients from this.

Resource focused therapy in practice

The experience of the therapeutic relationship itself (Chapter 7) and the educative nature of therapy (Chapter 6) will be familiar to therapists as the *means* for resourcing clients (e.g., the brain/mind systems and processes, and the polarities of the self-system). Here resourcing results from what the therapist does, what clients do, and what the relationship does, and is also both implicit and explicit, as well as verbal and non-verbal. The following vignettes bring a preliminary spotlight to these areas to illustrate ways to resource clients comprehensively within the context of the *means*; Chapter 8 will focus specifically on resourcing for trauma as an example of resourcing for more complex processes. These vignettes will also highlight the role of the dimensions to resource and exemplify the use of resourcing categories, orientations, types or styles.

Vignette: Ralph

Since the tragic loss of a friend in a boating accident when Ralph (now aged thirty) was an undergraduate, he had become aware of a gradual loss of meaning and purpose in life. Seeking support to come to terms with the loss, Ralph was concerned that he was since unable to regain a full sense of life satisfaction, and that he was frequently experiencing cyclical or recurrent depression.

As he reflected on the impact of this in relation to the dimensions, Ralph felt a lingering guilt that he was unable to do more to help John when his kayak capsized due to overloading on a group expedition. This, he thought, was related to his general lack of joy, or even hope in life (feeling), and largely responsible for his holding himself back from opportunities and feeling unfulfilled. He was also often unable to motivate (energetic, behavioural, physical) or imagine possibilities for himself (imaginal). This degree of disconnection from life (feeling, interpersonal, spiritual) left him feeling low for much of the time (feeling). And, even though Ralph was not witness to the accident on that August morning, he was plagued by pernicious thoughts of self-criticism and self-blame for being partly responsible for John's death by 'failing' to be in a position to help (thinking). Ralph's main resourcing tendency was to appear sociable by maintaining few connections and engaging in a limited range of activities (but not sea kayaking), and settling into an undemanding job with few prospects. Pseudo resourcing in this way kept him 'going but not fully living'. Exploration of these areas led him to resource the dimensions in the following ways.

'It's not your fault' and the 'negativity bias' of the brain/mind: Concern for our family and other significant people in our lives can give rise to relational guilt if something happens to them that we cannot protect them from, when we feel we ought to. At times like this we can feel an overwhelming sense of responsibility when things go wrong. Sometimes this gives rise to a feeling 'it's my fault', or as with Ralph, that somehow 'I failed'. The phrase 'it's *not* your fault' (from the film *Good Will Hunting* with Robin Williams as the therapist to Matt Damon as his self-blaming client) is also an intervention Paul Gilbert (2010) uses in his Compassion Focused Therapy to enable a person to work through feelings of self-blame, shame and guilt. Tilting this 'negativity bias' of the brain/mind (Chapter 3) towards the more positive recognition of feeling helpless was one of the aims of resourcing Ralph in the thinking and feeling dimensions, supported by timely and appropriate education on the 'negativity bias' (Chapter 6).

Mindfulness and self-compassion: Cultivating a mindful perspective on his depressive symptoms was a key resource for Ralph as this helped him witness (thinking) more his inner processes rather than become overly identified with these. By imagining (imaginal) locating this inner witnessing awareness in his breath (physical), he came to know that the breath itself was a steadying resource supported by the strongest innate resource, the (left brain) will (thinking). The practice of self-compassion (Germer, 2009; Neff, 2011) also enabled Ralph to reduce negative rumination in favour of increasing self-kindness. The mindfulness and self-compassion practices, then, helped Ralph to increase self-awareness and affect regulation (thinking and feeling).

Nurturing the development of self-care: As a result of therapy Ralph took steps to increase self-care (behavioural) which he built upon his existing regimen of physical health by walking and cycling (energetic and physical). Ralph also paid more attention to inner self-care, particularly through the practice of self-compassion and increasing self-awareness (thinking and feeling).

Establishing meaningful connections: During the course of therapy Ralph began to feel more connected to many areas of life, including sea kayaking, as if he was beginning to 'awaken from hibernation' from his almost forgotten life (feeling, interpersonal, spiritual), and concurrently the depression began to fall away (feeling).

Continuing the process of integration: Ralph found that writing a reflective journal helped him to keep track of his symptoms and to bring meaning to them, and was also a way to record the quality of life when it was going well. He viewed these symptoms as information to help him befriend them rather than to discard them as unwanted. Journal entries included descriptions and images, dreams, thought patterns, resourcing experiences like walking, cycling, restoring vintage cars, and even his love of kayaking, as well as quality time with family and friends. Recording the full range of experiences in this way was evidence that life was not difficult all of the time (thinking). He also found it useful during therapy and between sessions, to imagine breathing in the more positive experiences, such as his growing sense of optimism, while imagining the feeling of these soaking into him like ink on blotting paper. Thus he came to realise that imagination is a potent resource, and that to ruminate on 'the accident' was a negative use of imagination (imaginal, feeling, physical). Ralph found this exercise particularly useful when walking in the countryside (physical, energetic).

Furthering achievements: Similarly, Ralph was gradually able to recollect achievements and imagine more of what he sought in life (thinking and imaginal). Also, by recalling early memories of feeling inspired, hopeful and joyful, Ralph was able to draw strength from these and then absorbed them by imagining them sinking in with the rhythm of his breath (imaginal, feeling). During one visualisation he imagined these feelings filtering down from the top of his brain to the brainstem, then up from the brainstem to the top of his brain, then from the right hemisphere to the left and the left hemisphere to the right, and finally infusing his whole body (imaginal, physical, feeling).

Resourcing the dimensions as well as integrating top-down–bottom-up and right–left hemisphere experiences meant that, in dealing with his depression, Ralph was able to discard pseudo resourcing for a more expansive, authentic way of living, and thus be open to a wider ambit of resourcing experiences. This included considering career pathways more fitting with his values.

David Rosen (1993: 12) in writing on depression, notes that alongside cognitive and behavioural changes 'the affective component' is equally vital and often emerges in interpersonal relationships, such as in therapy. It is also interesting to observe how Rosen's holistic view of depression suggests confronting difficulties in the dimensions (he prefers the term 'factors') to overcome depression. He writes that while it is 'impossible to say exactly at what point depression may cease to exist as an unmistakable condition', taking the 'factors' into account as a unified co-influencing whole makes an important contribution towards this (p. 17). After all, developing the 'factors' embraces the quest for meaning in these areas, so often lacking in depression. Rosen identifies four 'factor groups', namely the 'biological factor', the 'existential/ spiritual factor', the 'social factor' and the 'psychological factor' (p. 16). In one way or another these 'factors' are represented in my framework of the dimensions, for example, the 'biological factor' is included in the physical and energetic dimensions, and the 'social factor' is included in the behavioural and interpersonal dimensions. Different aspects of the 'existential/spiritual factor' are to be found under the behavioural, imaginal, feeling and spiritual, and the 'psychological factor' embraces the thinking dimension.

Furthermore, there are similarities in feelings between depression and loneliness. Writing on loneliness, Mary Ellen Copeland (2000) notes that because depression can prevent clients from reaching out to others, feelings of loneliness can worsen depression, with the latter also deepening loneliness, perpetuating a vicious cycle. But many people, like Andrea in the following vignette, are lonely without being depressed.

Vignette: Andrea

For most of her adult life, Andrea (aged fifty-five) found herself avoiding relationships because of fear of abandonment. This also kept her feeling lonely. As she talked about her memories of abandonment in relationships she was reminded of the 'catastrophic' feeling of 'abandonment' on the death of father when she was only ten. Following a series of brief unsatisfactory relationships from the age of eighteen, Andrea decided in her late thirties to immerse herself instead more fully into her teaching career and her enjoyment of helping others to learn. Between term-times she walked long distance paths with a group of old friends as well as others whom she did not know, and enjoyed the companionship of her reading group. But in other areas of her life she felt the familiar well of loneliness, even when in the company of others.

Reflecting on the impact of this in relation to the dimensions, Andrea felt unfulfilled and distrusting of intimate relationships because of the distress they often brought (interpersonal). It was therefore easy to forget about relationships to focus instead on the 'relationship' with her career which was all-consuming and demanding (thinking, feeling, energetic and behavioural). But with time, loneliness began to fill the void where there was once intimacy (emotional and interpersonal), sometimes 'taking the edge of enjoyment from life'. Coming to therapy was an opportunity to reflect on her losses, especially that of her father, and also to explore her fear of abandonment and regain confidence to consider the possibility of relationships in the future (feeling, interpersonal). Apart from this, Andrea's passion for walking through beautiful countryside, brought a sense of connection with the routes she walked with her friends, and fulfilled her in many ways (physical, behavioural, energetic and spiritual).

Andrea's self-protective resourcing style in the interpersonal dimension kept her safe from her fear of abandonment in relationships and of being hurt, but it also distanced her longing for intimacy and therefore kept her lonely. However, the ripples of restriction in one dimension are also felt in other dimensions; for example, the feeling of loneliness is difficult to overcome with the feeling of satisfaction in teaching. To put it another way, deficits in one emotion regulating system cannot be fully compensated for by benefits in another; the joy of achievement does not satisfy the longing to belong (Hanson, 2013). Therapeutic exploration of these concerns led to resourcing in the following ways.

Gaining strength from the therapeutic relationship: Processing the hurts of losses, especially the loss of her father, and her related fear of abandonment was a continuing theme in therapy. The resourcing intrinsic to the experience of being in the therapeutic relationship (Chapter 7) enabled her to put to rest difficult feelings and limiting thoughts (interpersonal, feeling and thinking) and also to acknowledge the 'wisdom' of her self-protective side wanting to keep her safe (behavioural).

Contemplate life possibilities: As with Ralph, therapy with Andrea considered the outcome of imagination as a forceful life enhancer or limiter (e.g., the 'negativity bias' of the brain), and brought opportunity to reflect on possibilities for the relationship, while also to find ways to soften the activation of her fearful inner 'younger' part (imaginal) with the understanding that *neurons that fire together, wire together* (Chapter 1).

Reframing loneliness as aloneness: Andrea felt that loneliness was an 'infliction' rather than a measure of her longing for relationship and this became increasingly difficult for her. It was this felt intensity of 'infliction' which first brought her to therapy. In a sense it was the unfulfilled and largely unlived interpersonal dimension pressing for more expression. Through reflective communication we were both able to enter into the felt meaning of her loneliness, and as a result Andrea was able to begin to think about loneliness as less of an 'infliction' and more of an 'invitation' to find a way into an intimate relationship; in this sense loneliness was a measure of the *valuing of intimacy*. This breakthrough in understanding and ensuing acceptance felt like a loosening of the 'infliction' so rooted in old wounds. The acceptance of loneliness became a chosen aloneness, and Andrea was able to embody this as a temporary 'looked for achievement' rather than a state to which she was condemned (Whyte, 2015: 5; feeling, thinking, imaginal, interpersonal). As so often, transformation is present in the wisdom of acceptance.

Establishing meaningful connections through appropriate risk taking: Eventually Andrea began to open her eyes more fully to the felt quality of communications between people. Connections began to feel deeper and more meaningful, and it was as if she began to know some people in her walking group for the first time. For a long while participation in life was only partial for her until passion began to awaken in her and she felt more courageous in getting to know people (feeling and interpersonal). As David Whyte (2015: 39) writes 'Courage is the measure of our heartfelt participation with life, with another, with a community, a work; a future.'

Reparative processing in the resourcefulness of a safe relationship enabled Andrea to trust her capacity to let go of protectively resourcing her vulnerability in knowing there is strength from a more confident, accepting and emollient relationship with herself, while also cultivating greater openness toward others. There is more strength in being open than in being self-protective, and openness is also wisely protective.

If the 'voice' of loneliness is the longing to belong, then the experience of loneliness is the felt poverty of intimacy or connection. Loneliness comes to most people, even those who enjoy the quiet of being alone, for there is loneliness at the periphery of all experience. For some, the poverty of intimacy is profound. But the contrasting experience on the path of aloneness, be it temporary or more enduring, brings a restful stillness, often contemplative in feeling, which lacks the longing of loneliness. With Andrea it was only by sitting with the painful experience of loneliness week after week that the enabling resource of acceptance was able to arise. This also alleviated my own loneliness in the therapeutic relationship, since the client's experience of loneliness can create an almost unbridgeable distance that can engender the therapist's own felt experience of loneliness, allowing the therapist to empathise in an imaginative act. Equally, when the resourcing experience of acceptance arises, this is also felt by both in the relationship.

Experiences like depression and loneliness can undermine our felt resilience which we establish through factors like the genetic, developmental and psychological (Chapter 2). While resilience reduces the negative impact of something, persistent negative experience can erode resilience, as illustrated in the following vignette of Alice's struggle with self-doubt, despite her orientation towards growth facilitating or authentic resourcing.

Vignette: Alice

Alice (aged thirty-six) was a warm, open, affable and deeply reflective person and a GP, but self-doubt was a persistent struggle for most of her adult life. Like many people she made some mistakes in life, both in relationships and on her career path, and had learnt from these. At the time of coming to therapy she was looking for ways to trust more in her ability to make decisions about important things, especially in relation to her next step in life as she was frequently considering life's possibilities and musing on their consequences, sometimes negatively.

Reflecting on the impact of this in relation to the dimensions, Alice identified with the view that 'Worry's favourite shape is a circle' (O'Gorman, 2015:15) because intermittent bouts of rumination kept her in a persistent thinking loop of worry (thinking and imaginal), which meant that she felt 'somewhat directionless in life, even though on the whole life was good' (feeling and behavioural). Sometimes, because of the demands as a GP (energetic) she felt on the brink of abandoning medicine to train as a psychotherapist. Where relationships were concerned, Alice felt content and secure and was grateful for the loving people in her life (interpersonal), but she felt a void spiritually and often wondered about this (spiritual) although enjoying the pleasures and benefits of jogging (physical, energetic).

Alice's resourcing orientation was for the most part growth-facilitating and authentic, in the sense that she was resilient in many ways, though self-doubt diminished this at times. This also impaired her buoyant sense of optimism, and there were times when she was tough on herself for 'cogitating on the future, rather than getting on with things as they are'. Exploration of these presenting difficulties led her to resource in the following ways.

Strengthening growth-facilitating or authentic resourcing: Alice's attention was often drawn to her authentic resourcing orientation as a strength she should not take for granted. This helped her appreciate further this aspect of her nature, and allowed her to view self-doubt as a learnt tendency and be more open to it, rather than want to pull away from this. Exploration of the developmental roots of self-doubt was a core part of therapy, especially in relation to her lack of autonomy in early life due to an overly vigilant upbringing.

Coming into relationship with self-doubt: Alice learnt to step aside from self-doubt when it arose, even if only temporarily. This allowed her to regard the thought more objectively as something seeking sensory stimulation and embodiment. With the help of this observation she found that it diminished, thereby enabling her to regulate her negative thoughts. This brings to mind the myth of Perseus who avoids looking directly into the eyes of Medusa, but instead looks at her reflection on his shield for fear of being petrified should their eyes meet. Or in the myth of Psyche who gathers the wool from the ram with the Golden Fleece from the hedge at night, rather than approach the ram directly for fear of fatal confrontation. So, Alice also found that befriending self-doubt, by allowing it to be there, without becoming overly identified with it, helped her to trust more in her intuition, which self-doubt often masked. This was possible by differentiating the felt quality of self-doubt as *contraction* or *restriction* from intuition as *expansion*, thus putting more weight on the right hemisphere will, referred to in Chapter 4. Abandoning her fear of making a mistake enabled her to trust more in her inclinations in life, even if marginally. Thus self-doubt is often released by the open, expansive feeling brought about by trust, faith and optimism (thinking, Chapter 4)

Developing resilience through the use of embodied imagery: Given that imagination is a potent resource, one of the aims of using imagery in therapy is to facilitate a transformative experience. Robert Johnson and Jerry Ruhl (2007: 85), writing on the symbolic life, say 'that which is lived through the power of the imagination is an experience, and it changes us'. Angela found that guided imagery for increasing resilience, such as the following, gave her a practice to use between sessions.

> *First, recall an experience of courage, then locate this experience in your body while at the same time finding a position to rest your eyes that keeps the experience of courage in the forefront of awareness. Next, bring alongside the experience of courage a feeling of optimism. Take a few minutes to move to and fro between these experiences. Then, find a feeling of compassion towards another person, before applying that feeling towards oneself. Take a few minutes to move to and fro between the experiences of self-compassion, optimism and courage, noticing the distinctive experiences of each of these, and the transition from one to the other. Then allow an image of the union of these to arise within you. Notice where you locate that image in your body while gently breathing into that area. Then bring alongside this a feeling of self-doubt. Then let the self-doubt go and bring your attention back to the experience of unity between courage, optimism and self-compassion, and then find an image that arises from this, and locate this in your body, while continuing to breathe into this* (imaginal, Chapter 4; embodied imagery, Appendix).

> *Deepening resourcing through embodied writing*: Alongside this, Alice regularly engaged in embodied writing in relation to times when she felt sure of her direction in life, and confident in other ways, as well as her felt sense of her life aspirations. Embodied writing is an effective way of engaging clients' unique way of being. Rosemary Anderson (2011: 276) describes at least seven components to embodied writing, which invite the writer to engross themselves in creatively recording their felt sense experience of something *'from the inside out'*, as if re-living it (see Appendix). Alice found it useful to write in this way as it affirmed her more in her values.

Joseph Goldstein (2013: 163) informs us of two forms of doubt. The first, he argues, is helpful in that 'It is an aspect of inquiry and investigation, and it motivates us to examine things carefully' before accepting or rejecting them. The second is the sense of 'uncertainty, wavering, and indecision. It is like coming to a crossroad and not knowing which way to go.' This type of doubt 'paralyses us with indecision' and confusion (p. 164). Doubt often 'masquerades as wisdom' (p. 166) or truth, but two things may help to ease this: first, recognise doubt when it arises; second notice the experience of the absence of doubt by absorbing the experience of this absence and by noticing the gradual transition from doubting to no doubt (p. 166). Goldstein maintains that at the point of recognition of doubt, it begins to disappear temporarily, so that we can value the experience of its absence.

By cultivating more positive experiences such as being more optimistic, courageous, self-compassionate, and engaging with these in a bodily sense way, Alice was increasing her store of resourcefulness.

Re-sourcing core depth or 'soul'

Resourcing clients can sometimes access deeper areas of the psyche when strengthening 'ego' or 'self' processes to support the emergence of the depths. Meanings of terms like 'ego' or sometimes 'self' depend on who is doing the defining, and the use of these terms may not always be the same, as in ego-process and 'self-capacities' (Chapter 1). Resourcing these areas of the psyche includes the conscious and unconscious range of functions and processes of relating to tasks and other people, enabling self-regulation, increasing self-awareness, and maintaining a consistent and cohesive sense of identity through-out a lifespan. Within this view, increasing self-awareness and self-regulation are key processes for noticing the activity of inner life and establishing inner stability. Resourcing these is often the starting point for cultivating an even deeper sense of self, which we can metaphorically refer to as 'soul'. Here the term 'soul' is taken to mean three unique, though sometimes simultaneously occurring processes: first, 'soul' is similar to terms like 'higher self', 'core self', 'deep self', 'nonegoic core' (Washburn, 1994, 1995 [1987]) and 'Self' (Jung), and in this sense refers to an inner essence (e.g., Kalsched, 2013). There is a sense of something 'deeper' with which we identify as a vital part of ourselves, which often also has an affinity with something 'out there', be it life's Mystery, Nature, the Dynamic Ground, the Ground of Being or for some the divine. However, we mostly finish the conversation here, sometimes believing that 'soul' is a concept referring to otherworldly things and bearing no relevance to therapy or resourcing clients. My view is that this is a mistake, because identity may be more than only inner. If we view identity as whatever we link ourselves to, then our identity includes wherever we place our values. This can be centred on our roles in life, the values we embody, the place we live in, and even the experience of the forest which gives us refuge. Second, therefore, 'soul' refers to an energetic quality *within which we are embodied*, and in this sense means that we are *in* 'soul' (e.g., O'Donohue, 1999). Here we are beginning to shift the parameters of 'soul' away from 'mine', as something we possess, to something we live *within*. But, let us for a moment go a significant step further than this by, third, understanding 'soul' as referring to experiences or events arising out of encounters with the other (e.g., person, presence, aspect of nature, work of art, dream or the images we encounter in 'active imagination'); an event originating out of a cocreative participatory encounter with the other (Ferrer). In this sense 'soul' is the experience of the in-between, an experience of the liminal. It is Mystery presencing itself to us in experiences such as beauty, joy, awe or wonder, as well as in life trans-forming numinous experiences evoking fear or terror (Wilson, 2011). This tripartite concept of 'soul' offers the view that our deepest sense of self is not necessarily only confined within the brain/mind/body, but is fundamentally more fluidly expansive than this. If we widen our self-concept in this way we view ourselves consisting of both a relatively stable egoic part of consciousness and also a more expansive participatory part of consciousness, namely 'soul', which connects us to the potentials of the Dynamic Ground, Ground of Being, Other, Mystery or Nature from which we are not entirely separate. Deepening into 'soul', therefore, means widening the parameters of identity by participating more fully with life and its Mystery, knowing that where we put our attention, in many ways, is what we become, especially if we keep our attention there. This widening of identity is our capacity to create *experiences* that open us up, that expand our view of ourselves, of others and of life; a widening that can begin through the different faces of imagination. This may mean, for example, to imagine what it might be like to prefer 'this' rather than 'that', or to imagine creating space to relax into our love of time spent in the garden with all that wants to keep us there, especially the evening scent of honeysuckle. If we follow through these imaginings by acting on them (behavioural) we can embody more of who we might become. All this is part of what it means to deepen into 'soul' and to live with openness to life's callings in relation to our feelings (emotional), our senses (physical), the imagination, which includes dreams (imaginal), and spirituality (spiritual, interpersonal). Another aspect of this soulcentric journey is to embody our values more and to find ways of living from these (behavioural). Such qualities, as we have seen with Alice, may include being more grateful (Emmons and Stern, 2013), courageous (Tillich, 1952), compassionate and self-compassionate, selfless or altruistic, discerning, pursuing of truth, loving, and so on (feeling, Chapter 4). As James Hillman (1999: 11) notes 'We make soul by embodying adjectives that differentiate soul's prolific potentials.'

However, following the calling of 'soul' can also take us into the unknown, into the dark. For new growth mostly begins in darkness. This can involve 'archaeological excavations' in therapy by integrating something of the depths; perhaps even going down into the depths of the right brain by accessing memories in the limbic system. Robert Ryan (2002: 142) reminds us of Carl Jung's images of descent as 'entry into the earth, a cave or tunnel or by water – especially large bodies of water – or immersion in water or in a well'. Mythologies throughout the ages tell of the transformative journeys of descent (e.g., Virgil, Orpheus, Psyche), and the mystical tradition speaks of the dark night of the soul (St. John of the Cross). Paradoxically the grounding experience of descent opens up experiences of ascent, and avoids 'spiritual bypassing' (Welwood, 2000) when we also engage in psychotherapy.

To respond to the 'voice' of 'soul' is a wholing activity which returns us to a more wholesome connection in our right brain (McGilchrist, 2009). As we embody values, attend to dreams and engage in 'active imagination', we can embrace renowned ways of deepening into 'soul' including, regardless of setting or context, contemplation, prayer, meditation, entering into stillness, walking in nature, and so on. We can also imagine the anticipated soulcentric future and bring the feeling energy of this to the present moment and let it influence life. It is also often through the love of the other that we open ourselves beyond our egoic self. Knowing what or whom we love can be the first step to encountering 'soul', and surrendering to this is the second step. The ways of embodying 'soul' are plentiful, and the limit of our expansiveness is in some way also the limit we put on imagination (imaginal). Importantly, living from 'soul' is connecting to and living from depth; from an embodied sense of integrity. Developing, then, a soulcentric focus in therapy may be deeply resourcing for clients.

If the right brain hemisphere is the source of origin of the left with which it seeks deeper integration, then we might surmise that many clients project their longing for wholeness onto the therapist and to the therapeutic space itself. This projection only finds a place to arrive if the quality of the therapist's presence, and that of the therapeutic space itself, is able to facilitate this emergence of 'soul'.

Paradoxically while we resource clients to deepen into 'soul' it ultimately resources us in its power to transform, as it is a presencing of the Ground of Being, Nature or Mystery. This re-sourcing from the energetic ground is inherently integrative and meaningful as it locates our unique lives firmly in the context of a bigger participatory coinfluencing whole.

Resourcing at key stages in therapy

To increase self-regulation and self-awareness are core strengths throughout therapy, and assessment, beginnings, reviews and endings are opportunities for joint evaluation of development and maintenance of these inner processes. These are in many ways the foundations which resource other processes, such as: to not become wholly identified with the content of awareness; to widen the scope of watchfulness in the mind's activity; to increase self-understanding; as well as to manage one's relations with others. The key stages are also opportunities to evaluate the integration of areas of concern, or 'issues', and highlight further areas for therapy, discerning when to stop or refer on. The stages are also occasions for appraising integration of the dimensions and the egoic and deeper parts of the self-system as a self-resourcing whole.

Assessment or initial meeting

From a resource perspective, then, initial meetings with clients may take the following enquiries into account:

Evaluating clients' existing resources through the basic information gathering question 'What or whom resources or supports you?'
Discernment of resource orientation; pseudo, protective or authentic.
Discernment of quality of engagement with the dimensions.
Evaluating the strength of egoic processes such as self-regulation and self-awareness.
Discernment of the tendency to resource from the depths or 'soul'.
Evaluating readiness for therapy by virtue of available resources to support the process. For example, the absence of resources may be a contra-indication of readiness for therapy.

In terms of the wider resourcing context, as considered in Chapter 4, the therapist may ask the following: 'How did/does your relationship with [the name of the place] resource you?' or 'What is it about [the name of the place] that resources you?' or 'What was difficult for you about living in [the name of the place]?'

It is likely that there will also be a conversation about fees as a resource for therapy, and the policy of missed appointments, and the implications of fairness around this, given the commitment both are making to the process. For example, I view this as a delicate balancing of negotiating 'two freedoms'. On the one hand, clients are free to come and go from therapy more or less as they like within the therapeutic efficacy of the process, as is the therapist. Both are free to live and work. On the other hand, non-attendance may restrict the therapist's freedom to work if there is no forthcoming fee for the time. Lurking here is a danger of the therapist's altruism intruding by sometimes forgetting that, like compassion, altruism is only complete if it takes the well-being of oneself into account.

Beginnings

Resource focused enquiry continues into the beginning of therapy, if this is not also the initial meeting, frequently along the following lines:

Establishing an inner 'safe place' at some point near the beginning of therapy, particularly when processing trauma (Chapter 8).
Questions like 'What or whom got you through?' and 'What inner/outer supports are available to you?' help bring the resource focus to the fore.
We might sometimes remind clients that coming to therapy is in itself a resourceful activity.
There may be conversation about the use of resources, for instance, the cultivation of mindfulness or in the quietening movement of the breath.
There may be recollection of memories of resources, and by imagination bring these into the present moment (embodied imagery, Appendix).
Dreams often serve as resources when we know how to engage with these symbolically or imaginatively rather than try to find a literal meaning or interpretation.
Journal writing is a resource as it helps with the integration process by increasing self-reflection and self-awareness. Journalling is a self-valuing process because it carries the message that there is something worth engaging with. Journalling may also be a useful way of bringing values to the fore by writing about them (e.g., Emmons and Stern, 2013; embodied writing, Appendix).

Already the therapist will be gauging clients' openness for empathic connection (Chapter 7).

Therapists may consider a more extensive review of resources along the lines of my REMAP (Chapter 6) as one way of keeping track of the resourcing process.

Reviews

Reviews are opportunities to evaluate resource capacities. REMAP-ing at regular junctures in therapy keeps resourcing in awareness. This will invariably mean revisiting areas from earlier in therapy.

Ending

By the time we begin the process of ending therapy clients will hopefully have gained significant insight into themselves; be able to self-regulate, witness inner processes from a place of compassionate inquiry and curiosity, view the phenomenology of their person more as information than identity, and locate their identity in something more significant than egoic processes, and with this, draw upon an increasing range of resources. REMAP-ing may also be useful in the ending process, and a 'goodbye letter' as offered in Cognitive Analytic Therapy (CAT) with a resource focus emphasis may be an equally useful way of summing up the resources clients have cultivated, established and strengthened. Goodbye letters are ways for both therapists and clients to reflect on the learning from therapy, and for this to serve as a point of reference for the future. Finally, as well as conversation about what ending means for clients, and maybe for therapists too, consideration may be given to reflecting on the future maintenance of resources.

Concluding thoughts

While focus in one dimension will influence other dimensions (Wampold and Imel (2015 [2010]: 61) it is probable that the full expression of the dimensions is only brought about by specific focus on the unique requirements of a single dimension, within the wider context of an embodied self-system. David Rosen (1993: 77) in speaking to the client in us all, notes 'Your therapist ought to point out and support every ego strength you have, emphasising all your assets, capabilities, and talents, thus giving you a safe place to identify, confront, understand, and abandon ego deficits and liabilities' (cf. Flückiger et al., 2010). This is a project in its own right, and also paves the way for integration of content from the depths or 'soul' on our journey towards wholeness. Thus resourcing deepens our sense of integrity by bringing the resourcing parts together into a whole, and enables us to live in more expansive and deepening ways.

References

Anderson, R. and Braud, W. (2011) *Transforming Self and Others Through Research: Transpersonal Research Methods and Skills for the Human Sciences and Humanities*, New York: SUNY.

Copeland, M. E. (2000) *The Loneliness Workbook: A Guide to Developing and Maintaining Lasting Connections*, Oakland, CA: New Harbinger Publications.

Emmons, R. A. and Stern, R. (2013) 'Gratitude as a Psychotherapeutic Intervention', *Journal of Clinical Psychology: In Session*, 69(8): 846–855.

Flückiger, C., Wusten, G., Zinbarg, R. E. and Wampold, B. E. (2010) *Resource Activation: Using Clients' Own Strengths in Psychotherapy and Counselling*, Gottingen, Germany: Hogrefe Publishing.

Germer, C. (2009) *The Mindful Path to Self-Compassion: Freeing Yourself from Destructive Thoughts and Feelings*, London: Guilford Press.

Gilbert, P. (2010) *Compassion Focused Therapy*, London: Routledge.

Goldstein, J. (2013) *Mindfulness: A Practical Guide to Awakening*, Boulder, CO: Sounds True.

Hanson, R. (2013) *Hardwiring Happiness: The Practical Science of Reshaping Your Brain – and Your Life*, London: Rider.

Hillman, J. (1999) *The Force of Character and the Lasting Life*, New York: Random House.

Johnson, R. A. and Ruhl, J. M. (2007) *Living Your Unlived Life: Coping with Unrealised Dreams and Fulfilling your Purpose in the Second Half of Life*, New York: Jeremy P. Tarcher/Penguin.

Kalsched, D. (2013) *Trauma and The Soul: A Psycho-Spiritual Approach to Human Development and its Interruption*, London: Routledge.

McGilchrist, I. (2009) *The Master and His Emissary: The Divided Brain and the Making of the Western World*, New Haven and London: Yale University Press.

Neff, K. D. (2011) *The Practice of Self-Compassion: Stop Beating Yourself Up and Leave Insecurity Behind*, New York: William Morrow.

O'Donohue, J. (1999) *Anam Cara: Spiritual Wisdom from the Celtic World*, New York: Bantum.

O'Gorman, F. (2015) *Worrying: A Literary and Cultural History*, London: Bloomsbury.

Rosen, D. (1993) *Transforming Depression: Healing the Soul Through Creativity*, New York: Arkana.

Ryan, R. E. (2002) *Shamanism and the Psychology of C. G. Jung: The Great Circle*, London: Vega Books.

Tillich, P. (1952) *The Courage to Be*, New Haven: Yale University Press.

Wampold, B. E. and Imel, Z. E. (2015 [2010]) *The Great Psychotherapy Debate: The Evidence for What Makes Psychotherapy Work*, New York: Routledge.

Washburn, M. (1994) *Transpersonal Psychology in Psychoanalytic Perspective*, New York: SUNY.

Washburn, M. (1995 [1987]) *The Ego and the Dynamic Ground: A Transpersonal Theory of Human Development*, New York: SUNY.

Welwood, J. (2000) *Toward a Psychology of Awakening: Buddhism, Psychotherapy, and the Path of Personal and Spiritual Transformation*, Boston, MA: Shambahala.

Whyte, D. (2015) *Consolations: The Solace, Nourishment and Underlying Meaning*, Langley, WA: Many Rivers Press.

Wilson, M. (2011) 'Encounters with Nature as a Path of Self-Realisation: A Meaning-Making Framework', *Journal of Transpersonal Research*, 3(1): 11–29.

Chapter 6

Therapy as education

Education resources a person for life by providing a nurturing environment to encourage potentials and communicate accurate information to enable further growth. Meanwhile therapy, I believe, offers a person one of the most significant learning opportunities in life as it endeavours to reduce suffering, resolve dilemmas and difficulties, and encourage growth from a more authentic foundation; and this is uniquely accomplished within the specific therapeutic traditions and modalities. From a dimensions perspective we can see that these modalities differ in their dimensional emphasis for entry points into the process, and sometimes do this dogmatically. Thus the tendency for analytic therapies is to put emphasis on the thinking and interpersonal, or in humanistic therapies on the emotional, interpersonal and physical, or the thinking and behavioural in CBT, or the thinking, emotional, physical, imaginal and interpersonal in some transpersonal therapies and arts therapies, and so forth. Together with this dimensions bias, education in therapies can play an implicit part in the process of therapy, largely through the power of the therapeutic relationship, and a more explicit one through suggestions or guidance, including psychoeducation. I understand 'psychoeducation' to mean explicit psychological education grounded in evidence and which supports well-being. In other words, given that therapy is a form of education, therapies offer this in different ways on a non-directive–directive continuum. So therefore, as I suggested in the behavioural dimension in Chapter 4, therapy is not a value free process, and therapists bring their values to the therapy regardless of how non-directive the orientation. For modalities themselves are in many ways value systems and influence clients within a theoretical frame.

Before turning our attention to the implicit and explicit modes of learning in therapy, it is worth reprising our earlier view that *the development of neuro-structure is experience-dependent* and *experience-expectant* and that this affects the brain/mind/body as a unified energetic whole. The cultivation of positive experiences draws upon a number of evidence-based principles, as discussed in Chapter 1, which underpin those two modes of learning. Revising these again now in more depth, these principles are: *Neurons that fire together, wire together*, therefore, *use it or lose it* (if the 'muscles' are not used they deteriorate), *use it or improve it* (using 'muscles' improves these), *regulation* (or self-control), *specificity* (or target areas), *repetition* (which increases strength), *intensity* (or 'go that little bit further each time'), *time* (lasting change takes time), *transference* (development in one area often positively affects other areas). While these principles offer a neurobiological explanation for how the mind/brain/body recovers from physical trauma, I suggest these principles can also be applied to therapeutic practice in helping the therapist to be aware of what promotes growth and development in clients and to recognise them when supporting the explicit educative side of therapy. However, modes and principles are difficult to separate and so when writing about one I am also referring to the others. To illustrate the purpose of the principles I am giving them emphasis first in describing how they underpin the modes of learning.

Principles active in effective therapeutic education

Neurons that fire together, wire together: Whatever we bring our attention to creates more of that thing, especially if this is repetitious thinking or felt-sense experience, for instance in worry (Alice, Chapter 5), optimism (thinking, Chapter 4), or gratitude (feeling, Chapter 4), especially given that an experience is more transformative than a thought.

Use it or lose it: This principle can be usefully applied to increase clients' strengths by bringing their attention to them, discussing their qualities, and experiencing them through body-felt-sense practices. An example of this is Rick Hanson's (2013) Positive Neuroplasticity Training (PNT) which develops positive experiences by following a sequence of steps in the acronym HEAL. Within this perspective, clients are invited to remember, imagine or *have* a positive experience (e.g., 'that everything is alright now'), then prolong or *expand* this felt-sense experience before *absorbing* or imagining 'it sinking into you, while at the same time sinking into it'; simultaneously from the top-down and from the bottom-up. Finally, clients can be asked to connect or *link* a related, but optional, contrasting negative experience with the positive for a few seconds to positively influence the negative by linking the two (e.g., failure alongside achievement, strength alongside vulnerability). The view here is that the positive influences the negative but not the other way around, perhaps because of the brain/mind/body's innate trajectory towards healing. Hence Hanson offers a novel way of using the mind to change the brain to change the mind. In different ways mindfulness and contemplative practices also embody the *neurons that fire together, wire together* and *use it or lose it* principles. The entry point for these practices are largely the thinking, feeling, physical and imaginal dimensions. The more multiple dimensions are brought together to support a single practice, the more beneficial the practice will be.

Use it or improve it: This principle refers to our capacity for growth through effort. Again, mindfulness or contemplative disciplines embody this principle by supporting the increase of self-awareness through regular practice. Entry points for this principle lie across the dimensions given that each is an area of growth in its own right, and the cultivation of them spans their full potential range. Suggesting homework to support change in the behavioural, interpersonal or physical dimensions is familiar practice to many therapists, and is an explicit form of learning in psychotherapy.

Regulation: Again mindfulness and contemplative practices are effective applications of this principle as ways of regulating the mind and asserting self-control (e.g., Pollak, Pedulla and Siegel, 2004; Germer, Siegel and Fulton, 2013; Witkiewitz, Lustyk and Bowen, 2013). The regulation of thoughts and feelings is a significant shift away from therapy which encourages the 'becoming' of an experience (e.g., some humanistic approaches), but rather enables a client to notice, acknowledge and witness an experience while also allowing for a taste of it, though not necessarily a full immersion. The maxims here are 'surf the wave' and 'touch and go, rather than touch and stay', 'observe and notice' and 'witness rather than become'. Within this view, when combined with cognitive therapy, at least one study suggests 'the superiority of [Mindfulness-Based Cognitive Therapy (MBCT)] over psycho-education for clients with [major depression or] MD who did not achieve remission following antidepressant treatment' (Chiesa et al., 2015; cf. Johnsen and Friborg, 2015). My point here is that it is sometimes beneficial to educate clients to come into relationship with the content of their awareness in a contemplative rather than an absorptive way.

Specificity: This principle encourages development in specific areas. It invites bringing attention to a single area at a time to enhance restoration and capacity in that area. Trauma-focused therapies are an excellent example of this. For instance, those therapies which correlate eye positions with memories of traumas or negative experiences (e.g., EMDR, Brainspotting) maintain they are able to process these at specific points in the brain/mind/body where the experiences are rooted (e.g., Corrigan and Grand, 2013; Corrigan, Grand and Raju, 2015; Corrigan and Hull, 2015; see Chapter 8), thereby facilitating healing through multi-dimensions, especially through more right brain feeling and somatic dimensions.

Repetition: Repetition of practices across the dimensions releases benefits, for instance, in the repetition of practising self-compassion to increase self-kindness and minimise self-criticism (e.g., Germer, 2009; Gilbert and Procter, 2006; Neff, 2011) which engages thinking and feeling in particular. Other ways include regular practising being in 'right' relations with others (interpersonal), or practising the Emotional Freedom Technique to bring about change (energetic), or practising overcoming compulsive actions (behavioural), or practising Jungian 'active imagination' (imaginal), and so on. While these are examples of explicit modes of learning, clients implicitly learn from their experience when they are consistently and empathically met by the therapist (feeling, interpersonal).

Intensity: This relates to the neurological benefits resulting from magnifying or strengthening an experience, for instance, by engaging in intense activity in the dimensions and cultivating positive experiences by using practices such as PNT or embodied imagery (see Appendix). A particularly useful intense activity is exercise, of course, which like prescription drugs is an accepted ancillary to psychotherapy when working through depression, though more the role of the GP to suggest than the therapist. Nonetheless, out of concern that clients are neglecting their body, the therapist may want to recommend they engage more in gardening, or walking, or yoga, or massage, or another complementary therapy to take care of their body. There are numerous studies which affirm the benefits of physical exercise for the whole person (e.g., Miles, 2007; Kallings et al., 2008), including its support in increasing resilience (Wu et al., 2013; de Terte, Stephens and Huddleston, 2014), especially when conducted in nature. Exercising in nature is not only mentally restorative (Hug et al., 2009), but 'can also positively enhance perceptions of physiological, emotional, psychological and spiritual health in ways that cannot be satisfied by alternate means' (Brymer et al., 2010: 21).

Time: It goes without saying that the cultivation of positive change takes time and patience. Benefits accumulate over time. Unfortunately, few people are able to commit to the process of ongoing weekly (or more) therapy – perhaps because of cost, expectations of a 'quick fix', and so forth. Therapy is not always the answer, but it can be the gateway to well-being in many areas of life.

Transference: Because the mind/brain/body is a unified whole, benefits or strengths in one area produce gains in others, that is, gains in one area transfer to others. Although this may be the case neurologically, persistent effort is necessary across the dimensions for them to develop and to bring about maturity of a dimension in its own right.

Implicit learning in therapy

Learning is at the heart of therapy, not just in acquiring ways to resolve issues, problems and dilemmas, and relieve suffering, but also in the profound and transformative insights and understanding gained that can constitute a re-visioning of one's life. Therapy is potentially a meaning-making, coherence-forming, self-integrating and life-shaping activity.

Aspiring therapists will gravitate towards trainings that resonate with their interests, beliefs and values, and also do likewise when it comes to looking for a therapist for themselves. Hence we are also subject to influence by the values of our therapist. On a personal note, as a trainee psychotherapist in the 1990s, it took some time to realise that my first encounter in Jungian analysis was not a 'compatible fit'. Then a while later someone recommended a Jungian analyst who was trained at the C. G. Jung Institute, in Zurich, who was compatible, because, as I realised, there was no trace of Freudian reductionism when exploring dreams and spirituality. My analyst was female, white, non-British, and a Buddhist, and my learning, therefore, open to influence from at least two meaning-making systems, and a range of other values and qualities and ways of being. Thus I was in a life transforming therapeutic relationship with a person on a unique life journey herself, and in whom I came to put my trust. This was the context of my learning for about six years.

People come to therapy with hopes or expectations that it will make a positive difference to their lives. But they are largely unaware of the theoretical and methodological differences in and between modalities, the values, assumptions and beliefs embedded in these, as well as other values the therapists themselves may bring to the therapy to which they will be exposed (Chapter 4). These influences are often subtle and implicit in the therapeutic relationship and process, and yet will inform the learning. As Carl Rogers (1959: 232) reminds us, 'Psychotherapy is a pervasive learning which is not just an accretion of knowledge, but which interpenetrates every portion of his [the client's] existence.' I conclude then that this learning is largely communicated through the empathic quality of the therapeutic relationship which includes transference and other processes (see below and Chapter 7).

Explicit learning in therapy and psychoeducation

Learning can be made explicit through suggestions, guidance and/or psychoeducation. I am proposing that this embraces the following aims using my acronym REMAP, which stands for: *Review, Enable, Manage, Ancillary, Prevention*. First, the therapist and client together *review* existing resources that may be available. This conversation can be facilitated by questions like: 'What has helped you previously?', 'What does your body (or feelings, and so on) want to do?' I suggest that it is useful at this stage to draw on the wisdom of the dimensions rather than assume thinking alone knows best. Second, the therapist is wise to ensure that education is rooted in accurate information to *enable* further understanding of the presenting issue, dilemma, difficulty or symptom, while also being aware that alleged evidence-based practices may not necessarily do so (e.g., Shedler, 2015). Third, where appropriate, the therapist can support clients to *manage* the situation or symptom through increasing self-care. Fourth, again where appropriate, we can ascertain whether the education is *ancillary* to or sits alongside other treatments such as medication which clients might be taking, since it is useful to know the range of available resources without needing to be expert in these. Fifth, where appropriate, we can support *prevention* or reoccurrence of the situation or symptom through regular reviews of the resources which direct the process back to the beginning of the cycle. The acronym REMAP helps us to remember these aims (see also Cummings and Cummings, 2008). REMAP-ing works crucially across the dimensions rather than in the thinking and behavioural alone which often tends to happen, and takes into account the neurological principles described earlier.

Examples of psychoeducation include basic instruction in mindfulness (e.g., Pollak, Pedulla, and Siegel, 2004), guidance when working through trauma (Chapter 8), conversation about the stages or tasks of grief, about managing anxiety, anger-management, offering relaxation exercises, suggesting grounding techniques, teaching resilience (e.g., Seligman, 2011a; Seligman, 2011b; de Terte, Stephens and Huddleston, 2014), introducing Positive Neuroplasticity Training (PNT) (Hanson, 2013), and so on. Examples of explicit learning suggestions conducted outside the therapy session may include giving homework (Kazantzis and Dattilio, 2010) such as recording dreams, keeping a journal, embodied writing (Alice, Chapter 5; Appendix), reading a recommended book (bibliotherapy), or experimenting with an aspect of behaviour, increasing self-care, and so forth. The range of ideas is endless. But within the spirit of education, ideas are meant as suggestions arising from respectful negotiation and coming from clients ideally in response to a REMAP review or 'first step' enquiry, rather than offered as prescriptions. This can be the wise use of teaching in therapy.

Vignette: Robin

> After six months in therapy, Robin (aged twenty-six) found it easier to practise self-compassion in contrast to a lifelong tendency towards self-criticism resulting from frequent disparagement from both his parents through his life for failure to live up to their expectations. Apart from exploring his early life experiences, Robin frequently initiated conversations on the theme of mindfulness as a way of being. This led to my suggestion that he pursue his interest in a Buddhist setting – in my view, the ideal context to learn mindfulness meditation, now that it has become a form of consumerism rather than a way of being. Consequently, Robin began to engage in regular meditation practice in a Buddhist group while he continued to process the effects of his difficult upbringing in therapy. Working across the dimensions Robin found explorations in the imaginal, emotional and physical dimensions helpful, in particular through Hanson's (2013) PNT process with its underpinning neurological principles, and embodied imagery (Appendix). Psychoeducation, therefore, strengthened his resources for self-support, while we continued to work with and through his struggles. For the most part therapy was an empathic engagement (emotional, interpersonal) in the here-and-now, with occasional forays into dreams (imaginal) which was suggested as 'homework' in-between sessions, and the further suggestion that Robin learn mindfulness meditation (behavioural).

Therapeutic implications of explicit education

Inevitably the explicit use of education in therapy influences the transference dynamic (also a key aspect of implicit learning; Chapter 7), particularly when the therapist is perceived as or assumes the role of expert (possibly out of a rescuing transference response). Positive transference can become negative if the education does not help, or if clients find the therapist's offer of more direct support intrusive, or if they are not ready for explicit education. Conceivably transference may not be so important in brief therapy because the focus tends to be less on complex relational difficulties and more on day to day functioning; if you like, more issue-based than process-based therapy. But this is not always the case as transference is often present from the outset, regardless of whether therapy is brief or more open-ended, as is well documented (e.g., Molnos, 1995). However, openness regarding the sources of information can help neutralise the expert–client dynamic, minimising the perceived 'wisdom' coming from the therapist. This is where the *review* or first step enquiry in the REMAP-ing process can be useful, as *self*-resourcing is more empowering than suggestions from the therapist. But discernment, timing, a mature internal supervisor, as well as open conversation, are important ways of gauging whether clients are receptive to education.

Ethics of education in therapy

Naturally the ethics of education in therapy follow the same well-known principles formulated by Tom Beauchamp and James Childress (2013 [1979]) in bioethics and applied within a number of caring professions; these are: *non-maleficence, beneficence, justice, autonomy*. To these, therapy adds *fidelity, respect* and *self-care*, and other principles and values such as are embedded in professional codes (e.g., United Kingdom Council for Psychotherapy, British Association for Counselling and Psychotherapy). Ethics is a fascinating and enlivening field and is widely written about (e.g., Lomas, 1999: Bond, 2000 [1993]; Gabriel and Casemore, 2009). One of the aspects often discussed is the balance between therapeutic safety (in the sense of being bounded by the above principles, rather than safety-seeking which sometimes arises out of difficulties with trust) and creativity, in the sense of being innovative and spontaneous (e.g., Owens, Springwood and Wilson, 2012). Principles like these also assume a measure of humility in that we are always learning first from clients (e.g., Casement, 1985), who often know what is best for themselves. Therapists might put weight on this by facilitating clients to find their own way of self-resourcing. We will know from the temperature of the relationship and process when or when not to intervene. Ultimately, education is always first negotiated with clients, but to avoid the risk of breaking an empathic connection, education is usually best negotiated when the therapeutic process sits more in the left brain thinking dimension.

Concluding thoughts

Education is an intrinsic feature of therapy. While both people in this relationship are learning, the therapist's learning is largely for clients whose learning is largely for themselves. However, sometimes clients' own learning becomes of benefit to the therapist (e.g., by disclosing what is helpful or unhelpful in therapy), whilst at other times therapist's learning is only for themselves (e.g., when managing self-care; see Chapter 9).

Learning for clients is heightened when it is across dimensions, as this enables a holistic learning experience. This is grounded in the fact that more than thought dependent, the development of neurostructure is experience-dependent and experience-expectant. Therefore, the more dimensions that are brought together in the learning process, the more complete and deeper the experience is. Alongside this is the view from neuroscience of principles which help the therapist towards understanding the process of transformation. In practical terms, there are two modes of learning; implicitly in and through the therapeutic relationship as a learning experience in its own right, given that 'The therapeutic experience is the process of education' (Rogers, 1992 [1940]: 162), and explicitly both in and outside the therapy session to include psychoeducation. REMAP-ing offers a summary of key steps in the explicit mode. Finally, the reflective therapist will be vigilantly aware of the impact of explicit education on the therapeutic relationship, and wisely offer interventions with full cognisance of therapeutic ethics.

References

Beauchamp, T. L. and Childress, J. F. (2013 [1979]) *Principles of Biomedical Ethics*, New York: Oxford University Press.

Bond, T. (2000 [1993]) *Standards and Ethics for Counselling in Action*, London: Sage.

Brymer, E., Cuddihy, T. F. and Sharma-Brymer, V. (2010) 'The Role of Nature-Based Experiences in the Development and Maintenance of Wellness,' *Asia-Pacific Journal of Health, Sport & Physical Education*, 1(2): 21–27.

Casement, P. (1985) *On Learning from the Patient*, London: Tavistock/Routledge.

Chiesa, A., Castagner, V., Andrisano, C., Serretti, A., Mandelli, L., Porcelli, S. and Giommi, F. (2015) 'Mindfulness-Based Cognitive Therapy vs. Psycho-Education for Clients with Major Depression Who Did Not Achieve Remission Following Antidepressant Treatment', *Psychiatry Research*, 226(2–3): 474–483.

Corrigan, F., and Grand, D. (2013) 'Brainspotting: Recruiting the Midbrain for Accessing and Healing Sensorimotor Memories of Traumatic Activation', *Medical Hypotheses*, 80(6): 759–766.

Corrigan, F. M., Grand, D. and Raju, R. (2015) 'Brainspotting: Sustained Attention, Spinothalamic Tracts, Thalamocortical Processing, and the Healing of Adaptive Orientation Truncated by Traumatic Experience', *Medical Hypotheses*, 84(4): 384–394.

Corrigan, F. M. and Hull, A. M. (2015) 'Recognition of the Neurobiological Insults Imposed by Complex Trauma and the Implications for Psychotherapeutic Interventions', *BJPsych Bulletin*, 39(2): 79–86.

Cummings, N. A. and Cummings, J. L. (2008) 'Psychoeducation in Conjunction with Psychoeducation Practice', in *Evidence-Based Adjunctive Treatments*, W. T. O'Donohue and N. A. Cummings (eds), Cambridge, MA: Elsevier, pp. 41–59.

de Terte, I., Stephens, C. and Huddleston, L. (2014) 'Stress and Health', *Journal of the International Society for the Investigation of Stress*, 30(5): 416–424.

Gabriel, L. and Casemore, R. (eds) (2009) *Relational Ethics in Practice: Narratives from Counselling and Psychotherapy*, London: Routledge.

Germer, C. (2009) *The Mindful Path to Self-Compassion: Freeing Yourself from Destructive Thoughts and Feelings*, London: Guilford Press.

Germer, C. K., Siegel, R. D. and Fulton, P. R. (2013) *Mindfulness and Psychotherapy*, New York: Guilford Press.

Gilbert, P. and Procter, S. (2006) 'Compassionate Mind Training for People with High Shame and Self-Criticism: Overview and Pilot Study of a Group Therapy Approach', *Clinical Psychology and Psychotherapy*, 13(6): 353–379.

Hanson, R. (2013) *Hardwiring Happiness: The Practical Science of Reshaping Your Brain – and Your Life*, London: Rider.

Hug, S. M., Hartig, T. T., Hansmann, R. R., Seeland, K. K. and Hornung, R. R. (2009) 'Restorative Qualities of Indoor and Outdoor Exercise Settings as Predictors of Exercise Frequency', *Health & Place*, 15(4): 971–980.

Johnsen, T. J. and Friborg, O. (2015) 'The Effects of Cognitive Behavioural Therapy as an Anti-Depressive Treatment is Falling: A Meta-Analysis', *Psychological Bulletin*, 141(4): 747–768.

Kallings, L. V., Leijon, M. M., Hellenius, M. L. and Stahle, A. A. (2008) 'Physical Activity on Prescription in Primary Health Care: A Follow-Up of Physical Activity Level and Quality of Life', *Scandinavian Journal of Medicine & Science in Sports*, 18(2): 154–161.

Kazantzis, N. and Dattilio, F. (2010) 'Definitions of Homework, Types of Homework, and Ratings of the Importance of Homework Among Psychologists with Cognitive Behavior Therapy and Psychoanalytic Theoretical Orientations', *Journal of Clinical Psychology*, 66(7): 758–773.

Lomas, P. (1999) *Doing Good? Psychotherapy Out of its Depth*, Oxford: Oxford University Press.

Miles, L. L. (2007) 'Physical Activity and Health', *Nutrition Bulletin*, 32(4): 314–363.

Molnos, A. (1995) *A Question of Time: Essentials of Brief Dynamic Psychotherapy*, London: Karnac.

Neff, K. D. (2011) *Self-Compassion: Stop Beating Yourself Up and Leave Insecurity Behind*, New York: William Morrow.

Owens, P., Springwood, B. and Wilson, M. (2012) *Creative Ethical Practice in Counselling and Psychotherapy*, London: Sage.

Pollak, S. M., Pedulla, T. and Siegel, R. D. (2004) *Sitting Together: Essential Skills for Mindfulness-Based Psychotherapy*, London: Guilford Press.

Rogers, C. R. (1959) 'Significant Learning in Therapy and in Education', *Educational Leadership*, 16(4): 232–242.

Rogers, C. R. (1992 [1940]) 'The Process of Therapy', *Journal of Consulting and Clinical Psychology*, 60(2), 163–164.

Seligman, M. E. P. (2011a) 'Building Resilience', *Harvard Business Review*, 89(4): 100–106.

Seligman, M. E. P. (2011b) *Flourish: A Visionary New Understanding of Happiness and Well-Being*, New York: Free Press.

Shedler, J. (2015) 'Where is the Evidence for "Evidence-Based" Therapy?', *The Journal of Psychological Therapies in Primary Care*, 4 (May): 47–59.

Witkiewitz, K., Lustyk, M. and Bowen, S. (2013) 'Retraining the Addicted Brain: A Review of Hypothesized Neurobiological Mechanisms of Mindfulness-Based Relapse Prevention', *Psychology of Addictive Behaviors*, 27(2): 351–365.

Wu, G., Feder, A., Cohen, H., Kim, J. J., Calderon, S., Charney, D. S. and Mathe, A. A. (2013) 'Understanding Resilience', *Frontiers in Behavioural Neuroscience*, 15(7): 1–15.

Chapter 7

Therapeutic relationship as resourcing experience

Resourcing, as I am describing it, is the capacity to increase functionality or efficacy across the whole lifespan. It is also the ability to turn one's attention back to, and align with, inner deep-seated core strengths when things become difficult; to re-establish, re-connect, re-source the resilience we were 'given'. The resourcing themes in this chapter are illustrated by a single case: Matthew.

Therapy potentially strengthens, restores and repairs connection to this innate capacity through the unique experience of the therapeutic relationship. David Sedgwick (2001: 3) reminds us that at both conscious and unconscious levels, 'The emotional experience in the therapeutic relationship is what makes therapy feel therapeutic.' The experience of the moment-to-moment meeting with a sensitively attuned empathic therapist allows the 'voice' of feelings to arise and communicate something of our deepest nature – our energetic sense of wholeness, the inevitable felt compromises, the feeling narrative of our wounds, our hopes, fears, shame, guilt, and our whole relational history that brought us to where we now find ourselves. In this sense, effective psychotherapy is largely defined by the interpersonal and emotional dimensions and thus leans away from 'left brain explicit conscious cognition to right brain implicit unconscious emotional and relational functions' (Schore, 2014: 388); away from left brain thinking dominance to felt-sense relational processes, which includes the significant and transformative quality and process of the therapist's presence (Geller and Greenberg, 2012). This affirms our knowing that 'the deepest sense of one's being is continually formed in connection with others and is inextricably tied to relational movement' (Jordan, 1997: 343). I also refer to Robert Hobson (1985: 93) who points out, 'The *true voice of feeling* is a guiding ideal for psychotherapists. It is not a simple emotion but a complex ordering and re-ordering of experience in growing forms, especially by means of moving metaphors' which 'opens up depths of experiencing' (p. 61). Metaphor-making is 'the imaginative act of comparing dissimilar things on the basis of some underlying principle that unites them' (Siegelman, 1990: ix), as a way to bring something new into awareness. They are descriptive images of evocative felt experience, for example, 'emptiness', 'inner restlessness', 'not at ease with myself', 'heaviness inside', and so on, and embody multiple meanings. The nature of a metaphor is that it is moving, not static, and engages the feeling imaginations of both client and therapist. Psychotherapy, therefore, also employs the imaginal, feeling and thinking dimensions through reflective consideration of metaphor (imaginal, Chapter 4). More than this, psychotherapy also engages the physical, behavioural and energetic dimensions through communications between client and therapist, and the energetic movement in shifts of feeling, and in the 'voice' of body sensations, impulses and symptoms. At the same time, empathic meeting at depth sometimes activates the spiritual dimension as rare in-between cocreative events in this participatory therapeutic process.

Vignette: Matthew

> Troubled for most of his life with feelings of 'emptiness', Matthew (aged thirty-four) came to therapy following the breakdown of a long-term relationship. The youngest of six siblings in a tumultuous environment with emotionally unavailable parents, he left home at the age of sixteen to live with his 'big' brother while taking an office job in a large institution. Now living on his own, Matthew spoke at length of his early life during the first few months of therapy, and the impact of feeling 'empty connections' with both of his parents since the loss of his twin sister through meningitis when they were both four years old. Some years later he was unable to talk to his parents about the impact of this, or they about their loss to him. And so a deep 'feeling-void' was unexpressed for most of his life. Engagement with these metaphors of 'emptiness', 'empty connections' and 'feeling-void' was the focus of his early therapy. As well as this, the empty feeling following his break-up was processed through embodied felt-sense enquiry into these experiences within the contemplative feel of therapy; Matthew quickly responded to this. This relationship was to become an important resource for him in processing the themes of 'emptiness', 'void', 'absence', 'loss' and 'grief'.

The resourcing potential in the therapeutic relationship

Drawing upon my own experience as a practitioner, this section considers some of the key processes in the therapeutic relationship which I find resource clients and increase core strength, and cultivate a more spacious and therefore less restrictive, insecure identity.

Empathy

Sensitive empathic communication is a key defining and resourcing factor in the therapeutic relationship. 'Empathy is a complex cognitive-affective experience of joining in understanding, a feeling-resonance that leads to a more differentiated understanding of self, other, and relationship' (Jordan, 1997:

344). This 'joining in understanding' is a recognition of the other's uniqueness, and momentarily releases one from a sense of aloneness into an experience of kinship. This sense of recognition communicates cognitive understanding as well as affective, felt understanding, and ranges from explicit to implicit experiences; from the water's surface to its depths, which includes the sediment, the entire bathymetry (from the Greek meaning 'measure of the depths'). This 'feeling-resonance' then includes 'moments of meeting' (Hobson, 1985: 277) arising through sensitive attunement to clients' moments of depth encounter, and moments of 'relational depth' (Mearns and Cooper, 2005) as metaphors for connection at depth. Margaret Warner (1997: 130) points out that while this experience of recognition is of worth in itself as a form of connection, it also opens up possibilities for awareness and transformation in relation to implicit, bodily felt, unconscious aspects of experience. What is more, in the process of being 'recognised and received by another person, one becomes able to recognise and receive one's own experience' both in a wide-ranging sense and also in one's ability to receive one's moment-to-moment experiencing. This recognition at depth can be profoundly resourcing and facilitate a wider, more expansive, sense of self. In this way, empathy is a process which enables and liberates a person from full or partial obscurity. In addition, 'Empathy affirms the importance of the "in-between"' (Jordan, 1997: 350), in that it not only reduces experiences of aloneness, but also affirms the felt value of kinship, and acknowledges the truth and reparative potential of being in a wholly valuing relationship. This in-between is fundamental to understanding empathy because empathy is a cocreative process where two people come together with the aim of understanding the suffering of one individual, often at relational depth. And it is in these moments of meeting at relational depth that something of the Dynamic Ground (Washburn, 1995 [1987]) or Mystery can break through, arising as spiritual events (Wiggins, Elliott and Cooper, 2012: 150) in the in-between.

While empathic communications also include an understanding of cognitive processes, 'The empathic therapist's primary task is to understand *experiences* rather than words', in particular '*moment-to-moment experiences*' (Elliott et al., 2011: 47). This emphasis on experience is particularly significant because it is in and through experience that we come to know ourselves. It is also the embodied felt-sense experience (more than thinking) which brings about transformation, and it is moment-to-moment experience which 'makes therapy feel therapeutic' (Sedgwick, 2001: 3).

Empathic understandings are communications of the therapist's felt sense experience of clients' verbal and non-verbal, explicit and implied communications; this therefore often includes self-disclosures by the therapist (e.g., Wosket, 1999; Rowan and Jacobs, 2002). There are generally two types of self-disclosure. First, there are disclosures of experiences arising in the present moment to increase client self-awareness (e.g., 'I'm experiencing a wave of sadness right now'), and often disclosures of transference or projective experiences. Second, there are infrequently offered biographical self-disclosures (strictly speaking more sympathetic than empathic) as attempts to be more fully alongside clients (e.g., 'I too lost a parent at the age you were'), often to soften experiences of aloneness through highlighting universal themes. Empathic communications are also often educative because they give rise to new insights.

However, sometimes clients are unable to receive empathy. For example, 'in shame we lose the sense of empathic possibility' (Jordan, 1997: 346). Here we often meet with profound feelings of loneliness, or self-disgust or self-loathing. Loneliness is the lack of felt experience of empathy; the lack of meaningful connections (Andrea, Chapter 5). At times like this, our attempt to communicate empathy can feel intrusive, directive, foreign or overwhelming (Kennedy-Moore and Watson, 1999). It is worth remembering that resistance is the 'red light' which keeps us safe from these perceived intrusions, and can therefore be a resource in times of fragility. The paradox of resourcing is that there is strength in feelings of vulnerability and weakness, and it is important for clients to be reminded of this.

Likewise, breaking empathic connection, for example, by the untimely favouring of a more cognitive intervention, can activate feelings of being not recognised or not received, and this can feel deeply wounding. This is a further reminder of the potency in offering and receiving empathy or the absence of it. Mistakes like this are a part of therapy, and the capacity to view these as experiences of rupture in the therapeutic relationship, to be collaboratively worked through, requires commitment on both sides of the therapeutic relationship, and a willingness to engage rather than withdraw. Most difficulties in therapy arise through a breakdown in the empathic relationship (Owens, Springwood and Wilson, 2012), or an inability to work through or with transference because of the therapist's defensiveness or activation of projective identification (see below). Therapeutic efficiency is also reduced by empathic impairment as a symptom of empathy fatigue, vicarious trauma and burnout. Therefore, we endeavour to discern the depth and readiness of clients' capacity to receive empathy, and protect our own empathic ability by practising self-care (Chapter 9). The practitioner will learn from empathic communications something about clients' experiences in moments of meeting, and gauge which are their 'safe' parameters for empathy.

Attachment

Alongside attitudes of care, respect and consistently fair and benign boundaries, empathy is the basic attachment-forming factor in the therapeutic relationship, and helps to foster feelings of trust and safety in clients. Therapeutic modalities generally agree that 'the healing power of psychotherapy derives primarily from the therapeutic relationship', and 'potentially function[s] as a development crucible' (Wallin, 2007: 7) by enabling clients to bring into the containing supportive therapeutic space felt accounts of early life wounds, especially experiences of empathic failures and ruptures in trust. Our emotional growth and awareness of the unconscious are 'facilitated or inhibited' by our family and sociocultural contexts.

> Attachment outcomes [e.g., secure, insecure-avoidant, insecure-resistant] are thus the product of the interaction of both nature and nurture, the strengths and weaknesses of the individual's genetically encoded biological predispositions (temperament) and the early dyadic relationships with caregivers embedded within a particular social environment (culture).
>
> (Schore and Schore, 2008: 17)

Developers of attachment theory John Bowlby, and Mary Ainsworth who was responsible for coining the term 'secure base' (Wallin, 2007: 16), brought to our attention the complex dynamics and processes within relationships, and in particular the experiences of attachment (Bowlby, 1969), separation and loss (Bowlby, 1973), sadness and depression (Bowlby, 1980) as experiences arising out of relationship. And writing on psychotherapy, Bowlby (1973: 191) pointed out that the role of the psychotherapist was 'to provide our patient[s] with a temporary attachment figure', as well as a 'secure base' or 'affectional bond' within which to reflectively examine themselves and their relationships, past, present and anticipated future (Bowlby, 1988: 421). The therapist will want to remember this bond with clients, otherwise 'something is missing', writes Barbara Stevens Sullivan (2010: 43). Also, 'It is provoking to talk about seeing the familiar patient as someone new; it helps us to remember that patient is not a noun, but a verb' (p. 43); not a fixed object but dynamic subject. While this is undoubtedly the case, there is also potential information for the therapist in not remembering, as this may point to a significant theme of being forgotten or left behind in life by parents or in some other way.

Building upon attachment theory, Allan Schore integrates neurobiological perspectives into a contemporary theory of attachment which emphasises affect-regulation of emotion in the therapeutic relationship as one of the key aims of psychotherapy. And his thinking about the influence on brain plasticity in therapy is reminiscent of Ainsworth's discovery of the malleability of our biologically driven attachment system, when he writes 'The growth-facilitating relational environment of a deeper therapeutic exploration of the relational-emotional unconscious mind can induce plasticity in both the cortical and subcortical systems of the patient's right brain', thereby impacting all attachment styles (e.g., insecure, secure) (Schore, 2014: 394). The development of the mind in this way facilitates the processing of 'more complex right brain functions (e.g., intersubjectivity, empathy, affect tolerance, stress regulation, humour, mutual love, and intimacy)' (p. 394), essential for secure attachment.

Pat Ogden and colleagues (2005) also remind us that more than what the therapist says or does, and more than through conversations, it is a background of sensitive empathic engagement, or attunement, that enables clients to connect with, describe and ultimately regulate their experience, and which brings about a more comprehensive and integrated sense of self; that is, if we attune with clients they are able to increasingly regulate activation of difficult felt-sense experiences. This, says Schore (2011: 90), 'facilitates the repair and reorganisation of the right brain, the biological substrate of the human unconscious'. The experience of the therapeutic relationship, then, is potentially profoundly resourcing, enabling, reparative and self-integrating, and can bring about transformation in brain/mind/body.

Therapists may also reflect on the impact of their own attachment style on the clients' experience in the therapeutic relationship. For instance, obvious as it may appear, findings mostly confirm that 'the more secure the therapists are relative to the client, the better the working alliance' (Degnan et al., 2014: 60). This means that if the therapist's attachment style is more secure (even if still relatively insecure) than clients', then this probably enables a strong therapeutic relationship. However, it is possible that clients with high attachment insecurity (anxious, preoccupied or avoidant) establish better relationships with therapists who incline towards avoidant attachment styles, as this can be less threatening to clients than therapists with secure attachment styles (Petrowski et al., 2011). There may be a correlation here with my earlier point that some clients find empathy difficult, and that therapists might therefore usefully gauge 'safe' empathic distances with clients (Chapter 8). Also, in thinking about the experience of the insecure therapist, Katja Petrowski and colleagues (2013: 32) surmise that 'attachment insecurity may render therapists more vulnerable during therapy to the reactivation of their own attachment-related worries and defences and this might interfere with their counter-transference reactions', and possibly contributes to empathic breakdown. This points to the paramountcy of self-awareness in the therapist as well as for clients.

Increasing self-awareness

Self-awareness is the foundation for self-regulation, and is a significant part of therapy. We may say that self-awareness arises in three ways: through clients' felt-sense *intrapersonal* insights in therapy; through felt-sense *interpersonal* insights offered by the therapist in the therapist's use of self (e.g., Wosket, 1999; Rowan and Jacobs, 2002), for example, sensitive, fitting and timely empathic self-disclosures and transference communications (responsive deliveries and not reactive ejaculations); and through *transpersonal* insights arising from the in-between cocreative therapeutic dynamic as well as dreams, the deep imagination and intuitive moments.

Therapists also facilitate the process of increasing self-awareness in ways specific to therapeutic modalities, though there are often significant overlaps, for example, in sensitive empathic communications, pertinent self-disclosures and speculations arising from our experiences in the transference. Alongside these is the bourgeoning interest in mindfulness-based practice across the modalities, which both increases self-awareness and strengthens the capacity to self-regulate. Mindfulness practice encourages the development of a compassionate, non-judgemental, impartial, witnessing, non-elaborative, observer part of oneself, which is not easily hijacked by the turbulence of inner thoughts and feelings.

It is the present-centred quality of the therapist's presence which most effectively demonstrates mindfulness by their paying compassionate attention to their own bodily felt-sense experiences, and the movement and flow of thoughts that come and go, as they rest on the sensation of the breath in a single point of steadiness. We might refer to this as a contemplative practice, in the sense that we are contemplating the nature of our embodied felt-sense experience from moment to moment, with non-judgemental curiosity, while being aware of insights that arise. We are simply paying attention. Eventually, through benign invitation, clients may come to adopt this process of enquiry for themselves, and increase their own self-awareness of their experience in the present moment in a spirit of acceptance and knowing that acceptance is far from easy.

Regrettably, mindfulness has become more of a way of 'doing' rather than a way of 'being' to inform 'doing'; perhaps even a way of avoiding difficult feelings. I think many people (including many therapists) who profess to practise mindfulness barely go further than the surface of mindfulness practice and so fail to experience its full transformative benefits as they are largely unwilling to engage the tradition within which mindfulness makes most sense: Buddhism. This form of engagement is hardly mindfulness, and risks following a path that is less about increasing self-awareness and more about managing ordinary feelings without first enquiring into the meaning of these; a subtle form of disassociation from inner processes.

Polly Young-Eisendrath (2004: 129) reminds us that individuation or wholeness includes recognition of our inner conflicts, opposites and 'self-division', and that 'A person unable to feel self-division [or felt inner conflict] is not a "psychological individual" in Jung's terms, not capable of self-reflection and personal meaning' (p. 130). Rather, it is as if at times 'a person believes that meaning comes entirely from "the ways things are" and "the way we were born"', and may lack the reflective capacity to imagine otherwise; resignation without imagination. Or a person may lack 'aware[ness] of the subjective factors of their experience', or not take responsibility for their lives (p. 130). Forceful as this sounds, it may well be true. The experience in the therapeutic relationship is an invitation to increase self-awareness to enable becoming a 'psychological individual' (in part at least), and wrestle with the struggle that this may bring.

For most of his life, Matthew felt unable to acknowledge his 'emptiness' on his own, especially of loss so early on. By bringing felt-understanding to his experiences in the facilitating therapeutic relationship, he gradually came to appreciate the language of feeling as a half-forgotten part of himself, just like 'my twin is the half-forgotten part of me'. Enquiry into his feelings in this way deepened his sense of self as if he was getting to know himself for the first time, especially through felt-sense exploration of metaphors like 'empty connections' and 'feeling-void' which became the focus of therapy from the beginning. His deepening sense of self-awareness brought him growing confidence; he felt more secure within himself, and gradually in relationships, too. Not surprisingly, this amplified awareness of his inner life led to a curiosity about his dreams, of which he was becoming more aware. These were processed through embodied felt-sense enquiry, opening a window to other 'forgotten' parts of himself. 'Allow your body to know what it feels' became a type of mantra for him throughout the therapy, and by forging a relationship with his inner life he found that he was more able to regulate this and deepen his outer life.

Increasing self-regulation

Self-regulation relates to our capacity to ease, relax or soften turbulences in the feeling and thinking dimensions, and the correlating somatic activations. Achieving this allows us to feel more in control of our emotions, feelings and thoughts. But more than this, self-regulation brings with it a sense of peace or serenity, spaciousness, and secure feelings of connection with others. This capacity begins with affect regulation in infancy in relationship with a nurturing other. Therefore, emotional states and arousal are first regulated interpersonally before being regulated intrapersonally. As Schore (2014: 389) points out:

> Emotional states are initially regulated by others [e.g., the mother], but over the course of infancy it increasingly becomes self-regulated as a result of neurophysiological development and actual lived experience. These adaptive capacities are central to the emergence of self-regulation, the ability to flexibly regulate an expanding array of positive and negative affectively charged psychobiological states in different relational contexts, thereby allowing for the assimilation of various adaptive emotional-motivational states into a dynamic, coherent and integrated self-system.

David Wallin (2007: 109–110) puts it another way by drawing upon the concepts 'interactive regulation' (interpersonal) and 'self-regulation' (intrapersonal):

> In interactive regulation, one partner focuses on and 'uses' the responses of the other to manage his or her own internal states of emotion and arousal. (The infant seeking relief from distress, for example, may tune in to the soothing cadences of the mother's voice.) In self-regulation, by contrast, states of emotion and arousal are managed by turning *away* from the partner and *inward* toward the self (as shown, for example, in

the infant's gaze aversion, leaning away, oral self-comforting, and rocking). A balance of interactive and self-regulation is reflected in the kind of midrange tracking that predicts secure attachment.

He further emphasises that in therapy those with a strong leaning towards interpersonal regulation 'vigilantly track our every response and/or seem utterly reliant upon us to help them manage their difficult feelings' (p. 109). Clients presenting in this way may be communicating a preoccupied attachment style or communicate that their fear is lack of attachment.

> They behave as if they are hopeless, both about relieving this distress on their own and about the possibility of engaging help without making their distress overwhelmingly obvious to others. The problem for these patients (and their therapists) is not their dependency per se. Instead, it is the fact that their wary need for others monopolises their attention so thoroughly that they have little opportunity to know or make use of their own resources and desires. What needs reinstating in these patients is their ability to live, as it were, *inside* themselves rather than feeling that their centre of gravity lies *outside* themselves, in the minds and reactions of others.
>
> (pp. 109–110).

Naturally, there are many clients 'whose vulnerability resides in their over-developed capacity for self-regulation', often extrovertly, even compulsively, self-sufficient, and dismissive of relationship. 'Their deactivation attachment strategy leaves them distant from the awareness of any feelings or impulses that might bring them close to their disavowed needs to connect with others.' The therapist might be aware (in the transference) of a sense of feeling unhelpful, redundant or having little to offer clients, while also alert to supporting them to integrate their 'attachment-related feelings, impulses, and needs' (p. 110).

This may be the case particularly where there is a history of the absence of recognition, or where 'self-division' is too replete to self-regulate. Experiencing recognition through sensitive empathic engagement, while often resulting in an intensification of feeling, also brings the possibility to self-regulate. To come into relationship with feelings in this way allows them to become more fully integrated; 'self-divisions' become more tolerable, inner conflict more bearable, and the individual more psychological – though also more felt-sense embodied and relational. To increase self-regulation through therapy enables the client to become secure with another person or when alone. This security is a direct result of being able to self-regulate when subjectively engaged with another person, and when disengaged (Schore, 2014).

Further, as we come into compassionate relationship with clients, so the hope is that they will come into compassionate relationship with themselves. Practising self-kindness and self-compassion are further ways to promote self-regulation as these attitudes are rooted in mindfulness and contemplative practices, and therefore embrace the values of acceptance, allowing, patience and non-judgemental witnessing self-presence.

Matthew became more aware of other feelings besides those of 'emptiness', 'loss' and 'grief', such as anger towards his parents for not being more emotionally available as he was growing up, especially regarding the loss of his twin sister: Margaret. This was the first time he was able to say her name in therapy, and it was as if she was also present in these feeling moments. Reflective silences often followed; remembrances, though mostly vague, were bodily felt. Matthew was gradually more able to allow himself to value the felt-sense experience of these, by bringing his attention to rest in the areas of his body where the feelings were present, while at the same time gently imagining breathing in through these sensate areas (Gibson, 2008), thus resourcing himself to be with difficult feelings.

Transference, projective identification and self-disclosure

I return to our earlier theme of interpersonal insights arising in the therapeutic relationship. These are construed differently in different modalities but with the common aim of the therapist using themselves to increase awareness of conscious and unconscious processes in the therapeutic relationship (e.g., Rowan and Jacobs, 2002; Wosket, 1999). The therapist's use of self includes communications of empathy, as well as transference, projective identification and self-disclosure.

Transference

Transference is the felt-sense experience and response of the client toward the therapist *as if* they were, in some way, either positively and/or negatively their mother, father, lover, friend or some other significant figure (past and/or present). Likewise, countertransference (positively and/or negatively), is understood as the therapist's *as if* felt-sense experiences and responses to a client (Pearlman, 2012: 285). In this sense transference is a 'bidirectional' (Schore, 2014: 392) emotional communication and transaction; an unconscious dynamic between client and therapist of principally (though not exclusively) early life relationship dynamics and processes. In addition, given that the right brain is considered more dominant than the left in unconscious processing of emotions (Gainotti, 2012) which are mostly hidden, transference is a right-brain to right-brain communication. This means that working with and through the transference is mostly a felt-sense activity, where felt-experience is given priority over thinking about it.

However, the idea of 'counter' suggests that transference originates first with the client to which the therapist is 'counter' responding, thus appearing to put more emphasis on the client as activator. Although countertransference is now often taken to mean the whole of the therapist's 'emotional reactions toward the [client] regardless of the source' (Bride, 2012: 601), I find it useful also to understand transference within the cocreative, participatory view of the therapeutic relationship.

Within this participatory view, transference as a whole is understood as a cocreative phenomenon, arising from both sides of the relationship and in-between. Therefore, rather than assign transference as a response belonging only to clients, and countertransference as belonging only to the therapist, I prefer to think of them as interchangeable, and therefore find it more useful to refer simply to transference. Thus this participatory view honours more fully the complexity of this rather transient, yet fundamental phenomenon.

As the therapist brings transference enactments (e.g., experiences of affection, rejection, nurturing, punishing, judging, impingement, idealising, and so on) into awareness through speculative and joint felt-enquiries into the nature of these, clients learn about their experiences in relationships (as does the therapist). These communications often arise as ruptures in the therapeutic relationship, or moments of disconnection, thereby re-enacting relational disconnections earlier on in life, and can be the most distressing aspect of therapy; but also the most rewarding and fruitful. Exploring both positive and negative transference enables both client and therapist to understand something of its biographical root, the precipitating factors in the therapeutic relationship, as well as giving clients sufficient insight in noticing when these re-enactments occur in life. Again, developing self-awareness and increasing insight are the resourcing factors here, to (mostly) recognise future transference-dramas as these arise (given that transference occurs throughout life), and afford the freedom to potentially respond differently.

However, transference re-enactments are complex, and like the challenges brought by empathy, some clients (i.e., 'borderline' or 'narcissistic') find transference enactments difficult since they may not easily regulate the experience of the event, especially in the separation between sessions (Schore, 2016: 456). By putting 'borderline' and 'narcissistic' in parenthesis I take these to refer metaphorically to states, traits or parts, or aspects of a fragile-self process, rather than diagnostic tags or labels, although I also recognise the containing value of labels for some clients. For instance, in an excellent exploration of psychotherapy with 'borderline' clients, Charles Cohen and Vance Sherwood (1991: 17) suggest that it is the 'ability to wait', to 'become practised in the art of not intervening' regardless of demands, to let go of wanting to *do* anything other than to remain compassionately and receptively still (this is unlike an empty stillness or withholding, that can feel like a threatening void), while enduring the 'tension and uncertainty' that is likely to arise, that which will hopefully benefit clients. This is because the therapist must first establish that they are 'capable of being present without intrusion' (Cohen and Sherwood, 1991: 18), including empathic intrusions. More recent findings suggest a considerable part played, 'particularly in the early phases of treatment, by an engagement between the therapist and client that depends upon a conversation in which the elements of the emotional, non-verbal, and analogical "language" of the right hemisphere are prominent' (Schore, 2016: 333). Within this context 'An analogue of something is another thing that is like it but not a copy' (p. 331); similar, but different. Therapists therefore aim to come alongside the experience of clients through the use of 'facial expressions, tone of voice' (p. 331), and other non-intrusive verbal and non-verbal empathic responses. The main resources with 'borderline' clients are the therapist's constancy, and ability to be sensitively present and facilitative, discerningly transparent, and open to exploring inevitable therapeutic 'mistakes', in a whole mind/body relational way.

'Projective identification' or 'participation mystique'

'Projective identification' (Melanie Klein) or 'participation mystique' (from anthropologist Lucien Lévy-Bruhl) occurs when clients feel unconsciously unable to contain an aspect of their experience (positive or negative), which they perceive as overwhelming, distressing or uncontainable in other ways, and project this to the therapist as a way of dissociating from the experience. Mostly unconscious, the projection 'seeks' somewhere to 'deposit' itself, by way of something in the mind/body of the therapist, on which the projection can 'engage'. The therapist then comes to initially view this projection as if their own. The discerning therapist receives, contains and gives the experience meaning, then communicates this back to the client who is (hopefully) then able to accept it. Hence 'Projective identification is defined as an early developmental interactive process between two individuals wherein largely unconscious information is projected from the sender to the recipient' (Melanie Klein cited in Schore, 2016: 465). This receiving and containing of clients' experience is an opportunity for it to be felt and acknowledged, before being respectfully and tentatively offered back, with clients then (mostly) able to internalise this (see, e.g., Wilfred Bion, Melanie Klein). As Schore (2016: 465) points out in writing on the origins of affect regulation, 'The recipient allows the induced state to reside within, and by reinternalizing this externally metabolized experience the infant gains a change in the quality of his experience.' This profound interactive process of giving, receiving, holding and returning, allows clients to eventually come to accept a part of themselves. Ogden (1992: 14) reminds us, '*Projective identification does not exist where there is no interaction between projector and recipient.*' This provides an important indication that something of clients' experience in relationships may have been missed, unacknowledged, overlooked or not sufficiently held early on in life, and that occurrences of projective identification are often important signs of a reparative opportunity in the therapeutic relationship. Some writers (e.g., Rowan in Rowan and Jacobs, 2002) argue that this makes it distinct from countertransference where the experience comes *from* the therapist, but it is likely that similar to countertransference, projective identification is also a participatory cocreated experience. And like empathy the process of projective identification is a potentially transformative moment of recognition; a moment of further self-integration.

Self-disclosure

Unlike most communications, self-disclosure reveals to clients something of the therapist's own inner process as it arises in the present moment in order to benefit the therapeutic endeavour, though without necessarily revealing anything biographical about themselves. Alongside non-verbal communications, these are further glimpses of the therapist's authenticity. Such authentic moments are moments of revealed integrity arising, as they often do, from one's depths. Self-disclosures are instances of personal and relational truth, and demonstrate something of the clients' influence and impact on the relationship and the therapist's willingness to be open, transparent, genuine and appropriately bounded. Therapy, then, is also a joint commitment to authenticity.

Revelations of therapist authenticity open up possibilities for trust in the therapeutic relationship, and consequently in relationship with life itself, even the Dynamic Ground (Washburn, 1995 [1987]) or Mystery. These communications are valuing of clients because the therapist is offering part of themselves in trust – be these glimpses of their strength or vulnerability, feelings of joy or helplessness, or their non-defensive response to anger at the therapist's therapeutic mistake. This potentially both deepens the relationship and also increases feelings of respect and value.

With deepening trust in the therapeutic relationship Matthew brought more of himself to the process: the relationships with his siblings began to emerge, for example, his fondness for his 'big' brother (ten years his senior) who was the 'go-to' sibling, and the brothers in-between who were as tumultuous as he, and often getting into trouble. Margaret was his only sister. The full narrative of his life was unfolding. The resourcefulness of the therapeutic relationship was felt through processing unconscious communications, especially in the transference and projective identification. At times, more than a therapist, I felt as if I were the empathically amenable parent, who often held difficult feelings, before tentatively offering these back to him when Matthew was able to receive them – as if they were gifts returning via a receptive route to further enable his integration. The strong tendency toward wholeness and integration is a profound resourcing power underlying all other resources, that 'wants' everything to be complete. I am, therefore, convinced as Beebe (1992: 126) when he writes: 'each time a willing receptivity to the whole emerges, I know that integrity has surfaced out of its prior life in depth'. Therapy with Matthew continues.

Relationship defined by the three loves: agape, philia and eros

Empathy is a type of love, a compassionate concern for a person. But more than empathy, this love embraces qualities like humility, patience, non-exploitative and non-possessive kindness, hopefulness, an interest in promoting truth, and a steadfast commitment to the process of therapy. This kind of love is *agape* (Greek: commitment to the welfare of others) (Gordon, 1993: 245). Agape prevails even when the therapeutic process and relationship becomes difficult. 'So it is not just the love, it is the being with them when you don't love them [clients]; hence the agape' (Sedgwick, 2001: 89). Peter Lomas (1999: 97) points out 'The therapist's love or hate, care or indifference, will affect patients directly and emotionally, and will intrinsically modify the outcome of the undertaking.' Agape is a constancy of love which is able to withstand the full range of feelings and communications, so the vigilant therapist can contain many (or most) of their feeling responses to clients, viewing them as significant information about the therapeutic process.

Similarly, Sue Wiggins and colleagues (2012: 152) argue that 'therapeutic, humanitarian love' is similar to *agape* or *philia* (Greek: friendship or brotherly/sisterly love). However, philia is distinct from agape in that it is defined more by the qualities of intimacy and closeness, 'something akin to friendship' (Lomas, 1999: 94), and embraces qualities of warmth and genuineness. Wiggins and colleagues (2012: 152) point out that this may be difficult for therapists who 'keep a professional distance', which is more the stance of agape.

Alongside these expressions of love, therapy is not complete without the presence of *eros*. Rosemary Gordon (1993: 248–249) points out that for the Greeks:

> Eros meant magic, power, and ecstasy, which in its lower forms could degenerate into frenzy. Eros, many claimed, refers to impulse and desire; it involves attraction and reaction to physical beauty and a passion that can transport man above and beyond himself.

Adolf Guggenbühl-Craig (1980: 26) identifies that eros, as the god of love, is a love which 'includes the entire spectrum of emotional attachment, from sexuality to friendship to involvement with profession, hobbies, and art'. Thus, eros energy in therapy is the motivating power towards wholeness, at-one-ment, and the integration of parts, and the conscious coming together of the dimensions to support the wholing trajectory, as well as creativity and spontaneity. Eros is also the erotic power in the transference and countertransference (Mann, 1999; cf. Schaverien, 1995) through its seductive, alluring pull.

Love in the therapeutic relationship, then, is expressed in a number of ways, and is a combining or blending of agape, philia and eros. These expressions of love occur at any time in therapy, and offer valuable information on what is happening in the relationship, especially in the transference and countertransference. It is also through the experience of love that clients come to love themselves. For some, the primary process of therapy is one of learning to love oneself, and this is often first experienced as the loving presence of the therapist:

> Therapy's premier task then consists of gaining access to this hithertofore inaccessible love; that is, to actualise the love that is already a basic part of the person. Love's actualisation in therapy occurs through the mutually loving nature of the therapeutic experience.
>
> (Natterson, 2003: 513)

The therapist will also be alert to the shadow side of love. For agape, this can arise as a tendency for do-gooding, rescuing and taking pity (a subtle judgemental view of clients); while philia can feel intrusive, smothering or unbounded. Similarly, eros potentially crosses boundaries, and can be sexually exploitative. But love also underpins the process of trust in the therapeutic relationship, and the therapist's 'capacity to resist to the temptation to act out, and this may enable him to feel and submit to the powerful and at times almost overwhelming feelings evoked in the countertransference' (Gordon, 1993: 254).

This trusting process is one of the main resourcing factors in therapy. This is because trust increases capacity for openness and honesty, to take risks, or explore the depths of one's person, and to go beyond the limits of preconceived possibility in life. After all, it is through trusting another with our process that we come to trust ourselves, and through breakdown of trust that many difficulties arise in therapy. And so, by entrusting ourselves to relationship we open ourselves to the reality of its loss too.

Potential, consciousness and the transpersonal

Within the context of resourcing, the transpersonal (meaning 'beyond the personal') aspect of therapy consists of discerning and promoting the trajectory of clients' life towards optimal growth in the context of the bigger picture (a coinfluencing, cocreative participatory whole), and enables clients to align themselves more fully with this. This, in turn, empowers clients to be more open to the influence of Mystery or the Dynamic Ground (Washburn, 1995 [1987]; Ferrer, 2002), and supports them to cultivate trust in the Other, with which (or whom) guiding 'conversation' is also possible, be it a dream figure or the 'spirit' or atmosphere of place, or something more than this (Wilson, 2011). The transpersonal aspect of therapy thereby facilitates an expansion of consciousness, and a widening of identity.

Transpersonally orientated therapy is primarily a right brain activity facilitating in-depth dialogical engagement with the 'voices' of the feeling, right brain thinking, physical, energetic, imaginal and spiritual dimensions, but also engages the aspirations of left brain thinking (in so far as this serves the wholing trajectory), and potentially explores the wider field of the behavioural and interpersonal dimensions which impact upon clients, such as global and collective themes and concerns. Hence working from a transpersonal perspective supports full expression of the dimensions as paths in their own right, and finds ways of listening to the wisdom of these paths. Major ways of working transpersonally include engaging with deep imagination (e.g., Jung's active imagination, imagery), dreams, energy, and felt-sense embodied practices such as embodied mindfulness. The literature in this field is increasing (e.g., Rowan, 2005 [1993], 2010; Friedman and Hartelius, 2013; *Journal of Transpersonal Research*), but the therapeutic focus is not yet fully represented, especially from British and European contributors.

Resourcing from the shadow

Carl Jung defined the shadow as 'the thing a person has no wish to be' (1993 [1954], CW 16, para. 470). This refers to the unacknowledged parts of a person; their 'light' as well as their 'darkness', which are often present in unconscious processes such as transference and projective identification. Throughout his writing Jung refers to the importance of developing awareness of the shadow in psychotherapy, and its projections in the individual's life (e.g., 'it's you/them/theirs, not me/mine'). As Jung writes (1952, CW 11, para. 131):

> Everyone carries a shadow, and the less it is embodied in the individual's conscious life, the blacker and denser it is. If an inferiority is conscious, one always has a chance to correct it. Furthermore, it is constantly in contact with other interests, so that it is continually subjected to modifications. But if it is repressed and isolated from consciousness, it never gets corrected, and is liable to burst forth suddenly in a moment of unawareness. At all counts, it forms an unconscious snag, thwarting our most well-meant intentions.

Resourcing from the shadow pays particular attention to potentials, capacities and strengths that are not fully acknowledged by the client, and explores the 'snag[s]' which inhibit the growth and embodiment of these. Beebe (1992: 33) points out, 'However unattractive the ground we uncover through this inquiry, finding the truth brings relief. Only then do we feel secure in figuring out what we must do. Jung called this process facing and integrating the shadow.' Discernment of the truth is the process of authenticity; a painstaking excavation into the depths of our being to explore possibilities and limitations, distortions and the buried and often forgotten parts of ourselves and abilities. Of course, this applies to both people in the therapeutic dyad.

Meaning-making in the *thinking dimension* is not enough

Traditionally, meaning-making is understood as a left brain cognitive process, concerned with making sense of something, by bringing reason to it. But meaning-making from the thinking dimension alone is not enough as it pushes our centre of gravity away from meaning-making as a wholistic activity to a left brain only function. From a resource-focused perspective, meaning-making engages all the dimensions in a type of conversation. Engaging dialogically with the 'voices' of the dimensions, especially the feeling and physical (body, sensate) dimensions, pulls the tilt away from left brain rational thinking to include more right brain processes, and therefore wholistic meaning-making. Moreover, left brain thinking does not 'speak' for the other dimensions. Meaning-making, then, is an embodied felt-sense process of discerning the 'sense', 'fit', 'rightness', 'decision', 'authenticity' and the 'next step' of something, whereby the distinctive 'voices' of the dimensions are involved in the process of meaning-making. Eugene Gendlin's (1969, 1996) 'focusing' process as a way of meaning-making is a comprehensive example of this (Chapter 4).

Concluding thoughts

Being in the therapeutic relationship is a resource-making experience, consisting of what I refer to as multiple 'therapeutic events' in the healing process. These events include moments of meeting in the sensitive empathic relationship, integration of interpersonal factors in this relationship (e.g., warmth, acceptance, love), and meaningful insights gained through increased self-awareness and careful exploration and enquiry, as well as moments of mutual humour, joy, and clients' feeling of being recognised, acknowledged and accommodated by the therapist. Sometimes, too, it is what the therapist does with the boundaries of therapy that resources clients. For example, significant moments in therapy may include acts of generosity with time, or forgoing fees in times of austerity or struggle, or when the therapist discloses being thoughtful of a client when going through a difficult period. These genuine, mostly spontaneous, acts of kindness are often experienced as valuing of clients, and the therapist will consider the possible implications of these for the relationship, while also remembering that, for some generosity can feel intrusive. But clients can attribute significance to almost anything in the therapeutic process, relationship and environment – the welcoming display of freshly cut flowers, the wood burning stove, and the water that has just been poured into the glass, waiting. The summation of these factors is what we often mean by the healing power of the therapeutic relationship. Importantly, it is when clients are invited to notice the embodied felt-experience of a therapeutic event that they come to view this as resourcing.

References

Beebe, J. (1992) *Integrity in Depth*, College Station: Texas A&M University Press.
Bowlby, J. (1969) *Attachment and Loss: Vol. 1. Attachment*, New York: Basic Books.

Bowlby, J. (1973) *Attachment and Loss: Vol. 2. Separation: Anxiety and Anger*, New York: Basic Books.

Bowlby, J. (1980) *Attachment and Loss: Vol. 3. Loss, Sadness and Depression*, New York: Basic Books.

Bowlby, J. (1988) *A Secure Base: Parent–Child Attachment and Healthy Human Development*, New York: Basic Books.

Bride, B. E. (2012) 'Secondary Traumatic Stress', in *Encyclopaedia of Trauma: An Interdisciplinary Guide*, C. R. Figley (ed.), Thousand Oaks, CA: Sage, pp. 601–602.

Cohen, C. P. and Sherwood, V. R. (1991) *Becoming the Constant Object in Psychotherapy with the Borderline Patient*, Northvale, NJ: Jason Aronson.

Degnan, A., Seymour-Hyde, A. S., Harris, A. and Berry, K. (2014) 'The Role of Therapist Attachment in Alliance and Outcome: A Systemic Literature Review', *Clinical Psychologist & Psychotherapy*, 23(1): 47–65.

Elliott, R., Bohart, A. C., Watson, J. C. and Greenberg, L. S. (2011) 'Empathy', *Psychotherapy*, 48(1): 43–49.

Ferrer, J. N. (2002) *Revisioning Transpersonal Theory: A Participatory Vision of Human Spirituality*, New York: SUNY.

Friedman, H. and Hartelius, G. (2013) 'Transpersonal Psychology: The Participatory Turn', in *The Wiley-Blackwell Handbook of Transpersonal Psychology*, H. Friedman and G. Hartelius (eds), New York: John Wiley and Sons, pp. 187–202.

Gainotti, G. (2012) 'Unconscious Processing of Emotions and the Right Hemisphere', *Neuropsychologia*, 50(2): 205–218.

Geller, S. M. and Greenberg, L. S. (2012) *Therapeutic Presence: A Mindful Approach to Effective Therapy*, Washington, DC: APA.

Gendlin, E. T. (1969) 'Focusing', *Psychotherapy: Theory, Research and Practice*, 6(1): 4–15.

Gendlin, E. T. (1996) *Focusing-Orientated Psychotherapy: A Manual of the Experiential Method*, London: Guilford Press.

Gibson, R. (2008) *My Body, My Earth: The Practice of Somatic Archaeology*, New York: iUniverse.

Gordon, R. (1993) *Bridges: Metaphor for Psychic Processes*, London: Karnac.

Guggenbühl-Craig, A. (1980) *Eros on Crutches: Reflections on Amorality and Psychopathy*, Washington, DC: Spring Publications.

Hobson, R. F. (1985) *Forms of Feeling: The Heart of Psychotherapy*, London and New York: Routledge.

Jordan, J. V. (1997) 'Relational Development Through Mutual Empathy', in *Empathy Reconsidered: New Directions in Psychotherapy*, A. C. Bohart and L. S. Greenberg (eds), Washington, DC: APA, pp. 343–351.

Jung, C. G. (1952) *Answer to Job*, Collected Works 11, Princeton, NJ: Princeton University Press.

Jung, C. G. (1993 [1954]) *The Practice of Psychotherapy*, Collected Works 16, London: Routledge.

Kennedy-Moore, E. and Watson, J. C. (1999) *Expressing Emotions: Myths, Realities, and Therapeutic Strategies*, New York: Guilford Press.

Lomas, P. (1999) *Doing Good? Psychotherapy Out of its Depth*, Oxford: Oxford University Press.

Mann, D. (ed.) (1999) *Erotic Transference and Countertransference: Clinical Practice in Psychotherapy*, London: Routledge.

Mearns, D. and Cooper, M. (2005) *Working at Relational Depth in Counselling and Psychotherapy*, London: Sage.

Natterson, J. M. (2003) 'Love in Psychotherapy', *Psychoanalytic Psychology*, 20(3); 509–521.

Ogden, P., Pain, C., Minton, K. and Fisher, J. (2005) 'Including the Body in Mainstream Psychotherapy for Traumatized Individuals', *Psychologist-Psychoanalyst*, 25(4): 19–24.

Ogden, T. H. (1992) *Projective Identification and Psychotherapeutic Technique*, London: Karnac.

Owens, P., Springwood, B. and Wilson, M. (2012) *Creative Ethical Practice in Counselling and Psychotherapy*, London: Sage.

Pearlman, L. A. (2012) 'Vicarious Trauma', in *Encyclopaedia of Trauma: An Interdisciplinary Guide*, C. R. Figley (ed.), Thousand Oaks, CA: Sage, pp. 784–786.

Petrowski, K., Pokorny, D., Nowacki, K. and Buchheim, A. (2011) 'Matching the Patient to the Therapist: The Roles of the Attachment Status and the Helping Alliance', *The Journal of Nervous and Mental Disease*, 199(11): 839–844.

Petrowski, K., Pokorny, D., Nowacki, K. and Buchheim, A. (2013) 'The Therapist's Attachment Representation and the Patient's Attachment to the Therapist', *Psychotherapy Research*, 23(1): 25–34.

Rowan, J. (2005 [1993]) *The Transpersonal: Spirituality in Psychotherapy and Counselling*, London: Routledge.

Rowan, J. (2010) *Personification: Using the Dialogical Self in Psychotherapy and Counselling*, London: Routledge.

Rowan, J. and Jacobs, M. (2002) *The Therapist's Use of Self*, Buckingham, UK: Open University Press.

Schaverien, J. (1995) *Desire and the Female Therapist: Engendered Gazes in Psychotherapy and Art Therapy*, London and New York: Routledge.

Schore, A. N. (2011) 'The Right Brain Implicit Self Lies at the Core of Psychoanalysis', *Psychoanalytic Dialogues*, 21(1): 75–100.

Schore, A. N. (2014) 'The Right Brain is Dominant in Psychotherapy', *Psychotherapy*, 51(3): 388–397, reprinted with permission from APA.

Schore, A. N. (2016) *Affect Regulation and the Origin of the Self: The Neurobiology of Emotional Development*, New York: Routledge.

Schore, J. R. and Schore, A. N. (2008) 'Modern Attachment Theory: The Central Role of Affect Regulation in Development and Treatment', *Clinical Social Work*, 36(1): 9–20.

Sedgwick, D. (2001) *Introduction to Jungian Psychotherapy: The Therapeutic Relationship*, New York: Brunner-Routledge.

Siegelman, E. (1990) *Metaphor and Meaning in Psychotherapy*, New York: Guilford Press.

Sullivan, B. S. (2010) *The Mystery of Analytical Work: Weaving Jung and Bion*, London: Routledge.

Wallin, D. (2007) *Attachment in Psychotherapy*, New York: Guilford Press.

Warner, M. S. (1997) 'Does Empathy Cure? A Theoretical Consideration of Empathy, Processing, and Personal Narrative', in *Empathy Reconsidered: New Directions in Psychotherapy*, A. C. Bohart and L. S. Greenberg (eds), Washington, DC: APA, pp. 125–140.

Washburn, M. (1995 [1987]) *The Ego and the Dynamic Ground: A Transpersonal Theory of Human Development*, New York: SUNY.

Wiggins, S., Elliott, R. and Cooper, M. (2012) 'The Prevalence and Characteristics of Relational Depth Events in Psychotherapy', *Psychotherapy Research*, 22(2): 139–158.

Wilson, M. (2011) 'Encounters with Nature as a Path of Self-Realisation: A Meaning-Making Framework', *Journal of Transpersonal Research*, 3(1): 11–29.

Wosket, V. (1999) *The Therapeutic Use of Self: Counselling Practice, Research and Supervision*, Hove, UK: Brunner-Routledge.

Young-Eisendrath, P. (2004) *Subject to Change: Jung, Gender and Subjectivity in Psychoanalysis*, New York: Brunner-Routledge.

Chapter 8

Resourcing for trauma

Trauma experiences include pre-birth and birth trauma (e.g., stress hormones circulating in pregnancy, attempted abortion, the birthing process itself, ill health of mother, depression, death of mother, born into war/conflict), loss, deprivation, neglect, accidents, assault and rape (e.g., Steenkamp et al., 2013), emotional neglect or intrusion, physical, sexual or emotional abuse, genocide and other war-time atrocities (e.g., Herman, 1992; Beebe, 2003; Krippner and McIntyre, 2003), as well as disasters; in fact the spectrum ranges from emotional and developmental trauma to other life event traumas.

The numerous understandings of trauma make it difficult to define, but theorists and practitioners tend to side with the Diagnostic and Statistical Manual of Mental Disorders (DSM-5) definition of trauma as 'stressful events outside the usual range of human experience' (cited in Scaer, 2014 [2007]: 2), namely direct exposure to, or witness in a person of, actual or threats of serious injury, sexual violence, as well as death or the threat of death. That is, as Robert Scaer defines it, 'anything that represents a threat to our survival as a human being' (p. 6) or 'an extreme form of stress, one that has assumed life-threatening proportions' (p. 100). Most therapists who work with trauma will recognise the psychophysiological symptoms which follow trauma to include flashbacks, repetitive and stressful images, nightmares, and a range of somatic symptoms such as nausea or trembling, and know that trauma leaves an imprint on the brain/mind/body. For instance, Post-Traumatic Stress Disorder (PTSD) is often understood as 'produced by a threat, shock, or injury that occurred in a state of helplessness' (p. xvi), triggering fight/flight/freeze (mobility/immobility) responses and producing a 'high state of activation of the emotional brain, the limbic system, and both sympathetic and para-sympathetic parts of the autonomic nervous system' (p. xvii). This means that clients are in survival mode for much of the time and in a high state of alert for the possible re-occurrence of threat.

While acknowledging the vastness of the field and the evolving under-standing of the impact of trauma (on self and others) and its recovery (e.g., Levers, 2003; Briere and Scott, 2015 [2014]), it is only possible, here, to pro-vide a brief overview of this developing field. Reviewing the literature highlights the following as areas key to effectively resourcing clients when working through trauma, and is illustrated by a single case: Angela.

Vignette: Angela

> At the age of sixteen, Angela (aged thirty-two) entered the religious life in a North American convent, partly to run away from a neglectful home life, but also to find a place of safe belonging. She had not known her father, and her mother, too, was unavailable through regular and often drunken, and sometimes violent, encounters with random men in her home. Angela frequently found herself in the role of 'mother's nurse' and 'protector', and was often forced (for fear of punishment) to keep standing watch at night while her mother slept. Rarely were there meals on the table, other than the ones Angela was sent to get from the Take-Out. Being an only child, it was not until Angela began secondary education that she came to view her upbringing as neither ordinary nor safe. When she came to therapy she had recently taken a sabbatical from her community to study in England, but found that she was vexed by recurring nightmares of her early life, and finding difficulties in relating to members of her own community and establishing friendships outside, especially with women.

Creating inner resources and experiences of safety

Within this context we might say that there are two ways of thinking about the function of a resource, as 'protection' or as a 'facilitator of growth or development'; a third resource function in 'pseudo' resources is often coupled with protective resources in their contracting or life-restricting orientation (Ralph, Chapter 5). Protective resources are, in a sense, inner resting places where clients can regain a sense of strength; time away from the processing of traumatic memories – stabilising more than energising. On the other hand, resource orientation as 'facilitator of development' is more energising than stabilising. To put it another way, the protective tendency is toward contraction, whereas the growth tendency is toward expansion. While both tendencies are innate processes of the brain/mind/body systems, therapists must be aware of the purpose the resource serves for clients, and possibly inform them of this so that they are not locked into only contracting, but come to view contraction–expansion as a healthy continuum of experiencing.

Therefore, when working with trauma, at some point near the beginning of therapy, it is useful to establish an inner-protective resource, a 'go-to' safe place. As was the case with Angela, this will sometimes arise without the therapist prompting, but at other times the therapist may intervene. For Angela it was people who were not safe, rather than places, and she had found a sense of safety within herself, as well as within the monastic setting. My preference is always to wait and see what resources arise from the innate wisdom of the person rather than to intervene too soon. Frank Corrigan and

Alistair Hull (2015) note that these resources need to be embodied, felt-sense resources, rather than purely imaginal, in order for them to be truly supportive when processing trauma memories becomes difficult. Key ways of establishing embodied experiences of safety can be found in EMDR's 'safe place' experience (SPE) protocol, Somatic Trauma Therapy's (Rothschild, 2000, 2003) 'safe place/safe person' intervention, as well as the 'running technique' as the frequent method for accessing the 'safe place/safe person' in Somatic Trauma Therapy (cf. Levine, 2010: 119, 'the running escape response'). Other key methods include the focus on 'establish[ing] an environment of relative safety' in Sensory Experience (Levine, 2010: 75), and the embodied grid system, combined with imagery and embodied breathwork practices (Gibson, 2008) in the Comprehensive Resource Model (CRM; Schwarz et al., 2016), which are also integrated into Brainspotting (Grand, 2013). This is similar to Carl Jung's 'active imagination' (imagination with felt-sense) or embodied imagination and is a cornerstone practice in some Jungian and transpersonal psychotherapies. During therapy, Angela came to realise that running away to the religious life was one of her most self-resourcing actions, and considerable time was taken at the early stages of therapy to explore the felt-sense experience of this. Sometimes, out of concern to establish a 'safe place' for clients, therapists forget to ask 'What or who got you through (the trauma)?', and therefore bypass waiting for disclosure of the protective resource. The clients' innate capacity for resourcefulness often finds a way of keeping them safe, but the story is not always forthcoming.

While in many ways the religious community was Angela's 'safe place', a safer place was a known inner sunlit or moonlit opening in the woods under the open arms of a California oak, where 'Our Lady of Tenderness' would meet with her in bodily-felt imagination.

Eliciting safe experiences in these ways is, in a sense, a boundary-making activity where clients are able to begin to identify with a part of themselves that is safe from the impact of trauma. This is a place of refuge in the psyche, a resource place, while they engage in the difficult work of processing and integrating trauma memories. It is in such spaces that it becomes possible to relax into breathing again rather than in holding one's breath through fear. Hopefully in time the therapist, too, becomes the trusted other on whom clients can rely; therapy then becomes a safe process with a safe person. By introducing a 'safe person' into her 'safe place', Angela was already beginning to imagine a companion with her in this 'safe place' with qualities of tenderness and compassion.

Sometimes 'safety' is found in other ways. Angela's *unconscious* protective resource (in that it kept her safe) was her capacity for avoidance and dissociation, in particular the 'somatic dissociation' of trauma memories. Therapists will know that psychotherapy with clients 'must treat not only traumatic symptoms but also the dissociative defence' (Schore, 2012: 65). As Allan Schore (2012: 60) points out, it is now generally accepted that dissociation is 'the bottom-line *survival defence* against overwhelming, unbearable emotional experiences', and is 'the essence of trauma' (van der Kolk, 2014: 66). Robert Scaer (2014 [2007]: 67) also points out that dissociation 'reflects the state of consciousness in a freeze response', and notes that if this occurs at the time of trauma it is likely that this will occur during recollection of the trauma. He also informs us that dissociation occurs in 'emotional, perceptual, physical, and memory-related' forms (p. 72); for instance, when there is a lack of awareness of feeling, confusion or depersonalisation, lack of bodily connection or body recognition, or forgetting important information and appointments. In addition, as Donald Kalsched (2013) notes, dissociation is not the result of external events alone, but of inner, protective factors. Traumatic events are 'kept alive by inner factors or defensive powers that haunt or hallow the unconscious mental life of the trauma survivor' (p. 285), and can be 'triggered by an inner "voice", or somatic reaction' which will often activate the trauma memory as if it were occurring now (p. 286). Angela's dissociative occurrences were mostly somatic, but were more fully felt when embodied through therapeutic processing, which was why it was so important to establish a 'safe place'. For instance, moments of 'somatic dissociation' were occasionally visible at the beginning of therapy when Angela found herself bumping into the furniture when she came into the consulting room (Scaer, 2014 [2007]: 88), and at other times when she reported being temporarily unable to feel sensations in her legs during therapy. When trauma memories became present in this way it was necessary to process them in the moment by sensitive empathic attunement, and also to find ways to transition from *unconscious* (dissociative) to more *conscious*, embodied 'safe place' experiences, thereby engaging both the felt-sense embodied right brain and cognitive left brain. As Margaret Wilkinson (2006: 105) notes, 'For our dissociative patients it is important that the [therapist] engage the right brain in an empathic mode of working towards relational change but while, crucially, remaining able to think.'

More than a thought or an image, the 'safe place' is an embodied felt-sense experience utilising most of the dimensions to accomplish maximum coherence, and grounding. Ways to the 'safe place' are via a combination of the imaginal, thinking, physical, behavioural and emotional/feeling dimensions. This is similar to Peter Levine's (2010: 138–154) SIBAM model, which he originated in the 1970s, and which is also used in Somatic Trauma Therapy (Rothschild, 2000, 2003). Here the acronym SIBAM represents: *Sensation, Image, Behaviour, Affect, Meaning*. In Levine's model there is absence of explicit reference to the energetic, spiritual and interpersonal dimensions, though the interpersonal is implied by the therapeutic relationship itself. The energetic is also often present in affect and sensation, and therefore certainly present in trauma memories, though 'safe place' energy is qualitatively different. Elsewhere he acknowledges the 'intrinsic and wedded relationship between trauma and spirituality' (2010: 347). The presence of 'Our Lady of Tenderness' in Angela's 'safe place' was a benign spiritual presence.

The spiritual dimension is often viewed as problematic when working through trauma because of a tendency in some clients (often unconsciously) to use spiritual experiences to 'bypass' psychological processing (Welwood, 2000). Many therapists may therefore feel uncomfortable or out of their depth in this dimension, and even fear its linkage with dissociation or psychosis. Although the evolution of trauma modalities increasingly aims to integrate the spiritual dimension into therapy, this is not always convincing. The NeuroAffective Relational Model (NARM), for instance, while acknowledging the importance of spirituality argues that the 'spiritualizing subtypes [i.e., coping styles arising out of early trauma survival adaption] disconnect from bodily experience and personal relationships' (Heller and LaPierre, 2012: 38). Within this view, lack of embodiment paves the way for more energetic disembodied connection in that some clients 'can be quite psychic and energetically attuned to people, animals, and the environment' (p. 39). However, this perspective does not take into account Jerome Bernstein's (2005: 9) ground breaking work on 'Borderland personalities' who *personally* experience, and must live out, the split from nature on which the western ego, as we know it, has been built'. He notes further that 'They feel (not feel *about*) the extinction of the species; they feel (not feel *about*) the plight of animals no longer permitted to live by their own instincts, and which survive only in domesticated states to be used as pets or food.' Moreover, and importantly, rather than disconnecting from their bodies many Borderland personalities are deeply *feeling and embodied*, and open to experiencing the plight of the environment, and species. These experiences are 'non-pathological' (p. 11), especially if they are 'traits' rather than pathological states: '*Those contents that tend to be consistently and highly defended are likely to be pathological contents; whereas those transrational contents that consistently tend to be not defended are likely to be Borderland components*' (p. 142). For Angela, the presence of 'Our Lady of Tenderness' in a nature setting with the California oak was a felt-sense embodied experience in imagination; a measure of deep religiosity, a resource rather than a pathological state (cf. Jung's 'active imagination'). The dialogue between trauma and spirituality in the field of trauma therapy continues. Donald Kalsched (2013: 25) offers one of the most comprehensive accounts of psychospiritual development as it relates to trauma, citing a tendency amongst the pioneers of depth psychology, specifically, to describe the 'spiritual' phenomena as becoming 'suddenly visible *through a gap created by trauma*'. That is, something that 'breaks' us can also 'open' us up to the Other; breaking-up can lead to breaking-through. In this sense the spiritual dimension is a profound resource.

To move on from the spiritual, the 'safe place', can sometimes be reached through the physical dimension and the facilitative soothing quality of the breath itself. Breathing also brings attention back to the present moment, and is therefore a grounding experience (Chapter 2). However, focusing attention on the breath can be difficult when there is a lot of anxiety in the body. For Angela, imagining her back against the ancient oak, while breathing in the forest air with its scents and sounds, with both feet firmly on the forest floor, was a deeply connecting and resourcing experience. Sometimes the experience of feeling 'strong, grounded and present', or connected to 'the Body Resource' (Grand, 2013), guided only by the breath, was enough to establish this experience of safety, while also imagining the experience sinking into her like sap through a tree (Hanson, 2013).

Clients who are unable to imagine themselves in a 'safe place' may find a way to imagine a 'vulnerable' other person in a 'safe place', and bring this alive through describing the felt-sense image for this person. Clients may then find a way of being present to this person in the image, thereby gaining an experience of a 'safe place' by association. Alongside establishing a 'safe place' is the aim to grow a self-soothing capacity to regulate difficult feelings as they arise. Finding a 'safe place' and a self-soothing capacity can often coincide, and yet they are different processes. For regulation is not dependent on imagining a 'safe place', and self-soothing may be more consciously grounded in the present moment. Hence it is useful to develop these separately.

Increasing capacity for affect regulation and distress reduction

Coming into 'friendly' relationship with our body is a key to self-regulation. Without this we become dependent on 'external regulation' from medication, drugs and other substances, frequent reassurance, and 'compulsive compliance with the wishes of others' (van der Kolk, 2014: 97). The clients' key to recovery from trauma is to befriend the body (p. 100), that is, to establish a relationship with the body based on self-kindness, self-empathy, self-understanding, including compassionate enquiry into the language of sensation, symptom and gesture. By this befriending, clients become more aware of the felt-sense communications (e.g., tingling, tensing, warmth, pressure, feeling empty, as well as gesture and movement), and increasingly ground identity firmly within their bodies. This allows us to process trauma memories embedded in our bodies more effectively, and to establish a sense of inner safety, especially when clients find activation of felt-sense experiences unmanageable, and when these contain a sense of fear.

Part of the process of cultivating inner safety is to support clients to appropriately deactivate the amygdala in the right hemisphere. The right amygdala is 'responsible for the emergency response system in the brain' (Wilkinson, 2006: 25) and its priority is to keep clients safe, even in the absence of threat when they are already safe. Essentially, information about potential threat comes to the amygdala through the senses and through feelings. When the threat alarm system 'goes off' fight/flight/freeze responses immediately follow, and messages are relayed to one of a pair of hippocampi (also on the right) which evaluates the threat viability (the right amygdala and right hippocampus are located in the limbic system or 'emotional brain'). In the absence of genuine threat, the hippocampus delivers a message to this effect to the amygdala, which then relaxes. But amygdala deactivation is also a whole brain process drawing upon the more conscious left hemisphere to intervene when threat arises. Scaer (2014 [2007]: 180) suggests at least three ways to down-regulate the amygdala: through *ritual, hemisphere integration* and *empowerment*.

Down-activating the amygdala through use of ritual

Social healing rituals involve repetitive behaviours like drumming (cf. Szabo, 2004), singing, dancing, hypnotic trances, or eye movements as in EMDR or tapping in EFT with its linked repetitive affirmations. Devon Hinton and Laurence Kirmayer (2013: 615), provide a brief overview of the benefits of ritual when working with trauma, pointing out, for example, that some rituals and practices strengthen clients' ability to alter their focus of attention by drawing them away from ruminating on their difficulties, and encouraging more openness to their experience. For instance, 'Music and dance may directly convey the notion of the self as flexible, adaptable, vital, and vigorous through body movement, sung images, and the shifting inherent in various musical modes such as rhythms and scales.'

For Angela the most powerful ritual was the daily sung Eucharist, as well as repetition of the Jesus Prayer, reciting the rosary and singing. But these practices were not always embodied. During therapy Angela began to befriend her body, and notice more the experiences of her spiritual practices, particularly helped by embodied writing and embodied imagery (see Appendix). So coming into embodied relationship with herself not only led to a widening of identity, but also to a deepening of her spiritual practices.

Down-activating the amygdala through brain integration

Scaer (2014 [2007]: 180) also notes that, theoretically, integration of the right and left hemispheres also 'inhibits independent functioning of the right amygdala', suggesting that this may be 'achieved through alternating visual, tactile, and auditory stimulation, and might down-regulate the right amygdala while the client images the traumatic event, removing the arousal charge'. Frequently during therapy Angela was invited to 'notice, acknowledge and witness' her felt-sense experience in the spirit of curiosity while also being aware of what was becoming present at the edges of her awareness. Therapies like EMDR and Brainspotting (BSP) may also help to achieve this through the use of bi-lateral sound which pendulates slowly and regularly from side to side, between hemispheres, when recalling a traumatic memory. Another form of pendulation is to imagine the 'wide-sweeping beam of a lighthouse' (a metaphor for 'bringing attention to something') centred on the brain's surface at the top of the head, scanning from left to right, then back again. At the same time clients are mindfully aware of bodily felt-sense activation but try not to identify with its content by continually stepping back.

It is a now widely acknowledged that mindfulness decreases activity in the amygdala, and thereby increases control over the emotional brain (van der Kolk, 2014: 264; Lazar, 2013). But it is also important to be aware that some clients 'who are subject to intrusive thoughts, flashbacks, rumination, or easily triggered trauma memories are at greater risk of experiencing distress when meditating' (Briere, 2013: 215). This is probably because as we connect more fully to our inner experience, including trauma memories, meditation and mindfulness reduce our ability for avoidance. Furthermore, sometimes during these practices clients are unable to regulate easily felt-sense experiences as they arise. John Briere (2013: 215) also cautions that 'those experiencing psychosis, severe depression, a dissociative disorder, mania, substance addiction, suicidal thoughts, or proneness to relaxation-induced anxiety generally should avoid meditation-based mindfulness' practices. This is largely because meditation renders us more susceptible to the emergence of an indiscriminate range of experiences (including negative ones), by loosening repression. We will return to integration again below.

Down-activating the amygdala through empowerment

Finally, Scaer (2014 [2007]: 180) speculates that 'Empowerment is the ultimate goal of all trauma therapy – it removes the state of helplessness that is essential to the trauma experience.' He argues that this can be achieved 'through accessing the felt sense in somatic experiencing', which enables clients to allow traumatic memories to be embodied before bringing cognitive meaning to these in the present moment. This cultivates the capacity for maintaining dual-awareness of being both in the present moment while also processing felt-sense trauma memories. It is likely that empowerment increases when clients demonstrate their ability to down-activate the amygdala in the presence of a sensitively empathic therapist while also giving voice to and exploring their feelings.

Empowerment also increases through the educative part of therapy (Chapter 6) as the client gains knowledge and understanding of the body's stress responses. Scaer (2014 [2007]: xix) notes that 'Altering the threat of the unknown by informing and educating the patient changes the body's stress response and promotes healing.' This may include educating clients about the 'negativity bias' of the brain/mind, and how trauma in early life may increase sensitivity to stress responses to minor challenges in later life (Rutten et al., 2013: 14), dispelling beliefs that 'there's something wrong with me' and that 'it's my fault', and learning to 'put the brakes on' when activation threatens to overwhelm.

Guiding Angela to bring her attention more fully into the consulting room (e.g., 'describe the room you are in', 'describe what I am wearing'), and bringing awareness to her breathing in the present moment while remaining relatively relaxed (van der Kolk, 2014: 207), were resourceful ways of 'putting the brakes on' when fearful memories of being locked in a dark cupboard under the stairs became difficult. The use of 'somatic breathing techniques' (Gibson, 2008) was particularly effective in reducing her stress, and grounding her in the present moment. Gradually, her sense of empowerment grew as her capacity to self-regulate increased.

Increasing relationality

The therapeutic relationship is the clients' primary resource. In fact, establishing a safe relationship is 'a precondition for beginning to resolve the patient's trauma' (Wallin, 2007: 245). 'Safety and terror are not compatible', and convincing the brain/mind/body that it is safe to relax is important in the process of recovery, especially if the connection to this sense of safety is possible when trauma memories are present (van der Kolk, 2014: 210). In adopting the stance of *dual-awareness* clients increasingly put their trust in feeling safe, while simultaneously processing trauma memories. With Angela, phrases like 'be aware of the then, while gently reminding yourself that everything is alright now', or 'notice the then, while breathing in the now', or 'allow the then to find healing in the safety of the now', or 'that was then, this is now' were frequent reminders of the importance of holding dual-awareness.

The therapeutic relationship, then, both facilitates experiences of safety and enables self-regulation through cultivating mindfulness practice. This includes gauging 'safe' empathic distances with clients (Chapter 7). However, as we have noted in the previous chapter, to come into and deepen the therapeutic relationship also activates transference/countertransference and projective identification processes, as well as fears about being in relationship, and a tendency for dissociation, avoidance and repression of difficult thoughts, feelings and bodily sensations. The therapist must be open to working with these processes, as the healing of trauma must include processing all activations and enactments relating to trauma memories until recollection of these are free of negative bodily felt responses.

However, Levine (2010: 110) notes that 'Traumatised individuals are not made whole through the therapeutic relationship alone.' This is because when clients are 'locked in either the immobilisation [i.e., frozen or collapsed] response or the sympathetic arousal system [i.e., in fight/flight mode], the social engagement function is physiologically compromised'. Clients can struggle to read positive non-verbal communications from the therapist, and can be temporarily impaired from detecting the therapist's positive feeling communications. In this sense being 'locked in' means that the therapist is locked out. When this happens we can resource clients by finding ways to draw them out of their 'locked in' state, by first engaging with them at the point of their experience in-the-moment, and, second, discharging the activation. This creates connection and makes receiving support possible. When Angela found herself 'locked in' it was phrases like 'notice what you are sensing in your body right now', or 'ease yourself back into your senses, then tell me what that's like', or 'that's it, keep returning to your bodily felt-sense' that brought her out.

As well as dual-awareness, David Grand (2013) notes that *dual-attunement* is vital in the recovery from trauma. This means that clients simultaneously experience the therapist's largely non-verbal empathic attunement with their self-attuned processing of a trauma memory. This view is specific to Brain-spotting (BSP) where clients fix their attention on a point in the consulting room (e.g., mid-air) while recalling a trauma memory. Like daydreaming, it is as if gazing at a point on the outside synchronises with a point on the inside of clients (the 'brain spot'), but in profound embodied connection with the trauma memory, not dissociation. The view is that the therapist's gaze may help clients to focus their attention on bodily felt-sense experiences of a trauma memory (even if clients are looking away from the therapist's gaze as the client often feels 'held' by the therapist's benign presence) and promote integration of memories. At the same time, and not specific to BSP, the therapist's relational attunement is attentive to and tracks the verbal and non-verbal communications of clients' experience, including somatic and uncon-scious therapist–client in-the-moment communications. This mindfulness focus can bring about significant changes in the embodied felt-sense brain/ mind/body processing of trauma (Corrigan and Grand, 2013: 760). When Angela spoke about her early life experiences she would often find a 'gaze point' relating to the trauma memories. Greater tolerance of her somatic experiences meant that she was now able to process strong impulses, 'that arose during the trauma but were supressed in order to survive (van der Kolk, 2014: 218)'. Processing at the 'gaze point' brought up feelings of anger, as well as spontaneous movements like 'hitting' and 'pushing' (p. 218), as the innate bodily felt right brain processing of trauma took priority over 'talking about' it, and the ensuing left brain abstraction from the trauma experience that 'talking about' brings. With the simultaneous use of breathing exercises Angela was able to feel stronger and grounded to her bodily felt-sense experiences in-the-moment.

This brief discussion on increasing relationality would not be complete without a consideration of the resourcing impact of touch. As Gill Westland (2011: 25) points out, 'Touch is intrinsic to communication, and without it a relationship is partial.' While this is undoubtedly true, touch is perhaps one of the most difficult areas of therapy, because of its potentially intrusive, seductive and threatening associations, alongside its capacity (in relation to trauma) to facilitate safety, connection and grounding in the present moment; such as, for instance, the complex communications in transference/countertransference phenomena (Warnecke, 2011). Westland offers an overview on the use of touch as support across therapeutic modalities under the following themes in relation to: traumatised clients, emotional and physiological dysregulation, those with childhood developmental deficits and traumas, embodiment of aggression and pleasure, easing of emotional defensiveness, increasing the flow of energy, deepening the experience of being in relationship, and acknowledgement in the person-to-person aspect of the therapeutic relationship. She further suggests that one's own '*experiential* training' is the starting point for the use of touch in therapy, and emphasises that touch must be spoken about throughout therapy (e.g., beginnings, reviews) with frank explanation of its usage. She also highlights the importance that both persons in the therapy must be 'comfortable' with touch, and cautions against the use of social forms of touching (e.g., 'handshakes and hugs around the edges of sessions') unless it is possible to talk about these in the session. Writing about trauma in particular, Aline LaPierrre (Heller and LaPierre, 2012) has integrated touch within the NeuroAffective Relational Model (NARM), for healing developmental and relational trauma, as has Peter Levine (2010) in Sensory Experiencing and Pat Ogden (Ogden, Minton and Pain, 2006) in Sensorimor to Psychotherapy. Meanwhile other trauma therapies avoid the use of touch (e.g., Grand, 2013) believing that the processing of trauma is possible without this physical connection.

Integration of trauma memories

Recalling our consideration of positive neuroplasticity (Chapter 1) and the principles for influencing changes in the brain, we noted the principle that *neurons that fire together, wire together.* Scaer (2014 [2007]: xvii) reminds us that this principle also applies negatively, hence 'negative neuroplasticity', and that changes in the brain/mind bring about negative changes in the body. 'The trauma therefore changes the brain, which therefore changes the body' (p. 113). However, this bilateral influence is reparative by resourcing clients, especially when trauma memories are integrated, by increasing self-awareness, self-reflectiveness and capacity for affect regulation. Key to this integration, is making bodily felt implicit memories more explicit 'within the context of an increasingly secure and affect-regulatory therapeutic relationship', without being re-traumatised by these memories (Wallin, 2007: 254). Integration brings somatic memories more fully into the left-hemisphere and the prefrontal cortical area of the brain, that is, into conscious awareness, and 'confers a growing sense of mastery' (p. 253). Integration is helped by naming and labelling feelings and bodily sensations, and bringing thought to these to give them meaning, while also remaining grounded in the body. David Michael Levin (1985: 61) notes, 'Thinking is not a question of "bracketing" the body (...), but a question of integrating awareness, living well-focused "in the body"'. Mindfulness and contemplative practices are good ways of achieving this (e.g., Pollak, Pedulla and Siegel, 2004; Ray, 2008; Lazar, 2013), though are not without their challenges (Briere, 2013).

Journal writing (Progoff, 1992; Schneider and Stone, 1998; Jacobs, 2010) and writing in sessions (L'Abate, 1991) are other ways of integrating bodily felt-sense experiences. Louis Cozolino (2010 [2002]: 169) notes, journaling 'about your experiences supports top-down modulation of emotion and bodily responses', that is, writing increases prefrontal activation but reduces emotional activation of the amygdala. Somatic Trauma Therapy (Rothschild, 2000, 2003), for instance, offers an innovative example of writing in sessions, by first outlining the trauma under headings (initially without going into the felt-sense experience of these) like the contents list in a book, and giving the whole a title. The final heading will always embody the theme of survival. Then beginning with this last heading, to ground the fact, the headings are processed in any order, over a number of sessions, for as long as it takes.

Integration is also reinforced by communicating an interest in clients' somatic experience, as 'we convey that what the body *feels* actually matters, both in its own right and as a signal about the clients' emotional experience.' Likewise, to inquire about clients' bodily felt sense, to notice the body, and to offer non-verbal communications that we are 'hearing' the body, brings clients more fully into the present moment, and further enables integration of experience (Wallin, 2007: 6). Increased self-awareness, especially emotional awareness, that clients can describe in themselves and others, involves and increases their ability to reflect upon affective experience and is a cornerstone of affect regulation (Lanius et al., 2011: 333). During therapy with Angela phrases like 'try describing this sensation' or 'allow your sensation to voice what's there' or 'tell me how it feels so that I can feel it in my body', were ways of deepening integration.

Meaning-making as integration

Meaning-making has an important place in therapy, but on its own is not enough. As Scaer (2014 [2007]: 2) argues, 'the meaning of the experience may be as important to the traumatised person as what actually physically happens to that person'. This is a crucial point, because in therapy it is not necessarily only the trauma that is the focus of healing, but also the sense or meaning that clients make of this. Trauma focused therapy and trauma trainings sometimes overlook this and often focus exclusively on the deactivation of trauma memories.

Moreover, meaning-making is not only a conscious activity, for 'a dream can bring together affect and image to create *meaning*' (Kalsched, 1996: 62). Dreams often bring to the fore forgotten vestiges of trauma memory which are not always discernible or forthcoming through bodily felt-sense focused psychotherapy. While the 'body keeps the score' (van der Kolk, 2014), dreams can be further communications of the score, and integrate traumatic experience, which is one of dreams' functions (Bosnak, 2007: 41). Kalsched (1996, 2013) offers outstanding contributions in this area, and others too: for example

Robert Bosnak's (2007) embodied dream imagery, and Eugene Gendlin's (1986) focusing dream interpretation. Others (e.g., Domhoff, 1993; Barrett, 2001 [1996]; Cushway and Sewell, 2012) suggest ways of working through trauma by paying attention to felt-images arising from the unconscious (imaginal, feeling, Chapter 4).

One of Angela's recurring nightmares was sensing that there was a malevolent 'something' hiding under the bed in her cell, and finding that she was unable to move to escape this. Through embodied dreamwork and focusing on a 'gaze point' relating to the most energetically potent part of this dream, upsetting memories of abandonment came to the surface. Pacing the process, we were able to work with and through the felt-sense images and put the activation of these memories to rest, while continuing to reflect on their meaning during the months that followed.

Widening of identity

Where there is trauma, identity often becomes defined by it. While life may be expansive in some ways, in other ways it may feel contracted, especially in relationships. For clients, connecting to themselves and to others, including the therapist, may be difficult, and dissociation, avoidance, repression and being out of connection may become a default way of being. Clients may also struggle to receive empathy, or know what they need or whether their needs are worthy or able of being met. Trust may also be difficult, and they may find intimacy and openness virtually impossible, especially regarding sexuality. They may also struggle with autonomy, particularly in relation to boundary-making, and with authentically expressing themselves without fear or guilt getting in the way or finding themselves hiding behind an image or self-protective role.

In the healing of trauma, the dimensions serve a restorative purpose of establishing safety and enabling the processing and integration of difficult memories, in our embodied felt-sense experience of these in the present moment; a type of embodied mindfulness, perhaps. 'During the present moment, we continue to develop our constantly evolving sense of self, based on incorporation of the somatosensory components of the moment into the library of our autobiographical memory' (Scaer, 2014 [2007]: 91). To put trauma memories to rest allows potentials to emerge. Gradually the dimensions begin to 'awaken' to their bigger purpose as pathways for growth in their own right; openings for the expansion and the widening of identity. By working through trauma and resourcing clients, self-contraction gives way to a more expansive sense of self. For some this may feel like a birthing process, from being once 'locked in' to now beginning to experience themselves more spaciously, while noticing more the 'invitations' from life around them to live more fully; perhaps coming into compassionate relationship with their feelings and their bodies for the first time; and perhaps finding themselves thinking of possibility rather than ruminating on self-doubt and impossibility. As integrity deepens, clients may come to discern more their values, and find ways of embodying these (behavioural, Chapter 4).

The widening of identity engages the imagination. For imagination goes before us to investigate possibilities (imaginal, Chapter 4). Our openness to possibilities also opens us to our depths, for openness simultaneously goes *in* as well as *out*; just as being 'locked in' is also being 'locked out'.

Writing on the therapeutic process, Kalsched (2013: 8) stresses that *'for every self–other relational moment in psychotherapy, there is also an inner event'*. But not 'an inner event in the wiring or sculpting of the brain' but 'an inner event in the sculpting of the soul' as depicted in clients' dreams, in the space between the personality and the ground or depths of being. Within this view Kalsched (2013: 10) refers to 'soul' as a 'vital animating core of our embodied selves'; an experience of an 'essential *something*' connecting us, through love, to everything, including Mystery. As I have described in Chapter 5, opening up to 'soul' in this sense is an opening up to possibilities in the spiritual dimension, with its roots in the Dynamic Ground (Washburn). While the spiritual dimension is sometimes a refuge and resource for clients who suffer from the impact of trauma, lack of grounding can mean their spirituality is not fully embodied and discerning this might be difficult. Essentially, spirituality is a deepening of relationship to oneself, as well as a connecting to the elements of a spiritual path (e.g., meditation, contemplation, prayer, ritual, teaching, religion). Spirituality is also a turning one's attention with love and compassion to the wider community, and to the planet and universe; for *inner* without *outer* is not whole. Spirituality is a participatory activity. To deepen relationship with 'soul' is to reconnect consciously to the resourcing Ground of Being and to Mystery, in unique ways that make embodied felt sense.

In my twenty years' experience as a psychotherapist, and in my role as a counsellor before that, I have found that by adopting a soulcentric view on the therapeutic process, the integration of the spiritual dimension in therapy through exploring dreams, 'the spiritual life', and engaging in 'soul conversations' (e.g., about 'callings', potentials and longings, though not always associated with religious beliefs) has often brought about the greatest transformation of the individual.

Concluding thoughts

To summarise, resourcing the client in trauma, while grounded in the embodied quality of the therapeutic relationship (interpersonal), involves supporting emotional (feeling) and somatic (physical) processing of painful trauma memories, and the overwhelming energy often present in these (energetic), and draws upon imagination (imaginal) and thinking (thinking) to develop resources of safety, process dreams and meaning-making of traumatic experiences, and to put difficult memories to rest. Resourcing also uses rituals to relax the avoid-threat system in the brain/mind/body (behavioural), and is often supported by mindfulness and contemplative practices and the power of the Ground to create stability, and open up possibilities for new growth (spiritual).

There is no single method for healing trauma, and Bessel van der Kolk (2014: 212) wisely cautions that therapists who argue otherwise are 'suspect of being an ideologue'. Sometimes 'single method beliefs' prop up therapists' own vulnerability as practitioners by creating an illusion of being expert or superior. Also by asserting an expert role some therapists may even return some clients to a state of helplessness. At the very least, as therapists working with trauma, we must be able to resource clients to down-regulate the amygdala, enable them to 'lay traumatic memories and re-enactments to rest', and assist them to reconnect or deepen connections with others (p. 212) which includes the therapist. From surveying the field, resourcing for trauma is achieved by integrating top-down methods (to enable social engagement) with bottom-up methods (to relax the body), as well as left–right hemisphere connecting (to enable full integration of trauma memories), within the core resourcing relational framework put forward in this text, with particular emphasis on dual-attunement and dual-awareness.

References

Barrett, D. (2001 [1996]) *Trauma and Dreams*, Cambridge, MA: Harvard University Press.

Beebe, J. (ed.) (2003) *Terror, Violence and the Impulse to Destroy*, Zurich: Daimon Verlag.

Bernstein, J. (2005) *Living in the Borderland: The Evolution of Consciousness and the Challenge of Healing Trauma*, London: Routledge.

Bosnak, R. (2007) *Embodiment: Creative Imagination in Medicine, Art and Travel*, London: Routledge.

Briere, J. (2013) 'Mindfulness, Insight, and Trauma Therapy', in *Mindfulness and Psychotherapy*, in C. K. Germer, R. D. Siegel and P. R. Fulton (eds), New York: Guilford Press, pp. 208–224.

Briere, J. N. and Scott, C. (2015 [2014]) *Principles of Trauma Therapy: A Guide to Symptoms, Evaluation, and Treatment*, Thousand Oaks, CA: Sage.

Corrigan, F. M. and Grand, D. (2013) 'Brainspotting: Recruiting the Midbrain for Accessing and Healing Sensorimotor Memories of Traumatic Activation', *Medical Hypotheses*, 80(6): 759–766.

Corrigan, F. M. and Hull, A. M. (2015) 'Recognition of the Neurobiological Insults Imposed by Complex Trauma and the Implications for Psychotherapeutic Interventions', *BJPsych Bulletin*, 39(2): 79–86.

Cozolino, L. (2010 [2002]) *The Neuroscience of Psychotherapy: Healing the Social Brain*, New York: W. W. Norton.

Cushway, D. and Sewell, R. (2012) *Therapy with Dreams and Nightmares*, London: Sage.

Domhoff, G. W. (1993) 'The Repetition of Dreams and Dream Elements: A Possible Clue to a Function of Dreams', in *The Functions of Dreaming*, A. Moffitt, M. Kramer and R. Hoffmann (eds) Albany, NY: SUNY, pp. 293–320.

Gendlin, E. T. (1986) *Let Your Body Interpret Your Dreams*, Wilmette, IL: Chiron Publications.

Gibson, R. (2008) *My Body, My Earth: The Practice of Somatic Archaeology*, New York: iUniverse.

Grand, D. (2013) *Brainspotting: The Revolutionary New Therapy for Rapid and Effective Change*, Louisville, CO: Sounds True.

Hanson, R. (2013) *Hardwiring Happiness: The Practical Science of Reshaping Your Brain – and Your Life*, London: Rider.

Heller, L. and LaPierre, A. (2012) *Healing Developmental Trauma: How Early Trauma Affects Self-Regulation, Self-Image, and the Capacity for Relationship*, Berkeley, CA: North Atlantic Books.

Herman, J. L. (1992) *Trauma and Recovery*, New York: Basic Books.

Hinton, D. E. and Kirmayer, L. J. (2013) 'Local Responses to Trauma: Symptom, Affect, and Healing', *Transcultural Psychiatry*, 50(5): 607–621.

Jacobs, B. (2010) 'Writing for Emotion Management: Integrating Brain Functioning and Subjective Experience', *Journal of Poetry Therapy*, 23(1): 23–29.

Kalsched, D. (1996) *The Inner World of Trauma: Archetypal Defenses of the Personal Spirit*, New York: Routledge.

Kalsched, D. (2013) *Trauma and the Soul: A Psycho-Spiritual Approach to Human Development and its Interruption*, New York: Routledge.

Krippner, S. and McIntyre, T. M. (eds) (2003) *Psychological Impact of War Trauma on Civilians: An International Perspective*, West Port, CT: Praeger.

L'Abate, L. (1991) 'The Use of Writing in Psychotherapy', *American Journal of Psychotherapy*, 45(1): 87–98.

Lanius, R. A., Bluhm, R. L. and Frewen, P. A. (2011) 'How Understanding the Neurobiology of Complex Post-Traumatic Stress Disorder Can Inform Clinical Practice: A Social Cognitive and Affective Neuroscience Approach', *Acta Psychiatrica Scandinavica*, 124(5): 1331–1348.

Lazar, S. W. (2013) 'The Neurobiology of Mindfulness', in *Mindfulness and Psychotherapy*, C. K. Germer, R. D. Siegel and P. R. Fulton (eds), New York: Guilford Press, pp. 282–294.

Levers, L. L. (2003) *Trauma Counselling: Theories and Interventions*, New York: Springer.

Levin, D. M. (1985) *The Body's Recollection of Being: Phenomenological Psychology and the Deconstruction of Nihlism*, London: Routledge.

Levine, P. A. (2010) *In an Unbroken Voice: How the Body Releases Trauma and Restores Goodness*, Berkeley, CA: North Atlantic Books.

Ogden, P., Minton, K. and Pain, C. (2006) *Trauma and the Body: A Sensorimotor Approach to Psychotherapy*, London: W. W. Norton.

Progoff, I. (1992) *At the Journal Workshop*, New York: Tarcher/Perigee.

Pollak, S. M., Pedulla, T. and Siegel, R. D. (2004) *Sitting Together: Essential Skills for Mindfulness-Based Psychotherapy*, London: Guilford Press.

Ray, R. (2008) *Touching Enlightenment: Finding Realisation in the Body*, Louisville, CO: Sounds True.

Rothschild, B. (2000) *The Body Remembers: The Psychophysiology of Trauma and Trauma Treatment*, New York: W. W. Norton.

Rothschild, B. (2003) *The Body Remembers Casebook: Unifying Methods and Models in the Treatment of Trauma and PTSD*, New York: W. W. Norton.

Rutten, B., Hammels, C., Geschwind, N., Menne-Iothmann, C., Pishva, E., Schruers, K., Den Hove, D., Kenis, G., Os, J. and Wichers, M. (2013) 'Resilience in Mental Health: Linking Psychological and Neurobiological Perspectives', *Acta Psychiatrica Scandinavica*, 128(1): 3–20.

Scaer, R. (2014 [2007]) *The Body Bears the Burden: Trauma, Dissociation, and Disease*, New York and London: Routledge.

Schneider, M. F. and Stone, M. (1998) 'Processes and Techniques of Journal Writing in Adlerian Therapy', *Journal of Individual Psychology*, 54(4): 511–534.

Schore, A. N. (2012) *The Science of the Art of Psychotherapy*, New York and London: W. W. Norton.

Schwarz, L., Corrigan, F., Hull, A. and Raju, R. (2016) *The Comprehensive Resource Model: Effective Therapeutic Techniques for the Healing of Complex Trauma*, London: Routledge.

Steenkamp, M. M., Litz, B. T., Dickstein, B. D., Salters-Pedneault, K., and Hofmann, S. G. (2013) 'What Is the Typical Response to Sexual Assault? Reply to Bonanno', *Journal of Traumatic Stress*, 26(3): 394–396.

Szabo, C. (2004) 'The Effect of Monotonous Drumming on Subjective Experiences', *Music Therapy Today*, 5(1): 1–9.

Van der Kolk, B. (2014) *The Body Keeps the Score: Mind, Brain and Body in the Transformation of Trauma*, London: Penguin.

Wallin, D. (2007) *Attachment in Psychotherapy*, New York: Guilford Press.

Warnecke, T. (2011) 'Stirring the Depths: Transference, Countertransference and Touch', *Body, Movement and Dance Psychotherapy*, 6(3): 233–243.

Welwood, J. (2000) *Toward a Psychology of Awakening: Buddhism, Psychotherapy, and the Path of Personal and Spiritual transformation*, Boston, MA: Shambahala.

Westland, G. (2011) 'Physical Touch in Psychotherapy: Why Are We Not Touching More?', *Body, Movement and Dance Psychotherapy*, 6(1): 17–29.

Wilkinson, M. (2006) *Coming into Mind. The Mind–Brain Relationship: A Jungian Perspective*, London: Routledge.

Chapter 9

The resource focused therapist

One presumes that most therapists protect themselves from the challenges, pressures and strains of therapeutic practice by accessing resources which enable, restore and replenish their ability to participate effectively in the work. It is also probable that this is with a tacit understanding that self-resourcing is integral to codes governing effective therapy practice and a commitment to these. This chapter continues our theme from Chapter 7, on the therapeutic relationship as a resourcing experience, to highlight now some areas of difficulty for therapists, and how we can maintain our resourcefulness as effective practitioners. We may wonder whether this first depends on our commitment to increase our own self-awareness, for example, by routinely discerning into our bodily felt experience, given that our bodies will absorb everything of a therapeutic process. We may be especially vigilant for signs of empathy or compassion fatigue, especially since this reduces our capacity for concern or the ability to bear the suffering of others. This also has implications when experiencing trauma through the transference of vicarious trauma, and may even lead to burnout. Self-resourcing, then, is not only for clients, but also a continuing learning for the therapist, which straddles personal and professional life and is determined by needs inherent in our unique developmental journeys, with our distinctive traits, tendencies and struggles. As previously, the following will be illustrated with reference to a single case: Pamela.

Further reflections on empathy as the therapist's fundamental resource

The therapist draws upon many sources – theoretical and philosophical concepts and ideas, interventions and techniques – to both inform and facilitate a process which will hopefully and enduringly benefit clients; these are ways of 'being' and 'doing' in therapy. Vital to this process is the importance of the therapeutic relationship itself to effect change and to define in some way the qualities of this. This will mean embracing ideas about appropriate boundaries, and a range of values, attitudes and beliefs about how best to construe clients' difficulties and the way to agreed therapeutic goals. But the most fundamental resource is the capacity for empathy, which is the therapist's main instrument; 'not as a mere background characteristic [of therapy] but as a central variable in its own right' (Bohart and Greenberg, 1997: 5; Elliott et al., 2011). Alongside other factors (e.g., therapist acceptance, genuine care, techniques, client motivation and proactive engagement, giving homework) empathy is a key factor in therapeutic change, and is consistently viewed as the most significant forecaster of 'success' in therapy (Bohart and Greenberg, 1997: 3). Departure for our present discussion continues consideration (in Chapter 7) of empathy as the therapist's 'greatest gift'.

Empathy, then, is a way of being attentively receptive to the clients' experience and of establishing a rapport with them. This enables an open appreciation of their distinctiveness with a view of understanding them. Arthur Bohart and Leslie Greenberg (1997: 420) suggest that this 'kind of understanding may consist of what we typically think of as cognition (i.e., thinking and conception inference). Or it may involve more affective, perceptual, experiential, or tacit kinds of understanding.' More than experiencing the 'same emotion' as clients, empathy as a way of understanding also includes 'tacit, perceptual, and affective ways of contacting and being attuned to another's experience', as well as one's own experiencing in response to clients (p. 420). The importance of clients' perception of feeling understood is an obvious and robustly supported fact (Elliott et al., 2011). In our receptiveness we allow ourselves to be open to the complexity of clients' processes, their lives and those of others that they 'bring' with them into the consulting room, often unconsciously. We bodily and emotionally aim to position ourselves to be available to them, in non-defensive gestures of openness. Thereby we endeavour to be present to the client we commit to, in their commitment to themselves.

Empathy is also a way of engaging in 'sustained empathic enquiry or immersing of oneself in the experience of the other' (Bohart and Greenberg, 1997: 5). In this sense, alongside understanding, empathy also involves accurately attuning and responding to what our clients are experiencing (Elliott et al., 2011). This can elicit guesses or speculations as well as 'sensitive interpretations that help the clients access unconscious experience' (Bohart and Greenberg, 1997: 5). Empathy is the qualitative feeling-into the experience of the client, an immersion into bodily felt-sense 'language', where meanings are felt more than thought, sensate more than cognitive, certainly infinitely more than left brain. Within this, the accuracy of communications is tested by their felt-quality of resonant fit.

Bohart and Greenberg (p. 430) point out further that empathy also 'leads to [verbal and non-verbal] action and interaction in one form or another. This includes empathy as attunement or immersion, empathy as an active attitude, empathy as communication, and empathy as a basis for other therapeutic actions [e.g., the therapeutic use of silence or suggestion of techniques].' For example, therapy often includes a 'resonant grasping at the "edges" or implicit aspects of the [clients'] experience to [enable the emergence] of new meaning' (p. 5). Discerning implicit or peripheral aspects of experience are considered core to empathic responding, and are also communicated through speculations or guesses or interpretations. This includes inviting clients to increase awareness of their experiences in the moment, such as emerging values, feelings and objectives (Elliott et al., 2011). Empathy, then, is also the means by which content arises from the depths, often (if not mostly) led by the imagination, or more accurately felt-imagination. Discernment into the 'implicit' is to tune into that 'something' at the edge of awareness, and by an intuitive-imaginative leap of trust we find that we can 'speak its language' (verbal or non-verbal), possibly only tentatively, and maybe for the first time. This, in my view, is making an opening for the emergence of 'soul'.

Further, empathy is also a way of being together. It is a relational activity through which both people come to know something of the other; 'a fundamental mode of interpersonal knowing' (Bohart and Greenberg, 1997: 434). It is our entry point into relationship, the 'qualitative intuitive-feeler' of who it is we are sitting with. Indeed, McGilchrist (2009: 57) in writing on empathy, informs us that empathy is largely a propensity of the right hemisphere, 'the mediator of empathic identification'. Given that the right hemisphere experiences the whole rather than only the part (as the left hemisphere does), we may say that empathy is also a bridging capacity, envisioning felt-sense connections (often subtle) between and within others. The communication of empathy facilitates a wholing experience, in that it 'wants' for ever deeper experiences of connection, of the bringing together and integration of parts.

Empathy also validates, confirms, affirms (Elliott et al., 2011) and accepts the person for who they are. While not the same as acceptance (in the sense that acceptance is largely an attitude whereas empathy is a process), the experience of empathic understanding and connection can be validating. This is particularly so when empathic responses are not only affirming but also evocatively so. Robert Elliott and colleagues (2011: 47) coined the term 'empathic evocations' to refer to the therapist's attempt to bring clients' 'experience alive [by] using rich, evocative, concrete, connotative language [which] often [has] a probing, tentative quality'. Finding the 'voice' of experience in this way has a feel of going below the surface of ordinary awareness. We may also refer to this tentative probing or enquiring as a form of excavation. Therefore, we may put the process of 'empathic evocations' alongside that of 'empathic excavations', since both are attempts at empathic amplification to increase the experience of being understood at depth. For to evoke something is to bring or 'call' it to the 'surface', from 'darkness' to 'light', from the 'unknown' to the 'known', while remaining on the 'surface', whereas to excavate something is to go 'down' into the 'cave' of the psyche. Of course, with felt-imagination it is possible to do both, often simultaneously. This is validation at depth.

Just as an artist refines their ability by constant practice, the therapist increases their empathic capacity by continuous engagement in the process. Both require perceptive sensitivity, openness to the unknown, and the acceptance of vulnerability. However, to be sufficiently resourced these capacities need rest, resilience, an affirming life situation, sustenance, and a supportive and valuing practice environment. These resourcing conditions can render us susceptible to fatigue and impairment if they are absent or in some way undermined, for therapy is not possible if empathy is lacking or impaired. John Beebe (1992) reminds us that integrity in the therapeutic process and in the therapist's setting require safeguarding for therapy to occur. Regarding the latter, respectful, unobtrusive prioritising and prizing of the work are important environmental factors to take into account for this integrity to flourish. Matthieu Ricard (2013: 322) further points out that 'lack of empathy is caused by an emotional erosion linked to external situations of increased tension, which results in professional fatigue, or burnout'. The following vignette highlights the impact on a therapist of impinging factors contributing to 'empathic fatigue' and 'empathic strain'.

Vignette: Pamela

Body Psychotherapist, Pamela (aged sixty), came to therapy because of a growing sense of futility in her practice. Despite twenty years as a registered psychotherapist she was concerned about incipient feelings of incapacity in her role. This felt most pronounced within the therapy centre where she practised. Her experience here, while mostly positive, felt impinged upon by difficult systemic power dynamics of the organisation. Alongside this, Pamela was concerned about symptoms of 'empathic fatigue and strain' (which were familiar concepts to her), and was interested in her contribution to this sense of 'impairment'. Exploring this first in supervision brought to light the extent of this impairment and its implications on her practice, which then took her to consider this more fully in therapy. Working holistically with Pamela, including with dreams and the deep imagination in the use of imagery, she quickly gained a comprehensive understanding of her struggle, and was able to respond in ways that took the whole of her into account. This also confirmed her suspicion that she had embodied the 'failings' of the organisation, and that this was hindering her practice.

The effectiveness of the therapist, then, relies not only on comprehensive training, proficiency, experience and commitment, but also on unimpaired empathic ability. In the interdependent and mutually influencing therapeutic relationship, whatever positively or negatively affects the therapist is, in some way, also likely to influence the client, and whatever impacts the client may affect the therapist, including influence from outside the therapy. In this respect, we may say that empathy is the conduit through which everything passes. Thus, for instance, besides transference and projective identification processes, if the therapist does not feel supported by their setting, then it is likely that this will interfere with the therapy, even subtly, by the 'unsupported feel' that they may consciously or unconsciously bring into therapy, through distractions, concerns and other ruminations. Ironically, while therapy settings aim to support the work of therapy, some organisations are naïvely unaware of the toxic influence of administrative failings on treatment. Pamela was increasingly unable to protect herself or her clients from the unsupportive attitudes and difficult behaviour of administrators and management. When her frequent expressions of concern were not taken seriously she found that the only way to resolve the situation was to leave. Organisations may listen but not always hear; but Pamela's situation may be rare.

Professional codes of practice are the backbone of ethical therapy (Owens, Springwood and Wilson, 2012), but from time to time it seems that the content of these is thought to be for the therapist alone, not the organisation. As in Pamela's case, therapists can find themselves 'fighting' to uphold professional values and are powerless in the face of administrative indifference and myopic vision about things that matter. The role of administrators and management to either inhibit or generate stress is well documented (e.g., Huebner and Huberty, 1984; Wilkinson, 2006; Hardiman and Simmonds, 2013; Puig et al., 2014). Therapists might well be prudently aware of the signs of tokenistic adherence to professional codes and choose to opt instead for private practice. Despite the potential for professional isolation, this can be overcome through collegiality and peer supervision groups, so that private practice can be the 'safer' option, and may significantly minimise empathic injury.

When resource becomes depletion

In terms of the activity of the therapy itself, everyone responds differently to stress. Symptoms of emotional depletion can include disrupted sleep, withdrawal, lack of energy, feeling frequently run down or ill; basically, a weakening of physical, mental and emotional capacities. One study found that signs of impairment included 'irritability, depression, boredom, withdrawal, loss of energy, aggression toward clients, impulses to act out sexually, feelings of failure, or increased use of substances' (Coster and Schwebel, 1997: 12). Other literature suggests 'moderate depression, mild anxiety, emotional exhaustion, and disrupted relationships as the common residue of immersing ourselves in the inner worlds of distressed and distressing people' (Norcross, 2000: 710). But these symptoms are often offset by dependable availability of supervisory, collegial and environmental supports. Before they arise it is possible that empathy is already impaired, and that the therapist is 'impaired' in other ways, too, with the therapy only 'limping' along. It takes a number of persistent stressors for therapists to succumb to feelings of depletion, and a long time to recover.

Empathy fatigue, compassion fatigue or secondary traumatic stress

Like other forms of therapist impairment, signs of the synonymous terms 'empathy fatigue', 'compassion fatigue' or 'secondary traumatic stress' often arise not only when professional and personal resources are lacking, but when there is also disparity in the therapist's self-care system, especially when the therapist is exposed to excessive trauma. Feelings of helplessness, vulnerability, confusion and resentment towards our clients are typical indicators of fatigue or secondary traumatic stress. As Debora Arnold and colleagues (2005: 242) point out in their study on compassion fatigue, symptoms include:

> reflecting the re-experiencing of the [reported and empathically engaged with] traumatic event (e.g., through recurrent dreams or intrusive thoughts), avoidance/numbing (e.g., efforts to avoid trauma-associated thoughts or activities, diminished affect), and persistent arousal (e.g., difficulty falling or staying asleep, irritability, hypervigilance).

However, while the terms 'secondary traumatic stress' and 'compassion fatigue' are well known amongst therapists, it is more appropriate to talk about empathy fatigue, because it is the capacity to offer empathy that is impaired, not compassion. Compassion cannot be fatigued because, in my experience, true compassion always takes both sides of the therapeutic relationship into account. Compassion towards the other without the balance of self-compassion is sacrifice, not compassion, and may even be pathological. Sacrifice is not therapy but a form of do-goodism, which says more about the therapist than our clients, and sometimes disguises an attitude of sympathy or pity for our clients, which always contains a taste of superiority. Therapists effectively demonstrate true compassion by establishing consistent boundaries, including a commitment to the ethic of self-care (Owens, Springwood and Wilson, 2012). As Ricard (2013: 57–58) reminds us:

> far from leading to distress and discouragement, [compassion] reinforces our strength of mind, our inner balance, and our courageous, loving determination to help those who suffer. In essence (...) love and compassion do not get exhausted and do not make us weary or worn out, but on the contrary help us to surmount fatigue and rectify it when it occurs.

Compassion invigorates rather than depletes. Paul Gilbert (2010: 133) suggests in his Compassion Focused Therapy (CFT) that compassion combines many attributes including 'wisdom, strength, warmth/kindness and non-judgmental/ condemning'. Looking at these in turn, wisdom embraces our felt motivation for truth seeking, an ability to reflect on life's meaning, 'wise reasoning' to see things from different perspectives without judging or attributing fault, as well as emotions grounded in compassion and concern for others. Wisdom is also intuitive, in the sense of often knowing what is right or pressing (p. 134). Compassion is also an authoritative and fearless strength; while warmth includes qualities like 'tenderness, gentleness, kindness, concern, and playfulness' (p. 53), and 'non-judgemental/condemning' attitudes are inherently valuing (p. 135). Compassion is therefore also a resource. We may be able to embody some aspects, but not others, for instance: being kind while lacking in strength, or wise but lacking kindness, or kind to others but not to oneself. Indeed, while we may draw attention to compassionate strengths a client already has, and increase these, the therapist may not always embody these attributes for themselves. Without the resourcefulness that compassion brings we are more susceptible to empathy fatigue.

Experiencing trauma through transference

If empathy is like a conduit for what our clients bring to therapy, then the therapist's embodied felt sense of this is the container. As empathy is a core factor in therapeutically connecting with our clients, it is also the means by which trauma enters the body and consciousness of the therapist. Likewise, compassion is the proactive concern which arises out of empathy. Both are 'opening' processes. The therapist is therefore vulnerable to receiving and experiencing everything in the process of therapy; their own evoked processes and that of clients, as well as the qualitative 'energy' of the therapy setting or environment itself. While this is the case with both positive and negative experience it is particularly the case in the absorption of trauma through transference, perhaps because trauma is more difficult to manage given that it is often a more complex therapeutic process than other presenting difficulties.

It helps to notice how the telling and reporting of traumatic events is experienced in the therapeutic dyad, because transference 'is generally regarded as particularly powerful, complex, and problematic' (Arnold et al., 2005). Hence the astute therapist will monitor its impact and take steps to protect themselves accordingly, for example, by being vigilant to transference processes and responding rather than reacting, noticing in particular when this might activate their own trauma memories, sustaining attention in the present moment, and maintaining firm boundaries with compassion. Arnold and colleagues (2005: 241–242) point out that impairment or strain on empathy through transference responses to reports of trauma can be understood in at least two ways: (a) 'reactions involving withdrawal or repression of empathy (e.g., denial, detachment, avoidance, or minimisation of trauma material) and (b) reactions involving empathic enmeshment (e.g., over identification with or over idealisation of the client)'. That is, empathic retraction or empathic entanglement may give rise to 'feelings of self-doubt, anxiety, and insecurity about one's ability to be helpful to trauma survivors'.

Pamela found persistent feelings of self-doubt particularly difficult, as these were relatively unfamiliar to her self-view. However, as a Body Psychotherapist, she was also able to skilfully bracket her own process and work with and through the negative transference when these feelings took root in her body. But in her 'openness' the absorption of an often toxic therapy setting was more difficult to process.

Vicarious trauma

Absorption of our clients' trauma can often lead to vicarious trauma. Pearlman and Saakvitne (1995: 281) inform us that vicarious trauma results in a 'transformation in the inner experience of the therapist that comes about as a result of empathic engagement with clients' trauma material'. They argue that 'We carry our experience of vicarious traumatization far beyond our therapy space. Because it changes the self of the therapist, it will inevitably affect all of our relationships – therapeutic, collegial, and personal.' While transformation of the therapist is an inevitable part of the process of therapy, vicarious trauma does this negatively, and in ways that are distinct from empathy fatigue and trauma transference. Hence, vicarious trauma is defined as 'a negative transformation in the self' (Pearlman, 2012: 784) through empathic connection with traumatised clients and their reports of traumatic experiences.

Pearlman's (p. 784) review of the literature summarises signs and symptoms of vicarious trauma which include:

> social withdrawal, emotional dysregulation, aggression, greater sensitivity to violence, somatic symptoms, sleep difficulties, intrusive imagery, cynicism, anxiety, depression, substance overuse, sexual difficulties, difficulty managing boundaries with clients, and disruption of core beliefs and resulting difficulty in relationships reflecting problems with security, trust, esteem, intimacy, and control.

From this account you will be aware of the escalating intensity of symptoms of this condition compared with empathy fatigue and transference trauma, and the impact of this on professional and personal life. Babette Rothschild and Marjorie Rand (2006) have written extensively on the psychophysiology of both so-called compassion fatigue and vicarious trauma, and offer holistic ways to manage symptoms which support the brain/mind/body systems (see section on self-care below).

Therapist burnout

Ignoring signs of distress can lead to burnout; the brain/mind/body system's way of saying 'stop'. Alongside vicarious trauma and empathy fatigue, burnout is reassuringly one of the three least common conditions which impair therapists (Hardiman and Simmonds, 2013). Generally described as 'the deterioration and emotional depletion as a response to a range of work-related demands' (p. 1044), burnout includes most of the symptoms already considered. But more specifically, some research describes three distinct features of burnout as (a) emotional exhaustion (increased stress, tightness in body, frequent tiredness), (b) depersonalisation (e.g., withdrawing or leaving professional role, or lacking in empathy – withdrawing from clients – giving up on the process, losing faith in this), and (c) lack of personal accomplishment (e.g., feeling incompetent and unable to influence improvements for our clients, feeling frustrated with this and generally not feeling skilled enough). Job demands and related stress and over-involvement are frequently associated with emotional exhaustion (Pines and Aronson, 1988: 9; Lee et al., 2011).

Factors which help reduce emotional exhaustion include ongoing professional and personal support (e.g., supervision, colleagues, therapy, family, friends or restorative time alone), so that accomplishment and satisfaction in one's role is not lost (Lee et al., 2011). Regarding depersonalisation, while burnout reduces job satisfaction and increases thoughts of leaving one's job, or even the profession, commitment to one's practice makes this less likely to happen. It appears then that burnout is managed by committing to ongoing support, which eases emotional exhaustion and restores feelings of accomplishment. In any case, thoughts of leaving one's job or the profession come and go and are sometimes part of being a therapist. But as many health professionals may advise, it is wise to take note of symptoms if they persist, and increase ongoing support, rather than provide clients' care at the expense of ourselves (Rzeszutek and Schier, 2014). For care and compassion are not complete if they do not include oneself.

Interestingly, belief, perception and expectation may also influence burnout. For instance, one study found that *belief* in strong support on its own was more of a protective factor than received support. Paradoxically, there is also some suggestion of a positive association between over-involvement and personal accomplishment (Rzeszutek and Schier, 2014). In other words, these authors propose that this seemingly contradictory connection points to the possibility that therapists prize themselves in supporting clients as best they can, and that this is personally and professionally satisfying, although at the same time stressful. In this way the experience of burnout is offset by the experience of accomplishment. Another study suggested that practitioners' 'perceptions (...) may be the important factor in predicting burnout' (Hardiman and Simmonds, 2013: 1051), especially if there is a self-expectation of burnout. It is also likely that this is activation of the therapist's own 'negativity bias'.

Following on from this, there are at least two general antecedent categories of burnout. First, personal factors which contribute include 'demographics, personality characteristics, or coping styles' (p. 1045), and often age (p. 1051), and possibly gender (Maslach and Jackson, 1981: 985). While there are no obvious reasons to account for this, views point to the inexperience of the therapist (Maslach, 2001) and the idea of 'survival bias' when therapists exhibiting burnout survive those who succumb and leave their careers (Hardiman and Simmonds, 2013: 1051). Caseload may also be another factor (Maslach and Jackson, 1981). However, gender and caseload factors are not fully supported as contributing to burnout (e.g., Hardiman and Simmonds, 2013). Second, as I have described earlier, the practice environment itself is another contributor.

Fortunately, resilience is nature's most powerful resource or strength to enable recovery from difficulty. Even when working with trauma the brain/ mind/body systems seek ways to protect our resilience, for instance, through finding the positive in the negative. It may not be surprising, then, that there are possible benefits from working with trauma.

Therapist growth through working with trauma

We mostly associate empathy fatigue with negative experiences, yet some studies suggest benefits. Arnold and colleagues (2005: 243), for example, investigated the positive effects or 'vicarious post-traumatic growth' (VPG) of working with trauma. These benefits include 'changes in self-perception, interpersonal relationships and philosophy of life'. For instance, witnessing clients' capacity to find strength to survive difficulties can inspire self-confidence for further growth and development in the therapist themselves. This study also found that working with trauma 'led to enduring, trait-oriented changes' in the therapist, for example, by 'increase[ing] levels of sensitivity, compassion, insight, tolerance, and empathy' (p. 250). It further discovered a significant positive influence on therapists' spirituality in that it was broadened by greater acceptance of differences between people, in witnessing how people survive trauma, and the way spiritual commitment provides resourcefulness and support (p. 251). This points to the value of therapists nurturing the spiritual dimension.

Arnold and colleagues also found that many therapists, as a result of their encounter with victims of trauma, felt fortunate in having avoided traumatic events, were optimistic about the future, and also appreciated the strength and resilience of trauma survivors themselves. Working with trauma also brought a sense of vulnerability which gave many therapists a profound appreciation of life and a determination to live as fully as possible.

The cycle of self-care

Having identified the way strain, fatigue and impairment are triggered and exhibited, I now turn to suggest further ways therapists might resource themselves. Self-care is about self-resourcing through maintaining and increasing existing resources, and discerningly drawing upon others as necessary. It means paying attention to, and supporting oneself without criticism or judgement in the spirit of self-compassion. Self-care is not to be confused with increasing selfishness, self-preoccupation or rumination. Indeed, Ellen Baker (2003: 17) points out, 'Self-preoccupation is, in fact, more likely to occur as a result of inadequate self-care over time.' The theme for this section will be approached under four headings: increasing self-awareness, increasing self-regulation, embodying self-care and restoring equilibrium. The first step in self-care is coming into compassionate relationship with oneself as deserving of care and being vigilant for signs of empathy fatigue, vicarious trauma and burnout, and responding accordingly in ways described in this chapter. This recognition arises through increasing self-awareness.

Increasing self-awareness

Although not an easy and often a painful process, increasing self-awareness is compassionate self-reflection across the dimensions, and wherever possible without avoidance or distortion. It gives priority to oneself to increase wakefulness, layer by layer, insight by insight; to wake up to the fullness of one's person; to become familiar with the nuances and subtleties of one's existence, and the communications from all parts of oneself, past and present; to cultivate deep listening to the needs and wants of one's own 'voice' as expressed through the dimensions. As Baker (2003: 14) suggests:

> Only if we are aware of our needs and limitations can we consciously weigh our options in tending to those concerns, whether external or internal and whether related to personality, life stage, or circumstance. We can then consider our self-observations in tandem with information we gather from external sources, such as feedback from others received directly or indirectly.
>
> If we are not adequately self-aware, we risk acting out repressed – and thereby unprocessed and unmanaged – emotions and needs in ways that are indirect, irresponsible, and potentially harmful and costly to our self, personally and professionally, and to our patients, family and others. Unless we are aware of our self needs and self dynamics, we may unconsciously and unintentionally neglect our patients or exploit them to meet our own needs for intimacy, esteem or dominance.

Increasing self-awareness then, is a cornerstone to self-care, and is the process enabling other processes. Alongside therapy and mindfulness or contemplative practices, one of the ways to increase self-awareness is through the discipline of keeping a reflective journal. Ira Progroff's (1992) Jungian inspired method for journalling is perhaps the most comprehensive journal writing method available, engaging the writer to reflect fully on areas across the dimensions. Eugene Gendlin (1969, 1981 [1969]) offers another awareness-increasing practice in his 'focusing' process (Chapter 4) as a way to come into attentive relationship with one's felt-sense awareness in the present moment. Paying attention to dreams or engaging actively with the deep imagination is yet another way to increase self-awareness and to practise self-care, as it encourages us to look beneath the surface to what might need attention (Chapter 2). Practices are wide-ranging, and also include Integral Transformation Programmes (ITP) (Chapter 1), and so on. However, to increase self-awareness in itself is not enough. The other side of the coin is its application, use and practice.

Pamela took steps to increase her self-awareness and act on arising insights through making life decisions by more fully discerning her values and life aspirations, and trusting herself to align with these more. Paying attention to her dreams and the insights gathered from keeping a regular journal were ways she found particularly helpful in judiciously deepening into self-awareness.

Increasing self-regulation

Self-regulation increases the capacity to manage one's inner life, and is intrinsically linked to a growing self-awareness. Self-awareness increases when there is less activation and less distress. It is as if self-awareness can become blocked by the energy in distress, and so it becomes difficult to navigate beyond this. Thus the more proficient we become at self-regulating, the more 'openings' there are for self-awareness to be amplified. Self-regulation is also fundamental in the process of self-care as it enables the management of difficult feelings, impulses, urges, and so on, and is the key ability in cultivating affirmative feelings (e.g., optimism, self-kindness, patience, acceptance).

I find it useful to cultivate a 'map' of attitudes and feeling states to orientate myself towards self-awareness like a guiding rudder of a boat, or 'preferred ground' for one's identity, for example: the capacity to self-soothe (although sometimes difficult to achieve if not first learnt in infancy); or qualities of peace, satisfaction and contentment; or the cultivation of the practice of self-compassion (e.g., Germer, 2009; Neff, 2011); or those qualities inherent in contemplative or mindfulness practices which use breath as an object of stability. Alternatively, Rick Hanson (2013) encourages development of positive experiences in his Positive Neuroplasticity Training (PNT), and includes nurturing the experience of 'everything is alright now'. Then again, Marie-Louise von Franz (1980: 264–265) in writing on the symbolism and psychology in alchemy, outlines fourteen qualities considered to be necessary for personal transformation:

> The qualities are not only ethical but include all sorts of suppositions as to what a human being should have: health, humility, holiness (from the description that apparently means 'wholeness' or purity), chastity, virtue (effectiveness or efficiency), victoriousness (to be able to overcome, faith which has the capacity to trust, or to understand spiritual qualities which

cannot be seen), faith, hope (...), charity, compassion, goodness (a kind of benevolence), patience (which is very important), temperateness (a balance between the opposites), discipline or insight, and obedience.

Regardless of the pathways enhancing it, self-regulation is fundamental in self-care, and is particularly so when working with trauma. Developer of Somatic Trauma Therapy, Rothschild (2006), encourages therapists to find ways to control empathic visual images or felt-sense images arising through working with trauma, for example to imagine shrinking these images, or to convert them to monotone, or to cinematically zoom-out or zoom-in to anything neutral or positive in the images. To develop an ability to manipulate images in these ways is in itself resourcing. Another way of drawing upon the imaginal and energetic dimensions to protect the empathically attuned feeling dimension is to visualise empathy as a rose. When the rose opens it faces out towards our clients, when closed it turns to face inward towards ourselves. Or to imagine a duck-egg blue protective field of energy around oneself, or to put our hand gently over our solar plexus. Empathy can be imaginatively regulated in these and other ways. In addition, these symbolic gestures are not only effective in themselves, they are powerful self-communications of care.

Embodying self-care

Combining these largely internal practices with their external embodiment roots them more fully in identity. One study found that keeping a journal for recording experiences of gratitude gave rise to an increase in 'the positive states of alertness, enthusiasm, determination' and a general sense of well-being (Emmons and Stern, 2013). Other ways include developing a formal meditation practice, or engaging in any relaxing activity, such as going for a gentle walk while occasionally imagining breathing in the benefits that this brings, and so on. Other possibilities in the behavioural dimension include opening a window after a session to admit fresh air, or lighting some oils. In the interpersonal dimension, during particularly empathically challenging times, it is sometimes helpful to avoid empathic mirroring of body language temporarily (if one is consciously aware of the felt challenge). At the same time, we can remain attuned to our clients, and remind ourselves of their innate resilience, and in appreciating this, find appropriate opportunities to remind them of this. Likewise, in the thinking dimension, it is always important to remind oneself that the person has endured everything that has happened to them up to this present time, as we also listen carefully to their struggle.

Finally, the influencing factor of the spiritual dimension can often be ignored as resourcing and establishing support. However, cultivating spiritual support is highlighted in the literature as important in fostering a sense of protectiveness against burnout and vicarious trauma, thus enabling self-care (Hardiman and Simmonds, 2013). This is because spirituality is perceived to act as a 'moderator between trauma and life-stress' (p. 1052); a protective holding presence. From this perspective the therapist may imagine a greater power, presence or Mystery supporting both persons in the therapy, and participating in the therapeutic process. From a participatory perspective, spirituality is embedded in the here-and-now reality, rather than distant from it. Surrendering to this Mystery can feel supportive and is partly what is meant by the term 'trusting the therapeutic process'. Be that as it may, cultivating the spiritual dimension facilitates robust positive inner experiences (Rutten et al., 2013: 14).

Restoring equilibrium

The key aim of self-care is to achieve a sense of balance across the dimensions, so that thinking alone does not dominate as it is so often prone to do. Remembering that the dimensions deserve resourcing in their own right, it behoves us to listen to their respective 'voices' in order to establish a sense of equilibrium. 'Balance is essential in enabling us to tend to our core needs and concerns, including those of the body, mind and spirit; of the self in relation to others, and our personal and professional lives' (Baker, 2003, 16). Sometimes, too, it is useful to increase balance through diversity in one's practice, as this further reduces empathic strain (Norcross, 2000), so that offering therapy sits alongside activities of offering supervision, teaching, writing, and so on, providing, of course, self-care is present in these activities.

The metaphorical 'core', or 'centre' of one's experience is the embodied felt-sense experience of balance, and is integral to equilibrium. This point, or centre, is where gravity is not tilting one way or the other. Gravity is the centre; the centre is gravity. Weight is grounded in the middle where everything comes to a position of rest, peace, contentment and satisfaction; the wellspring of resourcefulness where something of our core strengths are able to arise. The aim in restoring equilibrium is to come consistently to this point, and is only possible by first increasing self-awareness.

If we view self-care as following a cycle we can say that increasing self-awareness is a process running throughout this cycle; noticing, acknowledging, witnessing whatever arises without judgement. Simultaneously, self-regulation manages the content of what arises, especially where activation occurs, in re-establishing rest or peace. Therefore, self-regulation is like bringing attention to something, to relax it, while also breathing (being self-aware). Embodying self-care is the practical application of insights gained through an ongoing 'conversation' between self-awareness and self-regulation. This more fully engages the dimensions. Then, restoring equilibrium is an opportunity to make adjustments, to listen more deeply to the whole, and to respond to whatever feels pressing, be it the 'voice' of feeling, the 'voice' of body or the 'voice' of energy, and so on.

The difficult ethic of commitment

As I have stated earlier the commitment of the therapist is first to themselves, then to their clients. Loyalty to oneself must always precede the allegiance to another because the care of the one is necessary for the resourceful and effective care of the other. But commitment is a difficult ethic, often because most therapists are accomplished in putting other people first, and sometimes find that, as a consequence, self-neglect subtly works its way into their self-care system, and is felt as fatigue (though this might also be a symptom of body-countertransference). Therapists may wonder in what ways they go beyond the boundary of generosity (e.g., in relation to time, availability, fee, or difficulty in saying 'no' to requests for therapy), or where felt-compromises are in their practice (e.g., comfort of space, working long hours, taking few holidays). Lack of self-care also creeps into the therapy itself, and sometimes manifests itself (often unconsciously, at times naïvely) by feeling resentment towards clients, by being too greedy in charging higher than average fees relative to their experience (greed displaces integrity in the therapy), by backing out of a therapeutic commitment, or by breaking relationship boundaries with clients through succumbing to 'be my friend' and 'be my lover' transferences, and so on. More than training or experience, this ethic of commitment is grounded in and arises from a comprehensive self-care system. This is why therapy is the first cornerstone of most trainings in psychotherapy (though not necessarily so for counselling), as it paves the way for greater self-care and self-knowledge. In some ways the more resourced the therapist is, the more resourced our clients will become, as something of this will be present undoubtedly within the therapy.

Fortunately, Pamela was resourced enough to avoid burnout, but might well have succumbed to this if she had not left the therapy setting. Her self-care 'radar', which brought her to therapy also guided her to self-resource, and it was by trusting her intrinsic wisdom that she came to prioritise herself more fully.

Concluding thoughts

Alongside the qualities of empathy, warmth, respect, humility, patience, integrity, and many others, the stance of the therapist is grounded in compassion and altruistic love. 'Compassion and altruistic love have a warm, loving, and positive aspect that "stand alone empathy" for the suffering of the other does not have' (Ricard, 2013: 60). If compassion embodies qualities of loving-kindness, peace and stillness, then it reinforces empathy and the ability to be with the suffering of another in a bounded way. Love and compassion take care of the whole, rather than only the other. Ricard (p. 64) writes, 'Empathy is indeed needed to trigger the arising of compassion, but the space of that compassion should be vast enough so that empathy does not turn into uncontainable distress.' Ricard suggests further, that therapists, and others in the helping professions, might benefit from specific training in altruistic love and compassion. Among other things it 'creates in us a positive space' to counter empathic strain, and 'prevents affective resonance from proliferating' to the point of exhaustion. 'Without the support of love and compassion', he argues, 'empathy left to itself is like an electric pump through which no water circulates: it will quickly overheat and burn' (p. 64). Empathy is resourced by the spaciousness of altruistic love, as well as the compassionate supportiveness of our personal life context, which includes people, nature, solitude and enriching experiences of all kinds, especially experiences which evoke feelings of beauty, joy and restorative rest. I suggest that more than empathy it is the immeasurable qualities of altruistic love and compassion which heal, both the client and the therapist, alongside those of joy and equanimity. Empathy arises from these qualities and brings with it many other qualities like humility, patience, optimism and respect.

The resource focused therapist then, draws upon a range of supports to ensure efficacy in their role. When these arise from across the dimensions there is a sense of steadiness in our practice which underpins our work. Depletion of empathy is a sign that there may be something in the therapeutic process that needs to be understood and worked through, or that the therapist needs to turn attention more to self-care, to strengthen their stance, and to find a way of balancing commitment to themselves and to the work.

If, then, we were to view suffering as, in some way, the experience of the absence of integration, then the wide embrace of compassion wants for everything to be whole. Certainly, there is a strong tendency and receptivity within us towards integration and wholeness (Kalsched, 2013: 166), and therefore facilitating and resourcing this process is one of the cornerstones of therapy. Something of the depths rises up to meet these edges of growth and support the further wholing of our lives when attention is brought to the wide range of available resourcing possibilities and pathways. It is then that we discerningly put our hope and trust in this transformative process. Resources are stepping-stones to wholeness.

References

Arnold, D., Calhoun, L. G., Tedeschi, R. and Cann, A. (2005) 'Vicarious Post-traumatic Growth in Psychotherapy', *Journal of Humanistic Psychology*, 45(2): 239–263.
Baker, E. K. (2003) *Caring for Ourselves: A Therapist's Guide to Personal and Professional Well-Being*, Washington, DC: APA.
Beebe, J. (1992) *Integrity in Depth*, College Station: Texas A&M University Press.
Bohart, A. C. and Greenberg, L. S. (1997) *Empathy Reconsidered: New Directions in Psychotherapy*, Washington, DC: APA.
Coster, J. S., and Schwebel, M. (1997) 'Well-Functioning in Professional Psychologists', *Professional Psychology: Research and Practice*, 28(1): 5–13.

Elliott, R., Bohart, A. C., Watson, J. C. and Greenberg, L. S. (2011) 'Empathy', *Psychotherapy*, 48(1): 43–49.

Emmons, R. A. and Stern, R. (2013) 'Gratitude as a Psychotherapeutic Intervention', *Journal of Clinical Psychology: In Session*, 69(8): 846–855.

Gendlin, E. T. (1969) 'Focusing', *Psychotherapy: Theory, Research and Practice*, 6(1): 4–15.

Gendlin, E. T. (1981 [1969]) *Focusing*, New York: Bantam Books.

Germer, C. (2009) *The Mindful Path to Self-Compassion: Freeing Yourself from Destructive Thoughts and Feelings*, London: Guilford Press.

Gilbert, P. (2010) *Compassion Focused Therapy*, London: Routledge.

Hanson, R. (2013) *Hardwiring Happiness: The Practical Science of Reshaping Your Brain – and Your Life*, London: Rider.

Hardiman, P. and Simmonds, J. G. (2013) 'Spiritual Well-Being, Burnout and Trauma in Counsellors and Psychotherapists', *Mental Health, Religion & Culture*, 16(10): 1044–1055.

Huebner, E. S. and Huberty, T. J. (1984) 'Burnout Among Rural School Psychologists', *Research in Rural Education*, 2(3), 95–99.

Kalsched, D. (2013) *Trauma and the Soul: A Psycho-Spiritual Approach to Human Development and its Interruption*, New York: Routledge.

Lee, J., Lim, N., Yang, E. and Lee, S. M. (2011) 'Antecedents and Consequences of Three Dimensions of Burnout in Psychotherapists: A Meta-Analysis', *Professional Psychology: Research and Practice*, 42(3): 252–258.

Maslach, C. (2001) 'What Have We Learned About Burnout and Health?', *Psychology & Health*, 16(5): 607–611.

Maslach, C. and Jackson, S. E. (1981) 'The Measurement of Experienced Burnout', *The Journal of Occupational Behaviour*, 2(2): 99–113.

McGilchrist, I. (2009) *The Master and His Emissary: The Divided Brain and the Making of the Western World*, New Haven and London: Yale University Press. Permission kindly granted by Yale University Press.

Neff, K. D. (2011) *Self-Compassion: Stop Beating Yourself Up and Leave Insecurity Behind*, New York: William Morrow.

Norcross, J. C. (2000) 'Psychotherapist Self-Care: Practitioner-Tested, Research-Informed Strategies', *Professional Psychology: Research and Practice*, 31(6): 710–713.

Owens, P., Springwood, B. and Wilson, M. (2012) *Creative Ethical Practice in Counselling and Psychotherapy*, London: Sage.

Pearlman, L. A. (2012) 'Vicarious Trauma', in *Encyclopaedia of Trauma: An Interdisciplinary Guide*, C. R. Figley (ed.), Thousand Oaks, CA: Sage, pp. 784–786.

Pearlman, L. A. and Saakvitne, K. W. (1995) *Trauma and the Therapist: Counter-Transference and Vicarious Traumatisation in Psychotherapy with Incest Survivors*, New York: W. W. Norton.

Pines, A. and Aronson, E. (1988) *Career Burnout: Causes and Cures*, New York: The Free Press.

Progroff, I. (1992) *At the Journal Workshop*, New York: Tarcher/Perigee.

Puig, A.Yoon, E. and Callueng, C. (2014) 'Burnout Syndrome in Psychotherapists: A Comparative Analysis of Five Nations', *Psychological Services*, 11(1): 87–96.

Ricard, M. (2013) *Altruism: The Power of Compassion to Change Yourself and the World*, (trans. Charlotte Mandell and Sam Gordon), London: Atlantic Books.

Rothschild, B. (2006) 'Controlling Empathic Imagery', *Self & Society*, 33(6): 15–21.

Rothschild, B. and Rand, M. (2006) *Help for the Helper: The Psychophysiology of Compassion Fatigue and Vicarious Trauma*, New York: W. W. Norton.

Rutten, B., Hammels, M., Geschwind, N., Menne-Lothmann, C., Pishva, E., Schruers, K., van den Hove, D. C., Kenis, G., van Os, J. and Wichers, M. (2013) 'Resilience in Mental Health: Linking Psychological and Neurobiological Perspectives', *Acta Psychiatrica Scandinavica*, 128(1): 3–20.

Rzeszutek, M. and Schier, K. (2014) 'Temperament Traits, Social Support, and Burnout Symptoms in a Sample of Therapists', *Psychotherapy*, 51(4): 574–579.

von Franz, M-L. (1980) *Alchemy: An Introduction to the Symbolism and the Psychology*, Toronto: Inner City Books.

Wilkinson, M. (2006) *Coming into Mind. The Mind–Brain Relationship: A Jungian Perspective*, London: Routledge.

Appendix

Embodied writing

Embodied writing is a way of writing from your felt-sense experience; from a sense of participatory embeddedness in life. It gives priority to right brain engagement and processing of experiences rather than cognitive, left brain processes.

Rosemary Anderson (Anderson and Braud, 2011: 268), one of the developers of this approach, argues that this way of writing gives opportunity to evoke the writer's distinctive voice, qualities and particularity: 'In the act of writing, slowing down and looking for resonance within one's own body seems to reveal the tangibly unique – and sometimes ineffable – qualities of the writer's experience and way of being in the world' (cf. Anderson, 2001, 2002a, 2002b). Further, 'As a style of writing, embodied writing is itself an act of embodiment' (Anderson, 2001: 83), a coming into one's senses, and deepening into the unique 'voices' of the dimensions.

Seven distinctive features of embodied writing

Of these distinctive features Anderson and Braud (2011: 269) point out that the writer 'might employ or emphasise some or most of these to render an account, but not necessarily all of them all the time':

1   *True-to-life, vivid depictions intended to invite sympathetic resonance in the readers or audience.* Try to make the telling of the experience(s) as full as possible, so that you become fully present in the writing, therefore inviting the reader to empathise with your experience, as well as possibly igniting a felt-sense response in the reader in relation to their own lives.
2   *Inclusive of internal and external data as essential to relaying the experience.* Include a balance of what is in your imagination, in your sensate experience (the inner), as well as what is observable, sometimes by others (the outer), for example, actions, behaviour.

3   *Written specifically from the inside out.* Allow your body to communicate through your words, allowing your 'voice' to rise up from deep within you.
4   *Richly concrete and specific, descriptive of all sensory modalities, and often slowed down to capture nuance.* Try to evoke a deep sense of your experience, perhaps tuning into your body's pace of unfolding the experience, while allowing yourself to include as much detail as possible, censoring nothing.
5   *Attuned to the living body.* Try to capture your sense of aliveness in the here-and-now, from moment-to-moment.
6   *Narratives embedded in experience, often first-person narratives.* Use the pronoun 'I', as this allows you to connect more fully to your experience. You might also write in the present tense, as if the experience is happening now.
7   *Poetic images, literary style, and cadence serve embodied depictions and not the other way around.* Allow your narrative to take the form of a creative piece of writing, like poetic prose. Feel free to experiment with varying the rhythms of your writing to achieve a full sense of your experience.

Allow yourself to re-live the experience in your felt-imagination, noticing how your body responds to this, for example, perhaps the experience contains sensations, sounds and smells. 'Write *from the inside out*' (p. 275), slowing everything down to your body's pace. Sometimes meditations on your experience help to deepen the experience.

Example

I find myself at the edge of a deciduous forest looking in. It is early spring, and the black branches appear lifeless as the March sun showers the forest floor with dappled light, making the carpet of blue wood anemones vibrant. The scene fills me with a sense of awe as my attention is drawn deeper and deeper, closer and closer, to what is unfolding in front of me. The occasional early bird breaks the silence. My warm breath meets the cool morning air creating a fine mist in front of me, as the forest draws me further and further into itself. Then suddenly, my whole body expands, or my whole sense of who I am expands to include the forest. At this precise moment a shaft of light flashes through the tall branches of the oak, illuminating, even more vividly, the blue anemones below. At this precise moment my awareness of who I am changes to include the experience of the scene in front of me. My body feels light, while at the same time I feel as if I have no body. I become one with the scene in front of me. My body is the tree, is the light, is the blue anemones. I feel the tree, I feel the atmosphere of place. The feeling opens my heart, or my heart opens my feeling. Expansive. Wide, wide, open space. I am a wide, wide, open space. Then a moment later I am standing looking into the forest, and I am feeling the chill of the air. The moment is gone.

Embodied imagery

Following the principles of embodied writing, embodied imagery seeks to immerse oneself in the experience of the image, thereby avoiding a tendency of viewing imagination as only a left brain activity.

Seven distinctive features of embodied imagery

1   *Bring attention into the body in the present moment through breath.* To bring attention to the breath helps us focus more on our bodily felt-sense experience in the present moment. For instance, breathing *as if* through any bodily symptoms (i.e., tensions, heaviness, numbness), or noticing the sensation of the breath and how the body moves to accommodate inhalation and exhalation, to bring deeper attention to the experience of our embodiment. The more areas of our breathing experience that we simultaneously notice, the deeper our connection with the right brain. For example, the sensation of inhalation at the back of your throat, the contrast in temperature between inhaled and exhaled breath, the rise and fall of your diaphragm, the subtle movement in your back, and so on.

2   *Locate the focus of bodily felt energy through enquiry.* To notice the movement of energy in the body brings further attention to our embodiment.

3   *Locate where the felt energy is more present in the body.* Open questions help to focus the attention on where the energy is mostly felt in the body. 'What feels pressing?' or 'What feels charged?' or 'Where is the greatest energy (positive or negative)?'

4   *Either evoke an image from the bodily felt energy or bring the bodily felt energy to an image.* Sometimes we evoke an image from a bodily felt-sense experience in the moment, or we evoke an image relating to an already held idea of something. *Therefore, notice the fleeting nature of images that may arise, or enquire to evoke these.* 'What is this?' or 'What is the image for this?' or 'What brings this?' *Alternatively, find an image of a looked-for state.* Evoking a bodily felt image of a positive state enables greater embodiment of this state, so that in time it can become a familiar trait. For example, evoking bodily felt images of safety, or the positive experience of optimism, resilience, gratitude, and so on, helps to strengthen these.

5   *Breathe into the experience of the bodily felt image as you imagine deepening into these, while at the same time locate yourself more fully in the image.* The image may arise as a situation or context where the quality is embodied. To create a scene in this way further helps to embody the image. Also, to discern distances between you and parts or objects in the image helps embody the image still further (e.g., you in relation to the safe space).

6   *Represent the image through describing it through the use of art materials.* This enables further engagement with the image, as well as provides a record of the experience.

7   *Bring meaning to the experience through more conscious reflection.* This integrates the experience more into left brain awareness by talking about it.

As with Alice in Chapter 5, it may be useful to bring Hanson's (2013) method of linking a positive experience with a negative one to influence the negative, before returning to rest only on the positive.

Example: establishing an inner safe place

Bring attention to your breath by noticing the global experience of breathing; the different sensations and movements in your body as you inhale and exhale. Be also aware of any tensions in your body, then gently breathe into these while letting the tensions go on the outbreath, as best you can. When you are ready, find an image of safety that you feel drawn to, taking time for this image to form in your imagination, and to get to know this image and what about it makes it feel safe. Take as long as you need for this. Notice, too, the feeling of being in this place, the sensation of being in this place, as well as any sounds and smells that contribute to the safe experience of being in this place. Take as long as you need for this. Notice, too, the distances between you and things or objects; getting to feel the scale and quality of this safe place that you are now in. When you are ready breathe in this experience of safety, noticing how your breathing wants to soak in the feeling of this place. Notice, too, where you hold this experience of safety in your body, as you continue to breathe its essence into you.

References

Anderson, R. (2001) 'Embodied Writing and Reflections on Embodiment', *The Journal of Transpersonal Psychology*, 33(2): 83–98.

Anderson, R. (2002a) 'Embodied Writing: Presencing the Body in Somatic Research, Part I', *Somatics*, 13(4): 40–44.

Anderson, R. (2002b) 'Embodied Writing: Presencing the Body in Somatic Research, Part II', *Somatics*, 14(1): 40–44.

Anderson, R. and Braud, W. (2011) *Transforming Self and Others Through Research: Transpersonal Research Methods and Skills for the Human Sciences and Humanities*, New York: SUNY.

Hanson, R. (2013) *Hardwiring Happiness: The Practical Science of Reshaping Your Brain – and Your Life*, London: Rider.

Index

abandonment, fear of 69, 95–6
Abram, David 14, 21, 81
achievement seeking system 4, 15, 19, 48, 51–2, 96
active imagination 31, 32, 34, 64, 68, 74, 101, 108, 131, 138
addiction 2, 12, 19, 143
ADHD (Attention Deficit Hyperactivity Disorder) 3
affect regulation 15, 16, 19, 21, 22, 29, 44, 48–9, 94, 127; and attachment theory 120; and trauma therapies 141–4; tripartite model of 48, *see also* emotional systems
affect-focused therapy 12
agape 129, 130
Ainsworth, Mary 120
Albrecht, Glenn 82
altruism 101, 103, 167, 168
amygdala 50, 141–4; down-activating 6, 142–4
Anderson, Rosemary 98, 171–2
anger/rage 9, 29, 30, 50, 51, 72, 111
anxiety/worry 2–3, 8, 15, 16, 28, 31, 46, 50, 68, 71, 97–8, 111, 143; and breathing 37, 56
archetypes 35, 36
Arnold, Debora 158, 159, 162
Art Psychotherapy 13, 68, 75
attachment seeking system 15, 48, 69
attachment theory 5, 119–21
Attention Deficit Hyperactivity Disorder (ADHD) 3
authentic resourcing *see* growth facilitating resourcing
authenticity 34–5, 54, 68, 78–80, 128, 131; and positive experiences 79–80
autonomy principle 1, 5, 112

autosymbolic processes 35–6
avoid-threat self-protect system 14, 15, 20, 48, 49, 69, 141–2; two systems in 50
avoidance 71, 95, 138, 143, 144, 148, 158, 159

Bachelard, Gaston 74
Baker, Ellen 163, 166
Baumeister, Roy 28, 29, 30, 50–1, 69
Beauchamp, Tom 112
Beebe, John 79, 128, 131, 156
Begley, Sharon 57
behavioural dimension 62, 78–81, 106, 165; and integrity/authenticity 78–9; and positive experiences 79–80; and resource focused therapy 93, 94, 95, 96, 98, 101; and values 80–1, 106
beneficence 5, 112
Berger, John 28
Bernstein, James 140
bibliotherapy 111
body 35, 109, 173; and left/right brain hemispheres 46, 63; symptoms/symbols of 64–5; and trauma therapies 139, 141, 143, 147, *see also* brain/mind/body systems; felt-sense; physical dimension
body ego stage 33
body intelligence (BQ) 3, 63
Body Psychotherapy 45, 156, 160
Bohart, Arthur 154–5
Borderland personalities 140
borderline clients 126, 127
Bosnak, Robert 32, 148
bottom-up–top-down loop 4, 5, 44–5, 48, 49, 56, 57, 91, 94
boundary-making 1, 2, 138